From Oil to Cities

DIRECTIONS IN DEVELOPMENT
Countries and Regions

From Oil to Cities

Nigeria's Next Transformation

 **WORLD BANK GROUP**

Contents

Boxes

Figures

Maps

Tables

Preface

The Nigerian Urbanization Review, *From Oil to Cities: Nigeria's Next Transformation,* is part of a global series of prototypes called the Urbanization Review and developed by the Social, Urban, Rural, and Resilience Global Practice at the World Bank.

The analytical program aims to provide diagnostic tools to inform policy dialogue and investment priorities on urbanization. It is based on the framework for urban policy developed in the *World Development Report 2009: Reshaping Economic Geography* and on the World Bank's Urban and Local Government Strategy, "System of Cities: Harnessing Urbanization for Growth and Poverty Reduction." To test the relevance and flexibility of the core diagnostic tools, prototype pilots have been initiated in several countries, including China, Colombia, Ethiopia, India, Indonesia, Malaysia, Tunisia, Turkey, and Vietnam.

This report serves the critical and timely purpose of focusing attention on the challenges and opportunities of urbanization in Nigeria. The Overview summarizes key trends of Nigeria's urbanization and sets out a framework to structure core urban challenges in view of underlying causes. Detailed analyses follow in the main report, which consists of four chapters. Chapter 1 presents and analyzes the dynamics of Nigerian urbanization, with particular attention to three key issues: the country's rapid urban population growth; the very large-scale urban expansion, notably on urban peripheries, accompanying population growth; and the stubborn persistence of high urban poverty, inequality, and regional disparity. Chapter 2 examines Nigeria's recent urban economic growth, focusing on the nature of the concentration of economic activity across the country's states and cities and on urban and regional economies' limited generation of higher employment and better business climates. Chapter 3 describes and assesses land management, urban planning, and housing provision procedures and systems, which face challenges in costs, affordability, capacity, equity, and efficiency. Finally, chapter 4 looks at the financing of urban development, focusing on urban public goods and services provision, which requires substantial finance and institutional and systemic reform.

The report should not be interpreted as a strategic or implementation plan or as a feasibility study. Further details, such as sector-specific targets, cost estimates, and investment requirements fall outside the scope of Urbanization Reviews. But they could be used to investigate opportunities for engagement and collaboration between the Federal Government of Nigeria—as well as state and local governments—and the World Bank on urbanization issues.

The study team hopes that the policy analysis and recommendations will be of particular service to the Nigerian government in taking the many existing opportunities to promote more efficient and equitable urban development and stronger urban economic growth and job creation in the country's fast-growing and expanding metropolitan regions, cities, and towns.

Acknowledgments

The Nigerian Urbanization Review benefited from the dedication and support of numerous actors. The work was coordinated and led by Sateh Chafic El-Arnaout (Program Leader, AFCW2) and implemented in two phases.

The first phase provided a series of background papers produced by a team of World Bank experts consisting of Somik V. Lall (Lead Urban Economist, GSURR); Dean Cira (Lead Urban Specialist, GSURR); Nancy Lozano Gracia (Senior Economist, GSURR); Salim Rouhana (Urban Specialist, GSURR); Hyoung Gun Wang (Senior Economist, GSURR); Tuo Shi (Urban Economist, GSURR); Austin Kilroy (Private Sector Development Specialist, GTCDR); Shuang Bin (Consultant to the World Bank); Bernadette Baird-Zars (Consultant to the World Bank) Ana I. Aguilera (Urban Specialist, GSURR); Alexandra Panman (Consultant to the World Bank); and Dr. Bolanle Wahab (Senior Lecturer in Urban and Regional Planning, Nigeria).

The second phase benefited from more analytical depth and the drafting of the final document. The latter phase was implemented by a consulting firm (ICF International) led by Robin Bloch (ICF) involving David Ryan Mason (Consultant to the World Bank); Michael Winter (Consultant to the World Bank); Matthew Crighton (ICF); Naji Makarem (University College London); Nikolaos Papachristodoulou (ICF); James Arthur (ICF); and Jose Monroy (ICF).

The team is grateful for the support received from World Bank Management, particularly Marie Francoise Marie-Nelly (Country Director for Nigeria at the time of completion); Sameh Wahba (Practice Manager, GSURR); Alexander Bakalian (Practice Manager, GWADR); R. Mukami Kariuki (Lead Water and Sanitation Specialist, GWADR); and Javier Sanchez-Reaza (Senior Urban Specialist, GSURR).

The report was enriched by extensive technical consultations with Kathleen Whimp (Senior Public Sector Specialist, GGODR); Shomik Raj Mehndiratta (Lead Urban Transport Specialist, GTIDR); John Litwack (Lead Economist, GMFDR); and Roger Gorham (Transport Economist, GTIDR); and benefited from the comments of both internal and external peer reviewers that included Stephen Karam (Program Leader, ECCU6); Mark Roberts (Senior Urban Economist, GSURR); Vincent Palmade (Lead Economist, GTCDR); Cecilia Briceno-Garmendia (Lead Economist, GTIDR); Asimiyu Jinadu (Professor of Urban and Regional Planning, Nigeria); and Waheed Kadiri (Lecturer in Urban and Regional Planning and Chairman of the African Planning Association, Nigeria).

Throughout the process, important contributions to the document were made by Somik Lall (Lead Urban Economist, GSURR) and valuable guidance was received from Roland White (Lead Urban Specialist, GSURR). The team also extends its gratitude to the editorial support received from Narae Choi (Urban Specialist, GSURR), Bruce Ross-Larson (CDI), and to the administrative support received from Ruth Adetola Adeleru (Program Assistant, AFCW2) and Roderick M. Babijes (Program Assistant, GSURR).

The team received generous support from the U.K. Department for International Development (DFID) and Cities Alliance, whose financial contribution comprised an important part of the report. The report also benefited from a series of background papers and research reports produced by the Urbanisation Research Nigeria program, a research component of the DFID-funded Urbanisation and Infrastructure Research and Evaluation Manager—Nigeria program.

Abbreviations

BRT	bus rapid transit
CAPDAN	Computer Allied Products Dealers Association of Nigeria
DCD	Development Control Department
DMO	Debt Management Office
DoH	Departments of Health
DPO	development policy operation
DRN	declared road network
ECA	Excess Crude Account
ECTDA	Enugu Capital Territory Development Authority
FA	Federation Account
FAAC	Federation Account Allocation Committee
FERMA	Federal Road Maintenance Agency
FMoH	Federal Ministry of Health
FMoT	Federal Ministry of Transport
GHS	Generalized Household Survey
ICT	information and communication technology
IDP	internally displaced people
IGR	internally generated revenues
ILO	International Labour Organization
JAAC	Joint Accounts Allocation Committee
LAMATA	Lagos Metropolitan Area Transport Authority
LQ	location quotients
LRT	light rail transit
LUA	Land Use Act
MAN	Manufacturing Association of Nigeria
NASSI	Nigerian Association of Small-Scale Industries
NHF	National Housing Fund
NHLSS	Nigeria Harmonized Living Standard Survey
NIAF	Nigeria Infrastructure Advisory Facility

NIAM	Nigerian Integrated Accessibility Model
NMRC	Nigerian Mortgage Refinance Company
NRC	Nigerian Railway Corporation
OYOWMA	Oyo State Solid Waste Management Authority
PHC	primary health care
PIT	personal income tax
PMI	primary mortgage institutions
PPP	public-private partnership
PSIA	poverty and social impact analysis
PSP	private service providers
RMFAC	Revenue Mobilization and Fiscal Allocation Commission
SJLGA	State Joint Local Government Account
SMoH	State Ministries of Health
SNG	Sub-National Government
SSA	Sub-Saharan Africa
SWM	solid waste management
TVE	township and village enterprises

Transitioning to a New Urban-Based Model of Economic Growth

Nigeria's economy is at a crossroads. For decades, it has relied mainly on oil extraction to drive growth and revenue. Outside oil and gas, tradable sectors have not been developed, leading to weak structural transformation and limited employment opportunities.[1] Consumption-based cities have arisen because of oil wealth, but these have not increased economic productivity or urban employment, or reduced poverty, as they have in many other parts of the developing world. Now, as declining oil prices reveal the economic weaknesses of the country, pressure for a new economic model is growing. Urbanization, which to date has *followed* wealth creation, can instead, if reformed, help *drive* economic growth and poverty reduction.

From 1980 to 2010, oil revenues contributed over three-quarters of the federal government's revenues, nearly 97 percent of total exports, and 35 percent of gross domestic product (GDP). But the growth they have created is not sustainable. Oil revenue per capita has grown more than tenfold since the mid-1970s, but GDP per capita only returned to the levels of that decade by 2008 (in real purchasing power parity). Although oil has created some positive spillovers in high-end services and finance, high oil revenues have also led to an overvalued exchange rate that makes other exports uncompetitive, lowering incentives, and the ability to invest in non-oil sectors, including manufacturing and agriculture. Tradable sectors, apart from natural resources, have not been developed. In particular, manufacturing development has resembled that in resource-dependent economies more than in most developing countries (figure O.1). Even in today's slightly more diversified economy, growth has been most rapid in nontradable services sectors, including real estate, financial intermediation, and information and communication technology (ICT).

The dependence on oil has in turn led to underdevelopment of other revenue sources and prevented improvements in governance. For 2012 the share of oil revenue in the national budget was 75 percent, and state governments received over 63 percent of their revenue from oil. Reliance on oil-based fiscal transfers

Figure O.1 Nigeria's Stunted Manufacturing Development Compared to Countries with Similar Urbanization

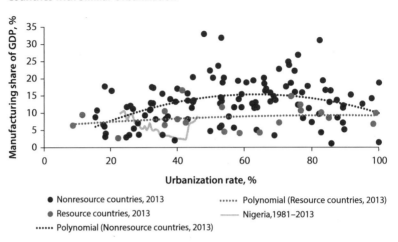

● Nonresource countries, 2013   ⋯⋯ Polynomial (Resource countries, 2013)
● Resource countries, 2013   —— Nigeria,1981–2013
⋯⋯ Polynomial (Nonresource countries, 2013)

Sources: World Bank, World Development Indicators; World Bank staff calculations.
Note: GDP = gross domestic product. Resource-dependent economies defined as those with 20 percent natural resource rents as share of GDP or higher.

to subnational governments provides few incentives to boost collections of local revenue and weakens urban planning and financing. Moreover, research on the "resource curse" demonstrates that developing countries with "Dutch disease" generally perform worse on the rule of law and good governance.[2] Nigeria is no exception, ranking extremely low on both, as well as on corruption indicators; Transparency International had ranked the country 136th place in their Corruption Perceptions Index 2014.

Oil dependence has also left the economy highly vulnerable to the drop in crude oil prices. The tax share of revenue averaged 30 percent over 2003–12, far below the 80 percent average in other countries at Nigeria's level of development.[3] The country's fiscal buffers—the Excess Crude Account and Sovereign Wealth Fund—are meant to finance countercyclical spending, but have been largely decimated in the past two years, mainly due to the decline in international oil prices.

The recent decline in oil prices has had considerably detrimental impact on Nigeria's economy, as did the previous episodes. Most notably, from the 1970s onward, oil revenues were used to develop urban and transportation infrastructure and to promote industrialization, which in turn fueled urbanization. But during the structural adjustment in the 1980s and 1990s, Nigerian cities simultaneously went through a phase of urban expansion alongside a decline in their physical condition: while they grew and absorbed newcomers, they often lacked the resources for appropriate infrastructure and services. This was closely linked to the collapse of oil prices, which meant that available resources for housing, water supply, security, and waste management in urban settings was undersupplied.

The triple impact—of a long-term drop in oil prices, low levels of non-oil-based internally generated revenues (IGR), and a growing infrastructure deficit—now pose an increasingly urgent investment challenge.

Oil dependence and poor governance have also left cities with limited job creation and access to basic services. Ideally, urban economies should help enhance productivity through economies of scale, agglomeration effects, and specialization. But oil dependence has decreased the competitiveness of the tradable sectors, particularly manufacturing, that usually tend to unleash these new sources of productivity. And at the same time it has removed the impetus to develop land management practices and a business environment that support these emerging sectors. Rural "push" factors have encouraged people to move to cities—particularly declining incomes in agriculture due to an overvalued exchange rate and high levels of conflict in northern and central regions—rather than urban "pull" factors, such as job creation. With poor land management and limited and mismanaged provision of infrastructure for services and mass transport, much of the urban population lives in settlements that lack access to basic services and, largely, to many jobs.

If Nigeria hopes to generate employment and reduce poverty, it must seek new sources of growth. Managed correctly, urbanization can provide such a path. Past efforts supported by the World Bank have focused on agribusiness and agricultural development. Such efforts are a key avenue for job creation in rural areas, but they are insufficient to provide a source of growth for the whole economy. Rather, metropolitan-based policies will be essential.

The density of cities offers the potential benefit of a high concentration of firms and households. Urban areas are natural hubs of economic density and productivity, and competitiveness accelerates when firms locate close to each other. Agglomeration facilitates the exchange of knowledge to improve productivity and ideas to spark innovation across sectors. For workers, cities increase opportunity through a higher concentration of jobs. And a better-planned spatial distribution of people can lead to efficiencies in public service delivery, presenting possible savings in water, sanitation, and road infrastructure, as well as making it easier to create efficient public transport networks.

These positive effects are not widely evident in Nigeria (figure O.2); instead, its relatively rapid urban population growth has occurred without structural transformation and, thus, without adequate job creation, infrastructure provision, affordable housing, or access to basic services. That pattern of rural push rather than urban pull is a key cause. Stagnating agricultural productivity and substantial conflict, particularly in the north, have spurred migration, not urban jobs or services.

Urbanization Can Help Economic Transformation, Creating Jobs and Reducing Poverty

A well-functioning urban system is needed to sustain growth and help Nigeria transform its economy and transition toward higher productivity—and this also helps rural areas. While urbanization is traditionally associated with economic

Figure O.2 Urbanization Has Not Led to Structural Transformation and Poverty Reduction in Nigeria

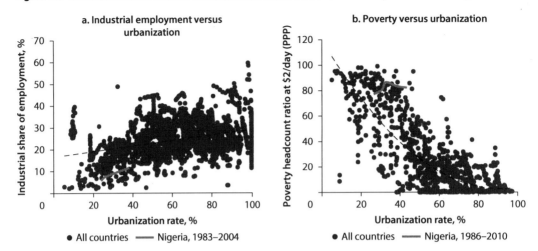

Sources: World Bank, World Development Indicators; World Bank staff calculations.
Note: PPP = purchasing power parity.

structural transformation toward manufacturing and services, cities are also central to improving agricultural output as the efficiency of agricultural production is tied to the urban system. Small cities, for example, are needed to connect farmers to input and output markets, and they perform a market aggregation.

Medium-sized cities, in turn, must be effective logistics hubs for the transport of goods, and are home to larger local markets. Finally, large cities, such as Lagos, have an important role to play in connecting the economy to the world; because of the agglomeration economies they provide, they also have the potential to become nodes for high-value services. In short, cities can support and facilitate efficiencies and productivity in Nigeria's economy, both in its transition to more productive agriculture, and in economic diversification toward higher-value activities.

At the broadest level, the greatest challenges in Nigerian urbanization today are too few urban jobs and that gains in urban living standards are small.

The first section of this overview discusses these challenges, highlighting the proximate causes of limited urban job creation—low productivity in labor-intensive sectors, lack of scale economies, a poor business environment, and market fragmentation. Much of Nigeria's urban poverty can be attributed to a lack of jobs. But additional challenges prevent urbanization from reducing poverty: in particular, the concentration of the urban population in settlements unconnected to trunk infrastructure crimps access to basic services, prevents household physical and human capital investments, and increases negative urban environmental externalities. High congestion and land-market inefficiencies prevent people from locating close to jobs and commuting to work.

The second section diagnoses these challenges and identifies interlinked underlying causes—insufficient institutions for land management, service provision, and urban finance; under provision of infrastructure; and ineffective targeted interventions for the poor and vulnerable. Combating these causes will yield reinforcing gains for both economic growth and poverty reduction; in other words, a double dividend. For example, reforming land management institutions will help generate an urban economy that can take advantage of economies of scale and specialization, and encourage the formation of settlements with increased access to basic services and proximity to jobs. Nigeria's economic potential is huge if it can get urbanization right, but tremendous costs await it under business as usual. The urban population is expected to reach 67 percent of the total by 2050 (United Nations 2014), and the economy will need to create 40 million–50 million jobs by 2030 (from 2010) as the population grows, translating to over 2 million more jobs a year, mostly taken up by new labor market entrants (World Bank 2014a). The vast majority of these new jobs will be in urban areas. Manufacturing makes up just 6.8 percent of GDP and is less productive than agriculture,[4] and half of working Nigerians are in low-productivity agriculture (World Bank 2016), offering considerable room for job creation and productivity gains from structural transformation. Yet, a continuation of current trends will undermine the enormous potential that is latent in cities to become hubs of innovation, in lagging regions to become part of a system of growth, and in small and medium firms to expand and compete regionally and globally.

Limited Employment Creation and Poverty Reduction Characterize Nigeria's Urbanization

Urbanization in Nigeria Is Occurring Rapidly—And on a Massive Scale

An estimated 85 million Nigerians now live in urban settlements—half the total population.[5] From urbanization of a mere 4.5 percent in 1921, the urban share rose to 30 percent by 1990 and 47 percent by 2014, much higher than the average 37 percent for Sub-Saharan Africa. And it continues to grow fast, increasing an average of 4.8 percent a year from 2000 to 2013—doubling in the past 15 years—and is expected to add another 85 million people within the next 30 years.

Inconsistent with global experience, however, Nigeria's rapid urbanization has preceded its economic growth, as noted, leaving it "over-urbanized" for its level of development. In 2007, real GDP per capita was the same as in 1977, but the urban population had increased fourfold as urbanization hit 46 percent in 2013 (figure O.3). GDP per capita was only US$1,056 then (constant 2005 US$), much lower than the average of US$2,675 for other countries at the same urbanization rate (figure O.4). Turkey reached the same landmark at US$3,836 GDP per capita, Thailand at US$3,390, China at US$2,403, and Guatemala at US$2,117.

Rapid urbanization amid low development is part of a broader pattern in Sub-Saharan Africa. That is, even though Nigeria urbanized faster than countries in the region that developed earlier, its experience is not unique. According to past data for Sub-Saharan African countries and based on its income level, Nigeria was expected to reach the urbanization rate of 35 percent in 2014,

Figure O.3 Urbanization Rate versus GDP per Capita, Global Benchmarks

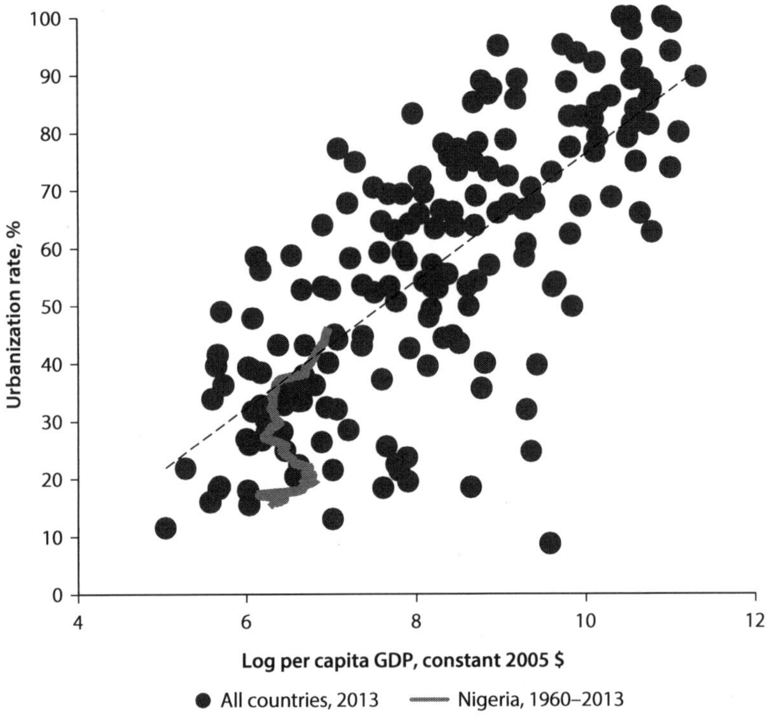

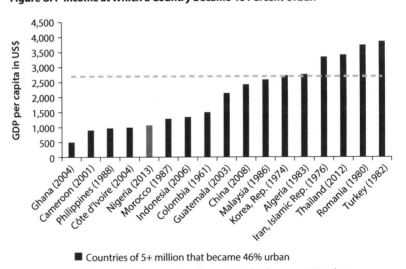

Sources: World Bank, World Development Indicators; World Bank staff calculations.
Note: GDP = gross domestic product.

Figure O.4 Income at Which a Country Became 46 Percent Urban

■ Countries of 5+ million that became 46% urban

▪ ▪ ▪ Average GDP per capita, all countries that became 46% urban

Sources: World Bank, World Development Indicators; World Bank staff calculations.
Note: GDP = gross domestic product.

whereas 47 percent of the country was urbanized in reality. Likewise, many countries in the region have urbanized rapidly in recent years at income levels that are similar to Nigeria's. For instance, Cameroon, Côte d'Ivoire, Ghana, and Mauritania all have higher urbanization rates than Nigeria at similar income levels.

Urban populations are growing at all levels in Nigeria: from Lagos and the other metropolitan cities of Kano, Abuja (the capital), and Ibadan to the other state capitals and smaller secondary and tertiary cities. Lagos is the sole megacity, with seven metropolitan areas of more than 1 million people, 15 large cities from 500,000 to 1 million, 19 medium-sized cities from 300,000 to 500,000, and hundreds of smaller towns. By 2020, another three cities are projected to reach metropolitan size (Uyo, Nnewi, and Aba), and by 2030 the number of cities with more than 1 million inhabitants will be 23, against just 41 in all of Sub-Saharan Africa.

Although relatively well balanced across city-size classes, the degree and pace of urbanization is not uniform across Nigeria. The population now concentrates in four city clusters. In the North, this is centered on Kano. In the South West, it is centered on the Lagos–Ibadan corridor and surrounding area, in the South East around Port Harcourt, and from Abuja to Jos along a newer agglomeration in a developing corridor. Spatial analysis indicates that as this continues it could lead to four mega-regions around the clusters—cities connected by physical infrastructure and tied economically to well-functioning markets—with the potential to reshape the urban and regional landscape.

That said, and contrary to common perception, Nigeria does not exhibit a high degree of urban primacy, meaning Lagos is not "too large" for the rest of the urban system. A more noticeable trend in Nigeria's present-day urbanization is heightened and accelerated spatial expansion, increasingly concentrated on the periphery of existing settlements. The growth of the urban population has been accompanied by both the intensification of development in already existing built-up areas, and by the appearance of new suburban development and the progressive absorption of adjacent, formerly peri-urban, settlements. This urban expansion, driven by urban population growth, is expected to continue and likely increase: urban land cover could double by 2030. This generalized pattern has been framed in Nigeria, as elsewhere in Sub-Saharan Africa (and globally), as "sprawl," but this term is too limited and descriptive to properly encapsulate the variety and complexity of spatial expansion.

A process of decentralization of both population and economic activity increasingly marked by a low-density pattern can thus be observed, notably on the urban periphery. The tremendous suburban development on the outskirts of cities throughout Nigeria in the last decade is diverse and manifested in residential, industrial, and commercial urban typologies: residential estates for the emerging urban middle class are frequently located alongside unplanned informal settlements and industrial and commercial uses—formal and informal—coexist with these planned and unplanned residential areas.

From Oil to Cities • http://dx.doi.org/10.1596/978-1-4648-0792-3

Nigerian cities are beginning to develop in a more polycentric pattern. The Lagos metropolitan area, for example, now encompasses a wide array of urban districts. These include the island of Lagos, Ikoyi (the seat of traditional administration in Lagos State), and areas planned in the past such as Apapa, Ebute-Metta, Yaba, Ilupeju, Surulere, and Ikeja, which are now marked by the increased presence of commercial activities and industries. Metropolitan Lagos also includes newly planned towns and estates including Festac Town, Satellite Town, Gowon Estate, Ipaja, Amuwo-Odofin and Anthony Village, Mushin, Iwaya, Iponri, Maroko, and Ajegunle, and older local villages incorporated into the urban fabric as the city expanded. These urban centers provide different functions. This polycentric structure is now emerging in many larger Nigerian cities such as Abuja, Kaduna, Kano, Enugu, Ibadan, and Port Harcourt.

Two additional developmental corridors in the Lagos region also deserve attention. One is the rapidly developing corridor to the west of Lagos—Badagry highway encompassing Amuwo Odofin-Mile 2-Festac Town, Okoko-Maiko, Agbara Badagry, and the transborder section from Seme in Nigeria to Cotonou in Benin. This development consists of planned sections—Festac Town, Agbara Industrial/Housing Estate—and the informal, low-income enclaves of Okokomaiko, Shibiri, and others.

East of Lagos is the Lekki Peninsula Development along the Lagos Victoria Island-Epe highway corridor. This is seen as one of the most dynamic growth areas in Lagos State, and is made up of several estates, gated residential developments, and areas allocated for a free trade zone.

Cities are also developing beyond their designated borders to form extensive urban corridors and conurbations. As Lagos expands, it has grown well beyond the borders of Lagos State, forming an extensive urban corridor reaching to and beyond Ibadan—and anchoring the South West conurbation.

Similar formations are emerging elsewhere, as noted, centered on Kano, Abuja, and Port Harcourt. Abuja is developing a polycentric metropolitan area due to the economic and residential links between the city and its satellite towns, as well as towns to the east in adjoining Nasarawa State. An urban transborder corridor has also emerged in the north of the country, connecting Maradi in Mali with Katsina and Kano in northern Nigeria, linking the two countries (OECD 2006). The K²M area, as it is known, concentrates a population of about 19 million, and with a population density of about 200 inhabitants per square kilometer, is one of the most densely populated areas in West Africa.

Urban Economies Suffer from Limited Employment Creation in Productive Jobs with Livable Wages

After two decades of economic stagnation, Nigeria in the past 10 years has been one of the fastest-growing countries in Sub-Saharan Africa, with GDP growth exceeding 7 percent a year. A recent rebasing of Nigeria's GDP shows that the country now has the largest economy in Africa, and with a revised gross national product of US$502 billion in 2013, it is the 26th largest economy in the world.

But this growth has not seen enough jobs created, with the economy failing to translate growth in output into lower unemployment. In fact, as growth has accelerated, unemployment has *increased* (figure O.5). According to data from the National Bureau of Statistics (NBS) in Nigeria, unemployment rose from 8.2 percent in 1999 to 21.4 percent in 2010. Much of this is probably best interpreted as underemployment, as the NBS does not follow the International Labour Organization's definition of unemployment. Still, the direction of the trend highlights a real problem: growing numbers of underemployed part-time workers in low-productivity and low-paying occupations.

Unsurprisingly, jobs are a central issue in public debate, particularly for youth. When asked to rank the main problems facing the country, more than twice as many people cited unemployment than any other issue, including poverty, electricity, crime, education, infrastructure, and corruption (figure O.6).

The weak growth of job opportunities has several interrelated sources:

- *The sectoral distribution of jobs.* Fast-growing sectors are capital intensive and use little labor, while labor-intensive industries have low productivity and slow growth.

Figure O.5 Changes in Unemployment versus Economic Growth

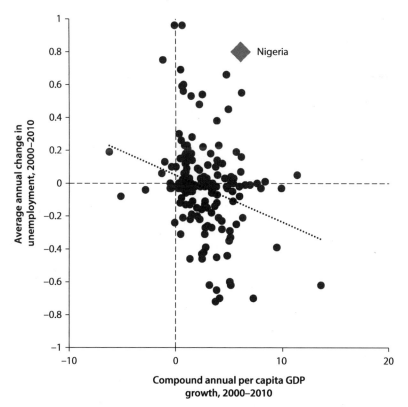

Sources: National Bureau of Statistics in Nigeria; World Bank, World Development Indicators; World Bank staff calculations.
Note: GDP = gross domestic product.

Figure O.6 Nigeria's Most Pressing Problems

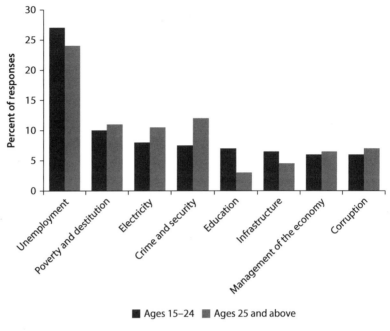

■ Ages 15–24 ■ Ages 25 and above

Source: World Bank 2016.

- *Informal firms struggle to enhance productivity.* Informal firms are less likely to grow than those elsewhere and take advantage of urban economies of scale and specialization. Uncertain property rights and limited access to land and the formal legal system weaken incentives to invest in physical and human capital, leading to lower productivity and slower growth.
- *A poor business environment.* Nigerian businesses face unreliable electricity provision, poor transportation and congestion due to insufficient road maintenance, high interest rates, precarious availability of finance, and red tape. These barriers affect business development across sectors, but have particularly pernicious effects on manufacturing firms.
- *Market fragmentation.* Limited connectivity within and between cities lift production costs in the tradable sector and prevent firms from expanding beyond local markets, diminishing potential for firm clustering and reducing agglomeration and localization effects.

Growth Sectors Are Capital Intensive; Labor-Intensive Sectors Lack Productivity

The past two decades have seen encouraging economic diversification, but expanding sectors have not created enough jobs, and job-creating sectors have lagged behind. All sectors have grown in real terms since 1990, and many have emerged from negligible levels, namely ICT, real estate, construction, and services—all predominantly urban sectors (figure O.7). With this rebalancing,

Figure O.7 Real GDP by Sector, 1990–2010

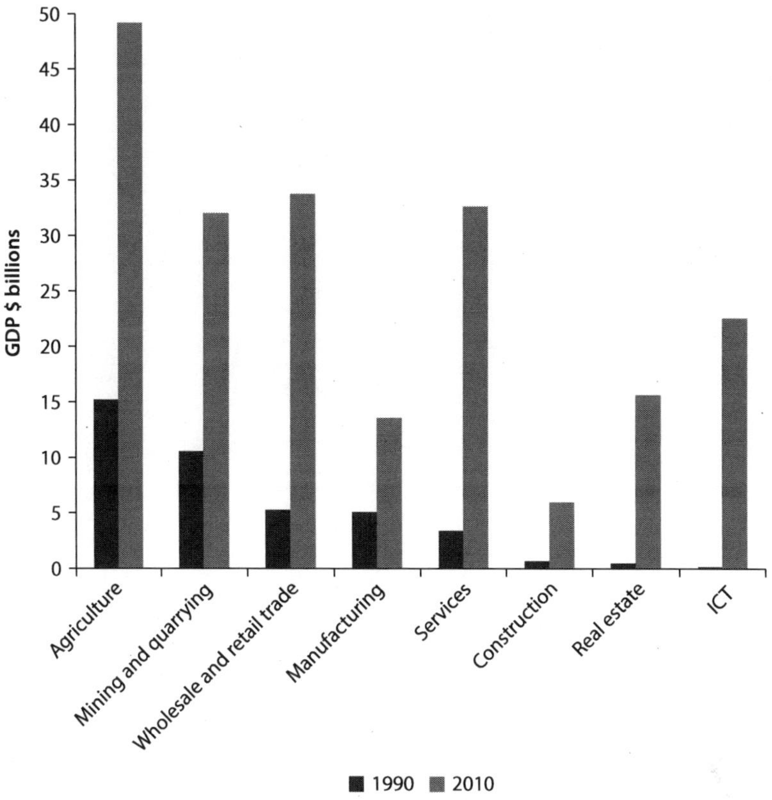

Sources: National Bureau of Statistics; World Bank staff calculations.
Note: GDP = gross domestic product; ICT = information and communication technology.

the share of agriculture and oil and gas contracted from 60 percent of GDP in 1990 to 40 percent in 2010. Oil exploitation has declined as a share of GDP, from 36 percent in 1981 to 15.8 percent in 2012 (rebased estimates).[6] However, over a third of 1990–2010 growth (36 percent) was driven by three sectors that employed a mere 1.4 percent of formal workers in 2010: ICT, real estate, and oil and gas. These high-productivity sectors contributed very little to aggregate employment.

Outside these urban, high-productivity, low-employment sectors, Nigeria's economy has felt little structural transformation. And although almost 50 percent of the population is urban, almost half the labor force is still employed in the low-productivity agriculture sector (figure O.8) (GHS 2011; World Bank 2016). Agriculture occupies over 90 percent of the 91.1 million hectares of the country, but primarily for small-scale production and subsistence farming (Oseni and others 2014). The average yield per hectare is estimated at 20–50 percent lower than in comparable developing countries (African Development Bank 2013).[7]

As employment in agriculture has remained high, the movement or agglomeration of urban workers into manufacturing has been minimal, stunting the

Figure O.8 Nigerian Job Concentration in Agriculture, Despite Urbanization

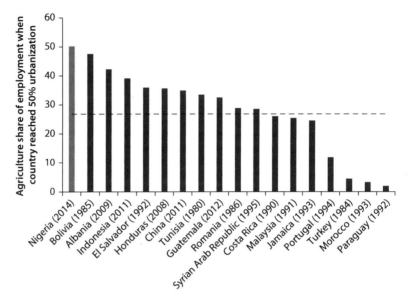

Sources: World Bank, World Development Indicators; World Bank staff calculations.

creation of scale economies. Manufacturing stagnated for decades, falling from over 10 percent of GDP in 1984 to only 2.5 percent in 2009. It contributed a mere 5 percent of output growth from 1990 and 2010. Despite signs of resurgence in the past few years,[8] manufacturing exhibits extremely low productivity, explaining the sector's lag.

Although some structural transformation toward manufacturing has characterized many countries in Sub-Saharan Africa, Nigeria's low manufacturing productivity is particularly pronounced. Labor productivity across sectors is lower than in comparable developing countries, including many in Sub-Saharan Africa, with the gap especially wide in manufacturing. A 2009 United Nations Industrial Development Organization study revealed that the manufacturing productivity of Nigerian workers was just 10 percent of that in Botswana and 50 percent of Ghana and Kenya (Iarossi, Mousley, and Radwan 2009). Productivity per worker in manufacturing is *less* than in agriculture (Bloch and others 2015).

Although wages in Nigeria are lower than in many of its competitors, low productivity means that Nigerian workers produce less on average than the country's competitors, reducing competitiveness. Despite recent improvements—labor productivity grew 3.4 percent a year over 2010–13 and now contributes 55 percent of GDP growth—Nigeria still lags behind other major developing and Sub-Saharan African countries. In 2013, output per worker was US$10,300 per year—57 percent less than the average of seven large developing economies. Wage differentials across Nigeria's sectors serve as a proxy for highly variable productivity (figure O.9).

Low productivity in manufacturing is a direct consequence of urbanization that has not taken advantage of scale economies and agglomeration effects.

Figure O.9 Wages Vary by Sector, Median Wage per Month, US$, 2013

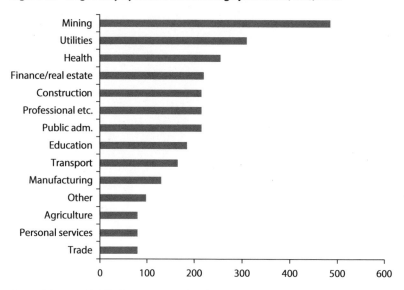

Sources: Jobs report, World Bank 2014a; estimates based on GHS 2013.

The sections below discuss three proximate and interrelated causes of the low productivity of the urban economy and low levels of urban job creation: informal firms struggle to scale up in urban areas, a poor business environment, and a failure to take advantage of agglomeration economies through densities and clustering. These are interlinked issues that have knock-on effects on each other.

Nigeria's Urban Informal Firms Struggle to Develop Local Scale Economies

The large majority of Nigerians work in the informal economy, largely in rural agriculture and urban services. Informal workers make up 53 percent of the active labor force: 54.6 million informal workers versus 48.5 million formal workers. Informal workers are grouped into seven categories (figure O.10). The majority, 62 percent, are proprietors and partners, but a staggering 17 percent are unpaid workers.

The informality of urban employment is associated with lower levels of productivity and lower tax revenue. Informal businesses are much less likely to grow in size given their lack of access to the formal legal system, reducing the benefits of scale economies that urban environments can provide. Further, informal enterprises avoid taxation and thus limit the funds for public use. Studies have found that, internationally, an increase of one standard deviation in the size of the informal sector corresponds to a 1–2 percentage point decline in per capita GDP growth (Oviedo, Thomas, and Karakurum-Ozdemir 2009).

The causes of informality are complex: although informality often emerges when formally registering a firm carries high costs, factors such as education and broader institutional frameworks also play a part. Indeed, research exploring the determinants of informality—drawing on a survey of micro, small, and medium

Figure O.10 Share of Informal Workers by Category
percent

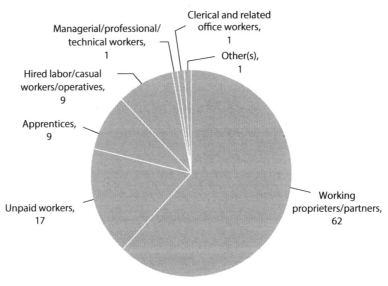

Source: National Bureau of Statistics 2011.

enterprises in Côte d'Ivoire, Kenya, Nigeria, and Senegal—confirms that corruption, which increases the cost of registration, is one. The research also found that higher-productivity firms, with better access to bank finance, are more likely to register and remain formal (Gajigo and Hallward-Driemeier 2012). Current economic conditions therefore provide few incentives for informal firms to grow, particularly given high corruption and little faith in the impartiality or effectiveness of the judiciary.

The problem here is not the informal nature of urban enterprises, but rather the regulatory and institutional conditions that prevent them from boosting investment and linking to other formal and informal enterprises. The experience of informal enterprises in other parts of the developing world demonstrates the high productivity that informal sector enterprises can achieve through local economies of scale generated by multiple small enterprises. In China, informal township and village enterprises, once their property rights were secured, increased investments in human and physical capital and linked with formal and informal enterprises. Local clusters of township and village enterprises in small urban regions generated local economies of scale with positive economic spillover, playing a critical role in China's economic development.

The relationship between government and the informal sector in Nigeria is complex: on the one hand, policy makers and authorities have sought to "formalize" the informal economy, treating it as social problem; on the other they have engaged with and recognized firms operating informally. The authorities' efforts to make the informal sector formal via fines and closures have been largely counterproductive, ultimately creating greater barriers to growth for them, rather than incentives for formality. The government has been far more effective when it engages proactively with the informal sector, particularly through local business associations. An example of this interaction between informal ICT firms is the Otigba ICT cluster in Lagos and the Lagos State government, which deals with them through the Computer Allied Products Dealers Association of Nigeria and even collects taxes from informal firms (Oyelaran-Oyeyinka 2014).

Already, evidence exists of successful informal enterprise clusters in Nigeria. The Otigba ICT cluster has been described as the Silicon Valley of West Africa. The cluster contains a variety of firms spanning the formal-informal continuum, from sole-traders dealing in laptop accessories, to retailers and small repair shops, and firms that make locally branded hardware products, including laptops and tablet computers, which are formally registered and even export internationally. In 2005, the cluster contained about 3,500 firms, which between them employed about 10,000 people. The numbers have grown since then. Moreover, in 2013, more than a quarter of businesses were estimated to be worth from US$6,200 to US$31,000, while more than a tenth of businesses were worth over US$620,000 (Oyelaran-Oyeyinka 2014). Other informal sector clusters include the Nnewi Automotive Parts Industrial Cluster, the Aba shoe and garment clusters, the Ilorin weaving cluster, the Kano leather tanneries, and the Onitsha Plastic Cluster (also known as the Osakwe Industrial Cluster).

Informal clusters in Nigeria share distinct characteristics that have contributed to their success. These include (a) the existence or establishment of active business associations and social and popular networks; (b) the contributions of skills, learning spillovers, and entrepreneurship in creating opportunity and innovation; (c) significant interfirm links, specifically with large firms; (d) specialization and division of labor among individual firms, which enhances productivity; (e) firms in informal clusters also engage in workplace training in the form of apprenticeships; and (f) sociocultural factors play an important role in the development of informal clusters in Nigeria, as a shared sociocultural identity provides a basis for trust and reciprocity in an informal setting (Meagher 2010).

The Poor Business Environment Hits Manufacturing Productivity through Multiple Channels

A poor urban business environment hinders the development of jobs. Nigeria ranked 175th out of 189 countries in 2014 on the World Bank's Doing Business rankings. Its ranking was particularly bad on dealing with construction permits, getting electricity, registering property, paying taxes, and trading across borders.

The biggest constraint to productivity in Nigeria is power. Almost all Nigerian firms experience power outages, averaging 8 hours per calendar day, causing indirect costs equivalent to 4.3 percent of sales for manufacturing firms and 5.3 percent for retail firms (World Bank 2011). In response, the majority of firms (88 percent) have installed their own generator, adding greatly to operating costs. Manufacturing firms reported that roughly 69 percent of their total electrical use comes not from the public grid but from their own generators, with large manufacturers more dependent than smaller ones. The cost of acquiring and maintaining a generator amounts to 9 percent of the total value of a firm's equipment and machinery and 13 percent of a firm's operating expenses (World Bank 2011).

In enterprise surveys, nearly 80 percent of firms identify electricity as a major constraint, well above the Sub-Saharan average of 50 percent (figure O.11). But against other countries in Sub-Saharan Africa, neither the cost nor skill level of labor is seen as a major problem, although some evidence suggests that wages in Nigeria are high relative to productivity, making firms less competitive (World Bank 2016).

Congestion costs also constrain business. Findings from a background paper for this report suggest that traffic congestion costs the Federal Capital Territory (FCT)/Abuja, Kano, and Lagos US$389 million, US$673 million, and US$2.8 billion a year in lost productivity, respectively.[9] Nationally, some US$5.51 billion is lost to congestion annually in the 14 largest cities—some 1.1 percent of GDP (figure O.12).

Setting up a business is very difficult; in particular, land transactions are very costly, lengthy, and complicated, discouraging buyers and sellers from formal procedures. To transfer real estate in some jurisdictions in Nigeria one has to pay stamp duty (2–3 percent of asset value), capital gains tax (2 percent of land value), transfer tax (8–30 percent of land value as set by states), and a registration fee (3 percent of asset value). Unusually, capital gains are taxed on the land value, not the gain; the transfer tax share is far higher than in other countries; and registration fees are a percentage of asset value, not a fixed amount (Butler 2009). The cost of merely titling land in Lagos and Port Harcourt is about 30 percent of the construction cost.

Figure O.11 Share of Firms Identifying an Issue as a "Major" or "Severe" Obstacle

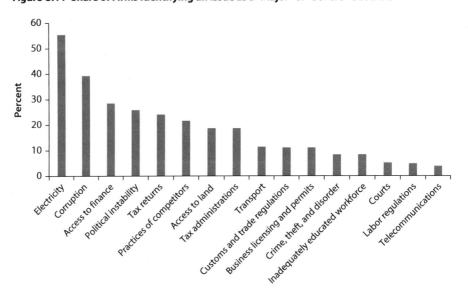

Source: World Bank Enterprise Surveys.

Figure O.12 Annual Cost of Congestion as a Share of Regional GDP (%)

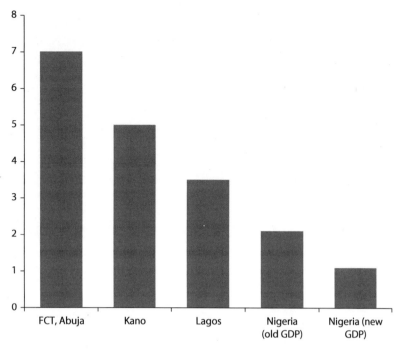

Source: FCT 2013 Travel Demand Survey/Kano 2012 Travel Demand Survey/Lagos 2012 Travel Demand Survey.
Note: FCT = Federal Capital Territory; GDP = gross domestic product.

Several of these obstacles are particularly pertinent to labor-intensive urban firms. Manufacturing industries are much more dependent on uninterrupted power than real estate or services firms. Congestion, expensive transport, and border barriers are most relevant for tradable sectors. In other words, while Nigeria's poor business environment affects all firms, it has a different impact on manufacturing firms' productivity.

Market Fragmentation Hinders Growth of the Tradable Sector

Nigeria has little specialization in tradable sectors. An analysis of location quotients reveals emerging industrial agglomerations and specialization across regions.[10] Growth in many of its fastest-growing sectors has been concentrated in specialized cities in the South West. The ICT sector, for instance, is highly concentrated, with over 26 percent of total ICT employment in Ogun State alone, and a further 18 percent in Lagos State. The professional, scientific, and technical services industry, largely offering high-end services to the oil and gas industry, is also highly concentrated in Ogun State, with a location quotient of 4.1,[11] and making up a staggering 10 percent of the state's employment, or 20 percent of the subsector's national employment. Finance and insurance are heavily concentrated in Lagos. These highly productive sectors have considerable spillover on local economies.

Concentration and specialization have tended to be in nontradable productive sectors in the south, with few employment-generation prospects. Manufacturing is more spread out across the country, with three major agglomerations: the Kaduna-Kano corridor in the North West, the Lagos-Ibadan corridor in the South West and around and in the South East, and a third evident agglomeration (not apparent in NBS employment data) in the south of the country, around Rivers State (map O.1). Lagos has the largest concentration of manufacturing small and medium enterprises (1,195), followed by the North West around Kano (map O.2). It also has the highest number of manufacturing workers, with 545,000 such jobs, accounting for 15 percent of total state employment. Other major manufacturing agglomerations are in Oyo and Ogun, making the South West the largest manufacturing agglomeration, with these three states accounting for 27 percent of national manufacturing jobs.[12]

The second-largest manufacturing agglomeration is in Kano, with 384,000 employees, and a location quotient of 1.23. This cluster is in Kano City, mainly comprising the textiles and tanning and leather subsectors. Jigawa and Kaduna are also major manufacturing employment centers, making the North West an important manufacturing zone. However, the manufacturing subsectors concentrated in the North West are in decline and are, moreover, in low-productivity activities. This is reflected in its low GDP per capita. Attempts to protect the manufacturing industry from imports have failed due

Map O.1 Manufacturing Employment Location Quotient by State, 2010

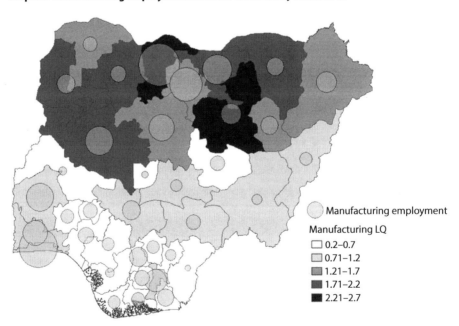

Manufacturing employment

Manufacturing LQ
- 0.2–0.7
- 0.71–1.2
- 1.21–1.7
- 1.71–2.2
- 2.21–2.7

Sources: Original map in URN 2014 Economic Development in Urban Nigeria; data from National Bureau of Statistics.
Note: ICT = information and communication technology; LQ = location quotient.

Map O.2 Location of Manufacturing SMEs at State Level, 2010

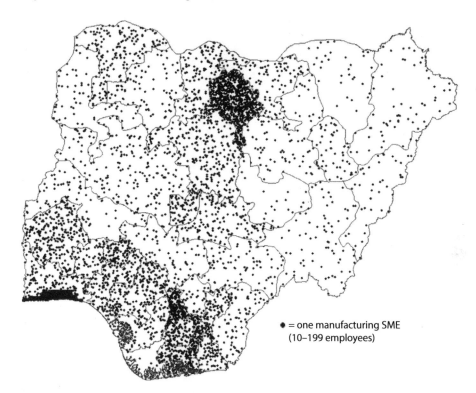

● = one manufacturing SME
(10–199 employees)

Sources: Original map in URN 2014 Economic Development in Urban Nigeria; data from NBS National MSME Collaborative
Survey 2010.
Note: Dots represent one firm in that state, not the exact location of a firm.

to an inability to regulate and protect the border, across which flood "Made in
Nigeria" imports from China.

The inability to capture the potential of cities to foster economic density is in
great part due to the thick borders between cities preventing firms from expanding beyond local markets. The economic distance between regions (especially
those connecting the north and south of the country) disconnects firms and
regional economies from national "home-market effects" and dramatically
reduces internal and external economies of scale and scope. Given the country's
population of over 170 million and its growing urbanized middle class, firms in
Nigeria, particularly manufacturing firms with tradable outputs, have a potentially massive home market. The middle class grew from 13 percent to 19 percent of the population from 2003 to 2013 (Corral, Molini, and Oseni 2015).[13]
Not tapping into them constitutes a major opportunity cost, manifested in rising
unemployment and informal employment.

Market fragmentation is evident in the price variations of eight basic commodities between Nigeria's six geopolitical zones, as well as price volatility.
Fragmentation is also seen in the market reach of firms: even though they have

access to a large consumer base throughout the country, most enterprises sell their products only in local markets (figure O.13). Manufacturing industries, however, are much more likely to sell outside the state: 43 percent versus 26 percent in agriculture and 24 percent in financial intermediation.

High transport costs pose a disproportionate challenge to the tradables sector, helping account for the lack of development of these sectors. Highway accessibility—measured as drive time to the nearest federal or state capital—shows large regional variation due to a mix of poor road conditions, urban congestion, and missing highway and bridge connections (map O.3). An estimated 40 percent of federal roads, 65 percent of state roads, and 85 percent of local government roads are in poor or bad condition and require rehabilitation or reconstruction.

The rail network offers scant alternative to roads. A legacy of the colonial era, it stretches across the country and links several major cities, but passenger and freight traffic have been in long-term decline amid deficient performance and erratic service. Traffic density is a tiny fraction of the already low levels found in other African rail systems (Foster and Puschak 2011).

Producers' inadequate access to markets beyond their immediate localities, especially those in large urban agglomerations, sharply lowers the internal economies of scale they can exploit. Such limits on the markets that producers can access reduce regional external economies of scale and scope. Cities and metropolitan regions cannot specialize and develop clusters connected to extraregional supply chains. This severely hampers firm capacities to focus on core competencies, to develop the capabilities and absorptive capacities to compete in broader and more competitive markets (including export markets), to upgrade to more productive activities, and to develop new products and services.

Figure O.13 Roughly 50 Percent of Firms Identify Local Markets (Locality, Town, or State) as the Main Sales Channel

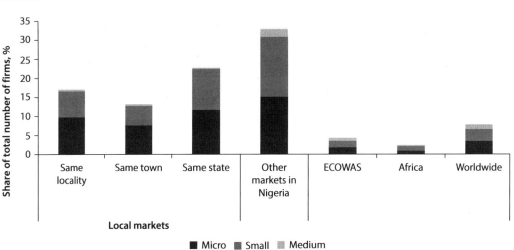

Source: World Bank calculations using SMEDAN 2010 survey.
Note: ECOWAS = Economic Community of West African States.

Map O.3 Highway Accessibility to the Nearest Federal or State Capital

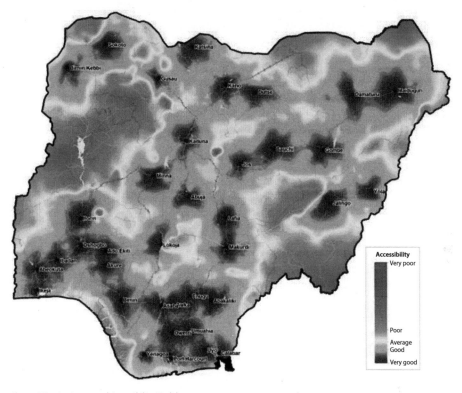

Source: Nigerian Integrated Accessibility Model.

Firms have the potential to overcome urbanization diseconomies and inefficiencies through clustering, but limited connectivity across and within regions has kept firms from relocating. Clusters generate positive agglomeration economies at the subregional level (localization economies) by concentrating specialized and interlinked firms within the region, either through conscious public or private initiatives (special economic zones) or spontaneously, as an initial concentration of firms attracts more workers and firms, generating a snowball effect. The proximity of specialized firms within an industry allows them to cooperate in pursuit of external economies of scale and scope, and to work together toward meeting market needs through product and process innovations and product differentiation.

Market fragmentation has particularly negative effect on the clustering of manufacturing industries. International experience suggests that at lower levels of development, manufacturing initially concentrates in large cities where it can exploit agglomeration economies. In China, for example, cities with more than 2.5 million people specialize in manufacturing, evidenced by a location quotient of 1.3. Medium and smaller cities do not show such specialization, having a location quotient below 1. With the agglomeration economies in large cities comes innovation, and, as time passes, the techniques that initially gave industries their advantage become standard, and economies of scale become more important than innovation. When this happens, manufacturing moves to medium-sized cities and later to small cities. But at the state level, the relationship between urbanization and manufacturing concentration is negative.

High interregional transaction costs are due to stark administrative differences between states and the high cost of transportation across regions. The freight costs for transporting a ton of goods inside Nigeria is higher than to ship the same load from Europe to China. Such high costs stem not only from the poor quality of roads and highways, but from institutional obstacles, including multiple road blocks (figure O.14). The cattle and leather trade, for example, along the Lagos-Kano corridor faces many unjustified charges and barriers, which raise transport and related costs by 18 percent and journey times by 23 percent (Coste 2014). Similarly, the Lagos-Kano-Jibiya corridor had 4.5 roadblocks and traders were required to pay an average of US$11.50 in bribes per 100 kilometers (USAID 2013), far higher than along other corridors in West Africa, even though many of them cross national borders.

Poor connectivity and market fragmentation have contributed to growing regional inequalities. Trucks running empty from the north to the south illustrate how traditional north-south trade routes have been undermined by the recent industrial decline of northern states and the poor infrastructure connecting the north to the rest of the country. Box O.1 outlines the rise and fall of manufacturing in Kano, the largest city and commercial capital in the north.

This growing inequality is reflected in the size of states' economies and per capita incomes (map O.4). Except for the FCT, GDP is largely concentrated in the south, while GDP per capita is notably lower in the north. The average GDP per capita of the northern states is just US$1,153, against US$2,432 for the southern states and US$5,612 for the FCT.

Figure O.14 Number of Roadblocks per 100 Kilometers (2011)

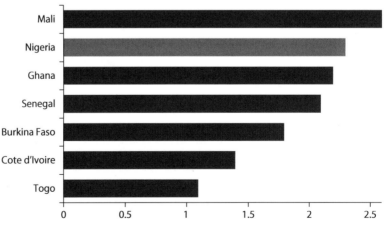

Source: Coste 2014.

Box O.1 Kano: Northern Commercial Capital

Kano is the commercial and administrative center of northern Nigeria, with a rich history dating at least as far back as the eleventh century, when physical planning of the city began in 1095 with the construction of its city wall. Since Nigeria's independence in 1960, its urbanization, population growth, and economic restructuring have been tremendous. Yet, today its gross domestic product (GDP) is smaller than its population share, estimated at about US$10 billion and equivalent to only 4 percent of national output.

In the 1960s, Kano was the most industrialized state in Nigeria. Run under strong business-civic leadership and entrepreneurship, it was the economic powerhouse of the north. The regional economy specialized in tanning and leather working, textile manufacturing, agricultural processing and, later, plastics. And although Lagos overtook Kano as the country's most industrialized city in the 1980s, it remained host to over 2,500 manufacturing firms.

Over the past two decades, however, the Kano economy has declined and deindustrialized. Kano State currently has just 350 large and medium manufacturing firms, many in Kano City. Most are operating at low capacity utilization, despite an increase in this metric in Nigeria as a whole.

By 2011, two-thirds of the tanneries had closed, for a loss of 16,000 jobs, and only five were still running in 2013. The same story of decline characterizes leather industries, with most factories having shuttered and survivors specializing in low-productivity, low-value-adding activities.

Once known as the Manchester of Africa for its dynamic textile industry, Kano today has seen that industry all but collapse. At its peak, the city employed about 350,000 textile workers in 175 businesses; 30 textile firms were operational in 1990 employing about 50,000 workers. Today a mere six factories have survived, with only three working at near full capacity.

The industry is highly uncompetitive due to its weak business climate, particularly inadequate access to electricity. According to the Growth and Employment in States program financed by the World Bank and the UK Department for International Development (DFID), the state experiences the equivalent of 16 days of electricity outages per month, making it the worst-hit state in the country. These weaknesses, among others, mean that local textile firms cannot compete with cheaper imports from China. Despite a ban on the imports of textiles, over US$2.2 billion of apparel is smuggled into Nigeria through Benin every year, according to the World Bank. Nigeria's production has declined to a paltry US$40 million a year, disproportionately affecting the economy of the north, and of Kano in particular.

Business surveys in the city also highlight the high costs of raw material and the lack of government support for business (figure BO.1.1). It takes 40 percent more time to start a business and enforce contracts in Kano than the rest of Nigeria.

Other problems revealed in business surveys are the cost of capital and difficulty in accessing financing for working capital, and more recently security concerns as the conflict with Boko Haram affects the city.

box continues next page

Box O.1 Kano: Northern Commercial Capital *(continued)*

Figure BO.1.1 Factors Affecting Business in Kano

Score	Factor affecting the business
2.1	Road conditions
3.1	Traffic congestion
3.4	Water supply
4.2	Electricity/power
2.9	Drains and drainage
2.9	Solid waste collection
3.0	Security in kano
3.6	Government assistance
2.2	Labor supply
2.3	Labor skills
2.3	Demand for products
3.5	Raw material costs
2.3	Transport to other cities
2.5	International connection
2.9	*Average for Kano*

■ Good in Kano
■ Neutral; neither especially good nor especially bad
▨ Bad in Kano

Source: Nigeria Infrastructure Advisory Facility Survey Kano, June 2013.
Note: N = 73.

The business climate is exacerbated by an inefficient and often dysfunctional political economy due to rent seeking, "elite capture", and corruption endemic to many regional economies in Nigeria.

On a positive note, a survey conducted by the Manufacturing Association of Nigeria and the Nigerian Association of Small Scale Industries in 2013 revealed that enterprises in Kano consider the city a good place for running a business and are optimistic about the future, as reflected in an increase in workers employed by them from 2011 to 2013, consistent with national growth of manufacturing from 2010 to 2013.

Source: Miles 2013.

Map O.4 GDP and GDP per Capita by Nigerian State, 2010

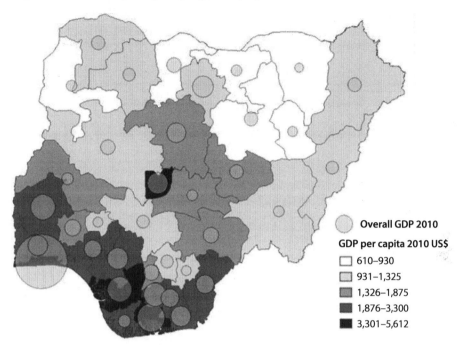

Overall GDP 2010

GDP per capita 2010 US$

- [ ] 610–930
- [ ] 931–1,325
- [ ] 1,326–1,875
- [ ] 1,876–3,300
- [ ] 3,301–5,612

Sources: Original map in URN 2014 Economic Development in Urban Nigeria; data from National Bureau of Statistics.
Note: GDP = gross domestic product.

Urbanization Has Generated Few Gains in Living Standards

Urbanization has not been a major catalyst for improving living conditions, largely due to the failure of urban economies to create widespread jobs. Much more needs to be done to promote more inclusive growth and to reduce urban poverty.

Some evidence suggests that poverty in Nigeria has declined sharply in recent years, but measuring poverty, particularly its incidence in urban and rural areas, is very difficult. Official survey data from 2010 showed that 62 percent of Nigeria's population lived below the poverty line of ₦53,674 per day (based on consumption of 3,000 calories per day), down only slightly from 64 percent in 2002 (World Bank 2014b). Nonetheless, some evidence suggests that these estimates underestimated consumption, and recent estimates suggest that the national poverty headcount may be only 33 percent.[14] It also suggests that while rural poverty remains above 44 percent, urban poverty is only 12.6 percent (World Bank 2016). However, as the urban-rural classifications behind these estimates have not been updated since 1991, the many people living in peripheral areas are categorized as rural poor, making it difficult to compare poverty rates between rural and urban areas.

Even though the impoverished and vulnerable share of the population has declined, perceptions of poverty have actually worsened and few citizens have entered the "global" middle class (defined in figure O.15). From 2003 to 2013, Nigeria's middle class, or nonvulnerable population, calculated as those having a less than 10 percent chance of falling into poverty, increased from 13 percent of the population to 19 percent (Corral, Molini, and Oseni 2015). Yet over this period, Nigeria still did not develop a global middle class (figure O.15). Indeed, perhaps the most important indicator of the slow pace of poverty reduction is that from 2004 to 2010 the number of Nigerians defining themselves as poor actually rose, from 76 percent to 94 percent. Thus given the difficulty in measuring urban and rural poverty, the focus here is on the more measurable aspects of urban living standards, rather than absolute income and consumption poverty.

Narrow gains in living standards are a consequence of limited access to basic services, high costs of urban transport that keep people from jobs, and deteriorating environmental conditions. These challenges face most of the 43 million people who came to Nigeria's cities from 1990 to 2010—and unless things change, will mark the rapid growth of the next decades, when the country's urban population is expected to rise to 55 percent of the total by 2020 and to 71 percent (278 million) by 2050.

Figure O.15 Share of Nigeria's Nonvulnerable and Middle-Class Populations (%)

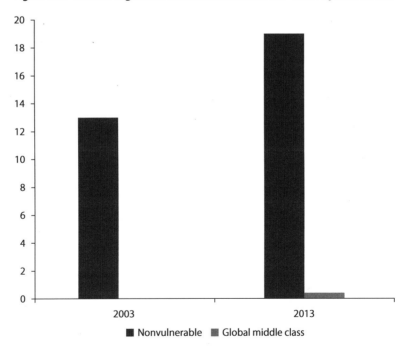

Sources: Corral, Molini, and Oseni 2015; World Bank calculations using ProvcalNet, an interactive computational tool for estimating the extent of poverty.
Note: Nonvulnerable is based on a threshold relating to the expenditure associated with a 10% probability of falling into poverty, calculated by Corral, Molini, and Oseni (2015). Global middle class is defined as US$10–US$100 per day consumption (Kharas 2010).

Urban Settlements Are Not Enabling the Transition to Better Living Standards
Despite an emerging middle class in many of Nigeria's cities, the majority of the urban population still lives in informal housing that has poor access to basic services. Informal housing consists of shelter conditions outside accepted legal and regulatory standards and is often self-financed and constructed by the owner. These areas also lack adequate infrastructure and are in urban peripheral areas. The poorest residents of Nigeria's cities, most of whom live in informal developments, face increasing marginalization and exclusion. A worrying finding from a recent survey in three informal settlements in Lagos revealed that a large percentage of respondents had lived there for more than five years, while many were born there, suggesting intergenerational immobility (Akinwale and others 2013).

Informality is the norm in housing markets, and most Nigerians in urban areas live in informal settlements. Although slums, conventionally understood as shanty towns, are actually quite rare, the word is often used to describe the unplanned, generally substandard housing where the majority of the population lives. The Government of Nigeria, using the UN Habitat definition of slums, estimates that the overall slum population had declined from 73 percent in 1990 to 60 percent in 2009; other estimates, however, put the number of slum dwellers as high as 80 percent. Formal housing is expensive to build and thus unaffordable to most of the urban population; informal housing is both easy to produce and affordable, but lacks access to basic services.

Housing interventions by federal and subnational governments have been unable to achieve even unambitious targets. Two federal government housing schemes between them supplied just 48,370 houses over seven years (table O.1). State governments have fared little better. For instance, according to the 2012 data from the Lagos State Ministry of Housing and Lagos State Bureau of Statistics, from 2001 to 2010, the Lagos State government constructed just 3,549 housing units. Informal housing is thus the only choice for the majority of urban residents.

The result is the incremental expansion of unplanned settlements on unoccupied land on the urban periphery, concentrating the poorest residents at city margins and increasing their risk of exclusion. These settlements are often characterized by slum-like conditions, which carries high risk of exposure to disease, violence, and insecurity. Educational outcomes also tend to be limited: indeed, Nigerian children living in slums are 35 percent less likely to attend school. The school drop-out rate for women living in slums is also high: 27 percent leave school early as a result of pregnancy and early marriage (ages 15–24) against 16 percent for nonslum dwellers.

Table O.1 Federal Government Housing Schemes

Period	Intended number of housing units	Number of units produced	Percentage completed
1981–85	200,000	47,234	23.6
1994–95	121,000	1,136	0.9

Source: Background paper for Nigeria Urbanization Review.

Urbanization often increases short-term disparities, but should help generate longer-term convergence (World Bank 2009). Instead, restricted mobility and too few urban jobs have led to persistent regional inequality, in terms of living conditions and economic activity, with poverty rates starkly higher in the North than in the South (map O.5). Recent NBS poverty data show that poverty has been reduced in the South West, South East, and South South zones and the North Central zone (including FCT/Abuja). But change is minimal in the North West, while poverty has increased in the North East, undoubtedly exacerbated by (and contributing to) the conflict with Boko Haram.

Limited Access to Basic Services

Few informal settlements are connected to trunk infrastructure, and the majority of urban households lack access to basic services. Informal settlements are not on the service grid and so residents must pay other providers, which is almost always more expensive. In Lagos State, the cost of buying informal water and garbage pickup is 1.3–3.0 times greater than the tariffs charged by the state.

According to the 2013 Nigeria Demographic and Health Survey, 76 percent of urban households had access to an improved drinking water source, compared with 49 percent in rural areas. But just 5.5 percent of urban households had piped water to the dwelling, and a further 9 percent had access to piped water in the yard or a shared public standpipe. The vast majority not connected to the water supply grid must use other sources such as boreholes, protected wells, or water tankers.

Just 35 percent of urban households have access to improved sanitation, against 27 percent in rural areas. Only Lagos and Abuja have sewage systems, however, and even in these two cities the majority of households are not connected, which means that just 6.1 percent of urban households have a pour or flush toilet connected to a piped sewer system.

Map O.5 Poverty Headcount by State, 2004 and 2010

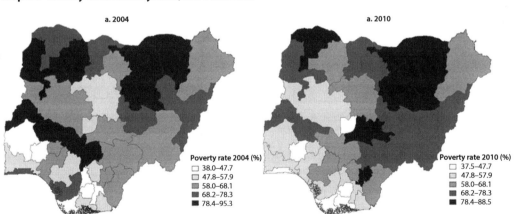

a. 2004

a. 2010

Poverty rate 2004 (%)
- 38.0–47.7
- 47.8–57.9
- 58.0–68.1
- 68.2–78.3
- 78.4–95.3

Poverty rate 2010 (%)
- 37.5–47.7
- 47.8–57.9
- 58.0–68.1
- 68.2–78.3
- 78.4–88.5

Source: Bloch and others 2015.
Note: Data are not directly comparable to General Household Survey results. They are presented just for illustrative purposes.

The majority of solid waste in urban settlements is disposed of or recycled informally, and therefore is not subject to public oversight, raising the risk of generating health hazards. State-managed waste collection services are often tied to land formality, excluding the majority of households living in informal settlements. Even where formal collection is available, high costs are a barrier. Many households and businesses therefore rely on informal-area dumps or collection by cart. Recyclables are collected by waste-pickers and scavengers, or are sold directly to local merchants and to a raft of micro- to medium-sized separation and recycling enterprises.

A relatively high, 84 percent of the urban population has access to electricity in Nigeria, but only 34 percent of rural dwellers do. And even in urban areas poor reliability and incessant power outages mean connection to the grid is no guarantee of supply. Many homes and businesses instead must rely on a generator.

High Costs of Intra-Urban Transport Disproportionately Affect the Poor

Transport costs and congestion deepen urban divisions: the poor spend over half their income on transport, and suffer most when land is developed without proper access to high-quality, high-capacity public transport. In FCT/Abuja, Kano, and Lagos, low-income households spend far more of their income on public transport than middle- and upper-income households (figure O.16).[15] The urban poor also spend more time travelling, thereby experiencing a poorer

Figure O.16 Household Public Transport Expenditure by Household Income, Three Nigerian Agglomerations (%)

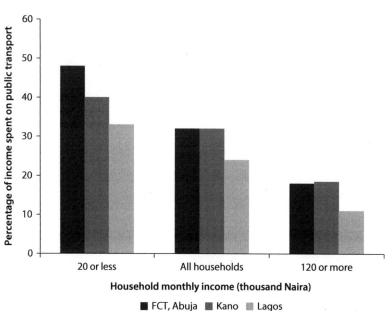

Source: FCT 2013 Travel Demand Survey/Kano 2012 Travel Demand Survey/Lagos 2012 Travel Demand Survey.
Note: FCT = Federal Capital Territory.

work-life balance and sleep deprivation. Lacking affordable transport, most urban residents walk to work, limiting their access to jobs.

Public transport trips in FCT/Abuja, Kano, and Lagos are longer than other world cities. Average trip length for vehicle drivers is 13.5 kilometers (km), 12.2 km, and 13.9 km, in the three cities respectively, compared with 16.1 km, 15.1 km, and 12.6 km for passengers on public transport (figure O.17). The average duration of trip is longer for those traveling on public transport (51–56 minutes) than for vehicle drivers (36–54 minutes) in all three cities, because of indirect routes and lower average speeds. For all journeys, public transport passengers moved at just 14–19 km an hour, compared with 16–23 km an hour for vehicle drivers.

Low-density planning that is not coordinated with the extension of transport networks raises costs to the poor. In the three cities, most poor people live on the periphery of the agglomeration, while employment, retail, leisure, and other activities are concentrated around the center. Especially in Abuja, this means that the urban poor travel longer and spend more of their income on transport than their more affluent counterparts. Metropolitan Lagos is more "polycentric" than the more monocentric FCT/Abuja and moderately monocentric Kano, with its 28 town centers and hundreds of residential settlements. Yet even in Lagos, poorer households are disproportionately affected, though to a lesser degree.

Figure O.17 Average Trip Length for Passengers on Public Transport, Selected Cities across the World (Kilometers)

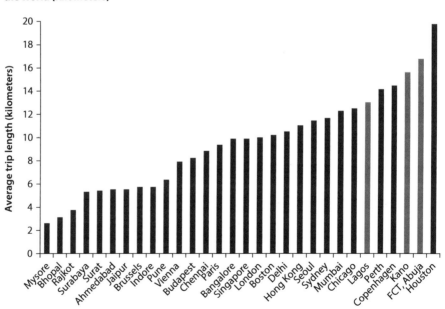

Sources: Data, Kenworthy and Laube 1999; UITP 2006; EMBARQ 2012.

From Oil to Cities • http://dx.doi.org/10.1596/978-1-4648-0792-3

Diagnosing Nigeria's Urban Challenges: Institutions, Infrastructure, and Interventions

Nigeria's current urbanization model is unsustainable. Not enough jobs have been created, productivity growth has been weak, and poverty remains high. Yet urbanization should be a catalyst for solutions, rather than a source of economic and social problems.

The previous section highlighted two general challenges for urbanization in the country and several manifestations of these challenges (table O.2).

The country's urban challenges can be tackled through solutions that focus on interrelated problems with institutions, infrastructure, and interventions. These include:

Institutions for land, service provision, and finance. At the heart of limited job growth is a poor business environment. This stems from institutional deficiencies in urban land management and uncoordinated institutional responsibilities for urban planning, rules for basic service provision, and inadequate urban finance. Clarifying land rights and management systems will let people move and trade more easily and allow cities to better plan and tax for sustainable expansion. Reforming the rules for basic service provision will enable services to reach the urban poor, helping improve living conditions and reduce poverty. Improving urban finance will enable local governments to generate funds outside oil revenue–based transfers, and thus to finance much-needed local infrastructure.

Infrastructure. Nigeria requires far more investment in infrastructure and urban services. Within cities, substantial investment is needed to expand utilities and enable them to reach all areas, including slums. Both within and across cities, systems suffer from a lack of connectivity. High market fragmentation

Table O.2 Urban Challenges and Their Underlying Causes

Urban challenge	Underlying causes
Limited employment creation and productivity growth	
Poor business environment	Weak land tenure and poor land management
	High costs of registration
	Poor infrastructure
	Heavy urban congestion
	High levels of corruption and poor judiciary
Market fragmentation	Lack of regional transport infrastructure
	Administrative/institutional inconsistencies
Few gains in living conditions in urban settlements	
Limited access to basic services	Poor land management and urban planning
	Lack of interjurisdictional coordination
	Insufficient infrastructure investment
	Inadequate local revenue sources
	Poorly designed intergovernmental expenditure responsibilities
Distance from jobs and services	Poor intra-urban connectivity
	Expensive public transport

From Oil to Cities • http://dx.doi.org/10.1596/978-1-4648-0792-3

reduces labor mobility, prevents clustering and attendant agglomeration effects, and increases transport costs within cities, keeping workers from jobs and people from services. Investment in interregional corridors and mass urban transit will improve connectivity, boost productivity, and help reduce regional disparities.

Interventions. Institutional reforms and greater infrastructure investment will go a long way toward generating a national urban system conducive to job-creating enterprises and poverty reduction. But additional targeted interventions will be necessary: within individual cities to improve living conditions in slums and within regions (particularly in the north) to make up for market shortfalls. The following three sections discuss these urban solutions.

Institutions for Land Management, Service Provision, and Urban Finance

Three strategic institutional reforms are needed to unlock growth:

- Clarifying land rights and management systems to let people move and trade more easily, and to allow cities to better plan and tax for sustainable expansion.
- Creating organizations to improve urban management and service delivery.
- Improving urban finance systems to provide resources for new investments and initiatives.[16]

Clarifying Land Rights and Management Systems to Facilitate Investment and Help Cities Plan

Nigeria needs clearer land rights and better institutions for land management. Once in place, they will help improve the business environment, simplify registration for firms, better manage growth of slums, and enable transport infrastructure to match urban densities. Uncertainty over land information and the high costs entailed in discovering the status of land add to costs and risks and slow land-market operations. Transparent systems for ownership, oversight, spatial regulation, and valuation of land parcels in and around cities could help reduce these costs, helping poor and middle-income families access secure holdings to grow their wealth, businesses, and housing.

Nigeria is far behind its peers—countries that show sustained growth—in its national and local institutions for urban competitiveness. Nearly every large country with similar GDP per capita is more advanced in all areas that touch on land institutions. Two key public tools to shape how cities urbanize—land management and planning, and land servicing—are underused. Only a small minority of urban parcels are regulated under any current and enforced land use plan, and a mere 3 percent of properties are estimated to be formally registered (Adeniyi 2011; Bimer and Okumo 2011). And stringent regulations on zoning and use are rarely reflected in implementation: in a 2000 study of Ibadan, for example, 83 percent of homes were noncompliant with city zoning regulations (Arimah and Adeagbo 2000). This points to the incompatibility of regulations with affordability and preferences.

Insecurity of land tenure deepens divisions. Households have little ability to sell their land and move on to greater economic opportunity. The constant risk of losing land makes families also less likely to make investments that could contribute to economic productivity. Because there is no formal system of guarantees, transactions are riskier, with high additional costs that reduce the fluidity of the land market and mobility for people. Transaction costs for land are high: formal fees alone are at 12–36 percent of property values.

Three core constraints prevent the development of healthy markets for affordable and serviced land and housing:

- Local and state governments have little information about the location, ownership, or use of specific parcels.
- Most land claims are insecure, as the legal system for rights does not provide robust protection for customary claims or titles granted by local governance areas, and even state-granted titles are often revoked.
- High barriers and costs to register land mean that few property owners bother registering.

The key constraint to the efficient delivery of land for urban development is that the current legal framework is unsuitable for urban markets or expanding suburban or peri-urban areas. The framework confers all powers of ownership of lands on the state governors and their Land Use and Allocation Committee, and effectively reduces all claims on land to leasehold status, vesting all ownership (freehold) in the hands of the government. In addition, the current legal framework fails to recognize the inherent value of land by only allowing for compensation based on above-ground assets. Consequently, landholders are incentivized to bypass the formal land market and transact directly, out of sight of the government.

Furthermore, procedures for land transactions and subdivision for development are complex, expensive, and time consuming, and state governments are ill equipped to manage and administer the process. Buying, selling, and subdividing land formally is costly due to insecurity of tenure, regulatory bottlenecks, and high fees. For this reason, much urban development is managed outside the formal system. Only 3 percent of properties across the country are estimated to be formally registered (having a certificate of occupancy), and more than 80 percent of growth on the periphery is estimated to be informal.

Clarifying land rights and land management will help urban planning. In the absence of elected municipal or metropolitan governments, state governments are responsible for urban planning and development. Under the Urban and Regional Planning Law, designated urban areas within each state are mapped and gazetted. However, the extent of urban areas as defined is somewhat arbitrary and generally unrelated to the areas subject to greatest development pressure. Urban areas are usually defined in terms of a circle described at 5, 10, 15, 20, or 30 kilometers from the urban center, depending on size or legal status and classification. Such boundaries also fail to match the jurisdictions for which data are collected.

Responsibility for planning within these defined urban areas lies with the urban development authority or board of each state. The absence of municipal or metropolitan authorities with specific and unique responsibility for urban areas seriously compromises the effectiveness of the urban planning system. State governments prepare their urban master plans under the provisions of the Urban and Regional Planning Law, which was designed to reinvigorate Nigeria's rigid planning system (as established through the Land Use and Allocation Committee) and facilitate urban land allocation, transfer, and development. However, the ability of the Urban and Regional Planning Law to enhance the planning system is constrained by its reference back to the planning structure established through the Land Use and Allocation Committee, and by weak institutions.

Most urban master plans are decades old and are too out of date to be used (exceptions include Lagos and Port Harcourt). Even if updated plans existed, the planning tools and capacity to administer, implement, and enforce them are missing. Existing urban master plans provide inflexible development frameworks, inadequate either to guide urban growth and development, or to respond effectively to the proliferation of informal urban expansion. Land use plans are overwhelmingly aspirational, envisaging fully serviced peri-urban developments that are remote from existing urban realities; and concentrate exclusively on high-end, multiuse developments.

The problem of urban planning is not necessarily one of density, but rather one of matching infrastructure and investment density with population density. Relative to the rest of Africa, Nigeria is very densely populated: the only countries in the region more so are small states such as Burundi, Rwanda, and the Seychelles. Nigeria is also fairly densely populated on a global scale, at 50 percent denser than other large developing countries such as Indonesia and Thailand, and it approaches the densities of Germany, Italy, and Pakistan. Cities such as Kano, Lagos, and Port Harcourt are considerably denser than other urban areas of similar population size such as London, Nairobi, and Dar es Salaam (figure O.18). However, Nigeria has very low infrastructure densities, as proxied by the low light-to-population ratio in Lagos (figure O.19).

Missed opportunities to coordinate new development at the city level lead to inefficient development, increase the costs of service provision, and burden commerce and industry with additional expenses. Metropolitan and wider regional plans should provide a framework ensuring that development is efficient and that allows service provision to be coordinated with land development. But few cities have active metropolitan-scale plans for land and service network development. Of those that do, not many are followed, as most development takes place informally and the plans lack regulatory instruments to enforce compliance. The lack of coordination between land use and development, and infrastructure and service provision, holds down growth and exacerbates the challenges of informality.

High-impact areas for policy reform fall along two axes of land and planning in Nigerian cities. First, transparent systems for ownership, oversight, spatial

Figure O.18 Density of Nigerian Cities Relative to Other African and World Averages

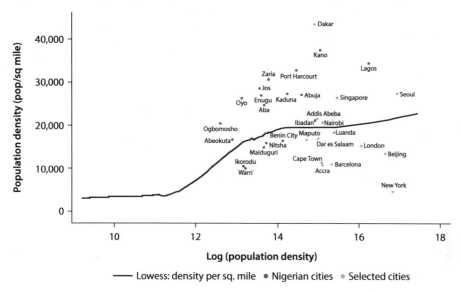

Sources: Demographic World Urban Areas (World Agglomerations) 2013 and own elaborations; World Bank staff calculations.

Figure O.19 Infrastructure-to-Population Ratio, by City Size and Income Group

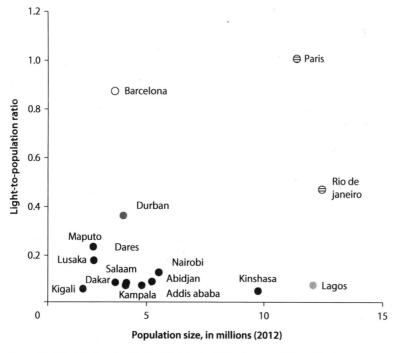

Sources: World Bank (forthcoming), Regional Study on Spatial Development of African Cities; data: VIIRS night lights.

regulation, and valuation of land parcels in and around cities could help reduce the costs of uncertainty over land information and of discovering the land's status. This will help poor and middle-income families formalize their land into secure holdings. Second, even when the status is clear, productive uses of land are hindered by a widespread lack of services and mismatches between infrastructure and land use. Greater coordination within and between public entities inside cities, and between local, state, and national authorities, would allow for more efficient provision of key urban services.

Creating Organizations to Improve Urban Management and Service Delivery

Three interrelated challenges hold back urban management and service delivery:

- There is a "missing" city level to plan effectively, coordinate land use planning with service provision, and develop and manage urban infrastructure and services systems.
- Lack of coordination across jurisdictions and existing capacity challenges within each unit of governance slows service expansion and hinders quality of service provision. At the lowest scale, local government administrations (LGAs) have responsibility for new urban functions but low capacity for performing them and little fiscal and administrative autonomy.
- Weak mechanisms for coordinating between local, state, and federal levels deter successful urban service planning, investment, operation, and maintenance.

Because Nigeria has no specific unit of government for urban areas, they are highly reliant on federal, state, and local governments. Except where metropolitan boundaries roughly (and fortuitously) coincide with state boundaries (such as in Lagos), Nigeria has no city or metropolitan governments with a mandate to provide public goods and services in cities or towns. Under the current constitution, no distinction is made between urban and other subnational governments.

In the absence of city governments, state and local governments are the principal providers of urban public goods and services. State governments (with the possible exception of Lagos as a city-state) are typically bigger than any one city and are expected to deliver statewide public goods and services. They have constitutionally defined functions (such as the provision of judicial services) and powers (such as legislative and regulatory authority) that go far beyond a municipal or metropolitan mandate. States are therefore typically less focused on purely urban priorities than are municipal governments. And the predominant role of state governments as de facto city managers, with a small role for local governments, raises concerns about local accountability and citizen engagement.

Without city or municipal governments, urban public goods and services are provided and financed in a largely ad hoc or residual way. State governments finance and deliver city infrastructure and services as part of a wider set of state-wide public goods and services; local governments (insofar as they are functional) do so within their much smaller jurisdictions and in very modest ways. In practice, state governments are responsible for the management of larger cities (as well as their wider jurisdictions); local governments, enjoy little autonomy and typically operate as deconcentrated arms of their state government.

Local governments have responsibilities for new urban functions, including service delivery, but low capacity and very little authority to implement their mandates in water, sanitation, solid waste, health, and education. States have a great deal of control for investing and expanding service networks, but these tasks are often scattered among multiple agencies, making upward and downward collaboration more challenging. State governments receive and distribute most funds for major infrastructure projects, and continue to subsidize water, sanitation, and waste services, but efforts are often bogged down because of the multiple agencies involved. At the federal level, oversubsidized national industries fail to deliver the supply needed for power, housing, and gas; undermine market operations; and do not appear to improve equity in outcome.

Blurred responsibilities across government levels hinder service network extension and operations. Local and state governments have mandates to deliver services in cities, but are hampered by low capacity, unclear division of responsibilities, and low coordination across jurisdictions. Nonaligned responsibilities at the state level make it difficult for the federal government to find a counterpart. Unclear responsibilities between agencies also mean fluctuations in who is in charge. For example, while local governments generally take responsibility for solid waste disposal, state governments may also step in, as with the Ondo State Waste Management Authority.

Moving toward universal access to basic services will require large investments (the financing of which is discussed in the next section on infrastructure needs in the cities), but these alone will not be enough—good planning is needed. Colombia exemplifies this. Between the early 1990s and 2000s, with a GDP per capita comparable to Nigeria today, it introduced policy reforms that allowed water fees to nearly cover costs, more than doubling the tariff per cubic meter. Because almost 90 percent of households were metered, increases to tariffs reduced excess household consumption, cutting existing demand almost in half, which in turn reduced the need for major new infrastructure (World Bank 2013a). Similarly for electricity, Colombia loosened regulations to permit more companies to join the market and recently became a net power exporter. Furthermore, to reduce the impact on the poorest of tariff increases, following a similar structure in Tunisia and other countries, fees were set to allow higher-income households to subsidize consumption for lower-income households within municipalities, keeping services affordable (World Bank 2014a).

Most important, Nigeria needs to improve institutional arrangements and institutional development. Even if there is very little likelihood of a "big urban bang" in Nigeria's institutional landscape, scope clearly exists for institutional change that may more effectively and efficiently bring about a greater focus on tackling urban issues and service provision. Options include:

- Exploring institutional options for city-wide and city-specific management and key service delivery functions.
- Providing support for city-wide and city-specific management boards, with a mandate to combine city-specific boards to achieve scale economies and the coordination of urban planning.
- Reviving local governments in cities to make them more meaningful actors in identifying and prioritizing public investments and services.

Taken together or singly, these options provide an entry point for engaging with urban development issues.

Improving Systems of Urban Finance to Match Expenditure and Revenue Capacity

Meeting Nigeria's urban development challenges requires substantial financing, particularly for the provision of infrastructure and basic services. The share of GDP spent on infrastructure should double over the next decade to bring current stocks up to satisfactory levels (this is discussed in the following section). Much of this financing will have to come from subnational governments. Assuming that subnational public infrastructure investments need to cover roughly 25 percent of all infrastructure spending, about US$50 billion will be needed over 2011–21. A significant share of subnational infrastructure financing will need to be targeted at investments in urban areas. Although capital financing is high on spending priority lists, it needs to be matched by investments in institutional capacity development and by funding operation and maintenance costs if new infrastructure is to be productive and to deliver urban services on a sustained and cost-effective basis. Putting all this together will be a formidable challenge.

The current intergovernmental fiscal system relies heavily on revenue-sharing allocations from a federally collected funding pool, the size of which varies depending on fluctuations in world energy prices. Between them, state and local governments have regularly accounted for over 50 percent of all public expenditure in Nigeria, but they rely on federal transfers for 85 percent of expenditures.

Subnational public expenditure and financial management performance is generally poor. Even without an urban planning framework, regular investment planning is inferior, public investment management is weak, and actual budget execution is generally far removed from planned budgets. In short, subnational governments do not deliver anything like value for money, and public resources are used inefficiently. In assessing subnational public expenditure on urban public goods and services, it is not just the amounts or institutions involved that matter—the quality of such spending by state and local governments also needs to be taken into account.

Current urban financing challenges relate to functional assignments of expenditure and of revenue. Functional assignments are clearer in some sectors than others. In the roads sector, for example, formal responsibilities are shared, but are relatively well defined and discrete for each tier of government. In other sectors, assignments are less clear cut, particularly for health and education. In practice, federal, state, and local levels often overlap, leading to inefficiency and little accountability.

Unlike many other countries, Nigeria has no municipal or metropolitan governments. Local governments have, for the most part, become marginalized bit players in urban finance, predominantly because the share of federally collected revenues allocated to local governments flows through their state government, providing the latter with the means to "deduct" charges from gross local government allocations. State governments also exercise control over their local governments through expenditure authorization powers, and local government annual budgets are subject to prior approval by state ministries of local government.

A number of factors help explain the generally below-par fiscal performance of subnational governments.

Tax assignments have not provided them with much revenue, and tax collection is very low. As a share of GDP, Nigeria's tax revenue averaged only 3.2 percent from 2003 to 2012, far less than the international average of 17.1 percent (figure O.20). Only 2 percent of GDP is collected through income taxes, against 6 percent in other low-income countries. Value added tax allocations to LGAs are now less than when they constituted a sales tax allocation. The current system allocates 15 percent of value added tax to the federal government, 50 percent to state governments, and 35 percent to LGAs (Khemani 2001).

States do not have the discretion to determine either the tax base or tax rate for any of their own-source revenues. They cannot therefore increase their revenues through upward or downward adjustments to the tax base or rate. The informality of firms and settlements also reduces potential for revenue collection, since a large number of potential tax payers are fiscally invisible.

State and local government tax administration and collection systems are often rudimentary and lack capacity, largely caused by flaws in the tax administration system. Such flaws include highly corrupt tax collectors, inadequate tax legislation and monitoring facilities, inefficient tax collection procedures, and

Table O.3 Revenues by Government Level and Share of Transfers by Source (₦ billion)

	2009	2010	2011	2012	2013
Federal government	2,642.98	3,089.18	3,553.54	3,629.61	4,031.83
State government	2,590.50	3,162.50	3,410.10	3,572.60	3,836.90
- *Transfers from federal government (%)*	74	67	82	77	83
Local governments	1,069.30	1,359.20	1,636.20	1,648.10	1,810.10
- *Transfers from federal government (%)*	96	97	96	94	98
- *Transfers from state government (%)*	2	1	2	1	1
Total revenues	6,302.78	7,610.88	8,599.84	8,850.31	9,678.83

Source: Central Bank of Nigeria.

Figure O.20 Tax Collection as a Share of GDP

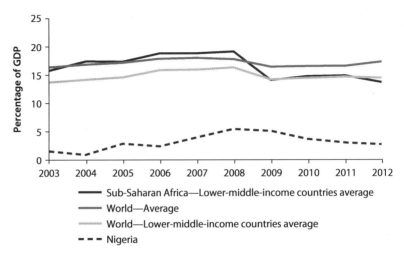

Source: World Bank, World Development Indicators.

outdated data and information systems. All these factors create strong incentives for individuals and corporations to evade taxes, although some states have improved their tax administration (such as Lagos and Edo) over the years.

Large amounts of revenue derived from federal transfers scuttle most of the incentives to increase locally generated revenues. With few exceptions, state and local governments are fiscally dependent on their shares of federally collected revenues, which in turn are highly dependent on oil. In the past five years, transfers from the federal government have accounted for about 67 percent of state government revenues and about 94 percent of local government revenues. The preponderance of revenue sharing in subnational government revenues provides a substantial source of finance, mobilized with minimal fiscal effort, which does little to encourage subnational governments to collect what they could as internally generated revenues.

State and local government dependence on their shares of federally collected revenues exposes them to fiscal uncertainty and fluctuations. Because 75 percent of federally collected revenues are derived from oil and gas revenues (World Bank 2013b), all three tiers of government are highly vulnerable to fluctuations in world energy prices. Although subnational fiscal reliance on transfers from central government is not entirely exceptional, what is unique about Nigeria is its subnational governments' dependence on federal revenues that are largely determined by global energy prices. Federally collected revenues are subject to the same kind of fluctuations as global oil prices, exposing subnational governments to the same unpredictability in revenues. Nigeria was one of the top-five countries for volatility of real government revenues per capita over 2000–2005, at 2.5 times the volatility of 1991–2000 (Addison 2007).

Urban finance systems can be reformed in several ways:

• Coordinate between governments to mobilize resources and manage invest-ments and services delivery. Nigeria should align functions and finance with urban jurisdictions to strengthen accountability and maximize resource mobi-lization. In particular, it should consider institutional arrangements that strengthen the fiscal position of local governments. Local government provides a framework for improving accountability and enhancing local voice, as well as for directing finance to where it is needed. Hardwiring local governments into the framework of city-specific authorities (such as Enugu Capital Territory Development Authority would be one way of doing this.

• Provide earmarked finance for urban development. Subnational govern-ments enjoy much discretion in budget choices: their allocations from feder-ally collected revenue pools amount to unconditional grants, and they are free to spend their IGR as they wish, as long as this is broadly consonant with their constitutionally defined mandates. Improving the extent to which sub-national governments address urban development challenges may therefore require providing them with access to funds earmarked for that purpose. Another way would be to craft and foster single-purpose or sector-specific urban authorities (such as Lagos Metropolitan Area Transport Authority or the Solid Waste Management Authority in Oyo State) and then earmark finance for these types of authority.

• Strengthen own-source revenue (OSR) collection and administration. Although the current system of sharing federally collected revenues provides few incentives for greater subnational fiscal effort, the IGR performance of a few states points to room to substantially increase own-source revenues. External lending (through instruments such as Development Policy Operations can be used to leverage greater fiscal effort at the state level. Much can also be done to modernize and upgrade subnational revenue collection and adminis-tration systems. More own-source revenues not only add to the pool of avail-able financing, they also provide state governments with more leverage to borrow domestically and externally.

• Promote public-private partnerships. This would likely help financially stretched subnational governments, especially in urban areas. Reducing the transaction costs of establishing and managing such partnerships should be a consideration.

• Improve state and local finance managerial skills. This requires providing state and local governments with support. There is much to be done, most of it via technical assistance and capacity development. A relevant model is the Nigeria Infrastructure Advisory Facility, which has a good track record of providing federal and state governments with assistance for infrastructure development.

- Restructure the transfers system. The revenue-sharing formula has knock-on effects on the resources to finance urban development. A large proportion of subnational government revenues is determined by the sharing formula that drives federal allocations. The formula for horizontal sharing is heavily weighted toward "equality" of states and local governments, such that each state or local government (irrespective of its size or other characteristics) receives an equal share of 40 percent of the funding pools. This means that smaller states and local governments get much higher per capita allocations (Boex and Alm 2002).

Current revenue allocations give little consideration to the needs of each subnational government entity and fail even to consider performance in service delivery, including access rates. Other countries have tried various structures to increase the transfer system's effectiveness and efficiency. China, for example, has piloted a performance-based grant system providing fiscal incentives for provinces and municipalities to reduce fiscal gaps at county and township levels. Grants are distributed based on the fiscal performance of local governments. Tunisia has piloted a grant system in which the central government provides fiscal incentives to local governments that increase spending on areas such as education, health, and water (World Bank 2014a). Many countries, including Bangladesh, Ghana, Nepal, Tanzania, and Uganda, have already implemented a performance-based grant system nationally.

But in Nigeria, revenue sharing is often seen as an entitlement rather than a transfer, making the linkage of revenue share to performance politically infeasible. A starting point would therefore be to apply such linkage to earmarked funding from federal to state budgets.

Infrastructure Needs in the Cities

Nigeria's cities face a formidable challenge in addressing their massive public infrastructure needs. McKinsey (2014) estimates that, compared with India, Nigeria has one-seventh the roads per kilometer and less than one-fifth the electricity generation capacity per person. Infrastructure investments are needed across a range of sectors: transport, water supply, solid waste management, and housing.

Much more needs to be done to bring Nigeria's infrastructure stock up to a satisfactory level, in coverage and quality, even if the country has relatively advanced power, road, rail, and ICT networks that cover extensive areas. A recent report (AfDB 2013) estimates that infrastructure investments across a broad spectrum of sectors for 2011–20 need roughly US$350 billion to meet the objectives set out in the government's medium-term Vision 20: 2020. According to the report, spending on infrastructure amounted to 4.6 percent of GDP in 2011, should peak at 12.6 percent in 2016, and then decline steadily to about 9.6 percent by 2020. Of this, about US$193 billion will be needed for public infrastructure and US$92 billion for private infrastructure. Current investment of 7 percent of GDP in infrastructure is above the average for Sub-Saharan Africa, but below that of other developing countries, such as China.

There are four critical areas for such investment:

- Utilities infrastructure, including electricity, water distribution, and sewerage, which are essential for business development and urban livability.
- Housing, the supply of which is considerably below demand.
- Interregional corridors, which can dramatically reduce economic distance between regions and cities, lowering barriers to firm growth, value-added activities, and city specialization.
- Mass transport in cities, which can be the best way to relieve congestion and lower transport costs, which will benefit the poor especially.

Expand Utilities Infrastructure for Business Development and Urban Livability

A priority for utilities infrastructure is improving reliable access to electricity. As already noted, Nigerian businesses identify the lack of reliable electricity as the greatest obstacle to their operations.

Lack of sanitation hurts productivity. Abuja and some areas in Lagos aside, no urban community in Nigeria has a sewerage system, largely because of the dearth of investment and the lack of coordination among the three tiers of government. The World Bank's *Doing Business* report shows that the absence of basic sewerage raises costs for commercial construction, as these needs must be addressed nonsystematically by the entity responsible for building.

Rapid annual urban population growth has made it difficult to meet piped-water demand. From 2004 to 2013, while Nigeria's urban population grew from 38 percent of the total to 46 percent, urban access to improved water sources stagnated at 79 percent. According to the WHO/UNICEF Joint Monitoring Program (JMP) for Water Supply and Sanitation, it is estimated that, country-wide, house connections to urban water supplies declined from 32 percent in 1990 to only 8 percent in 2010 (JMP 2012). Either way, growing numbers of Nigerians in urban areas face water scarcity. The African Development Bank estimates that the cost of upgrading and improving urban water supply will be about US$13 billion over 2011–20.

The public sector has rarely been successful in meeting more than a small portion of the demand for water and sanitation. Many households, often the poorest, must purchase water from private vendors much more expensively than from the public supply. Water supply services, where they exist, are still unreliable, of low quality, and unsustainable. Many water supply systems have extensive deterioration and poor utilization of existing capacities due to undermaintenance, poor operation, and inadequate power supply (World Bank 2014c).

Nigeria's water supply and sanitation sector suffers from an absence of policies to enable efficient and sustainable service provision. Water tariffs do not reflect the cost of services; nonrevenue water is considered costly, perhaps by 50 percent or more; overstaffing in water utilities is rife; no autonomous state water boards exist; perpetual operating deficits deprive the state water boards of funds for maintenance and new investments; and power shortages cause intermittent water services and damage to electromechanical equipment (World Bank 2014).

Lack of financial autonomy is also fundamental to the poor performance of all water utilities, coupled with frequent changes in management. One possible source of financing expansion of basic infrastructure—direct cost recovery from tariffs—is weak and underdeveloped. Most services operate with an uneven stream of national subsidies, channeled through states. Very few have cost-recovery mechanisms or draw on local or state revenues for expenditures. Nonpayment rates of up to 90 percent and widespread illegal connections are major factors.

Similarly, power tariffs are low and poorly collected. The Power Holding Company of Nigeria's household tariff is below cost recovery, and half of revenue is not collected. Illegal connections (and lack of a customer census) are major issues, as with water (Okojie 2009).

Unlocking private capital and competition to fuel expansion in basic services hinges on the public sector stepping up to build frameworks for partnerships as well as "stepping back" from involvement and policies that crowd out potential new entrants. Public-private partnerships or private sector participation can help engage nonpublic actors to assume risk and increase efficiency in delivery or development of services. States and LGAs can be more effective partners with capacity and greater autonomy.[17] For services where cost recovery is possible, decreasing operating and tariff subsidies, dismantling national monopolies, and granting more autonomy to private entrants entail disestablishing government monopolies, as in the power sector.

Investments in infrastructure must be accompanied by investments in institutional reform and capacity development. The recently approved Third National Urban Water Sector Reform Project, for example, is predicated on the need for upfront institutional reforms as a prelude to further infrastructure investments. Getting the institutional framework "right" in urban water supply is an essential precondition.

Make Housing Affordable to Improve Urban Livability

The formal housing deficit is estimated at 20 million–30 million units.[18] Nowhere is the problem more acute than in Lagos, which alone accounts for 31 percent of the estimated national housing deficit. The number of urban poor is set to continue rising and the housing shortage worsening as immigration from rural areas persists.

The chronic housing problems go beyond undersupply of new formal units. The existing housing stock—largely informal—provides shelter for the majority of people because it is the most affordable alternative. The quality of this stock, its connections to infrastructure, and overcrowded conditions must be ameliorated.

Most of the population lacks the means to afford formal housing. At current prices, 55 percent of Nigerians cannot afford a house. Another 25 percent (with daily incomes of US$1.25–2.00) need financial products to increase their investment capacity, and the remaining (richer) 20 percent require the development of financial products to be able to invest in housing (table O.4).

The wide supply gap stems from high housing prices that exacerbate affordability problems. In addition to land planning and bureaucratic bottlenecks, the high costs of housing reflect high construction costs (Centre for Affordable Housing Finance in Africa 2014). Although the price of cement has remained stable in recent years relative to other building materials, a situation helped by government interventions, 90 percent of the components for construction are imported.

The national government has been unsuccessful in increasing the supply of publicly provided affordable housing. Out of the initial target of 60,000 housing units from 1975 to 1980 (Third National Development Plan) and the revised 1976 target of 200,000 housing units, only 28,500 units (less than 15 percent) were provided. A substantial proportion of these units (8,500) were built in Lagos. Similarly, the national housing policy of 1991 planned to provide 121,000 housing units nationwide from 1994 to 1995, but only delivered 2,000 units (Ebehikhalu and Dawam 2015).

The federal budget for housing is low and falling. The Ministry of Lands, Housing, and Urban Development was allocated ₦18.5 billion for 2014, 40 percent less than 2013, amounting to 0.39 percent of the national budget. Of this, ₦5.0 billion is for recurrent expenditure, leaving only ₦13.5 billion for capital expenditure on housing and urban development. If spent on building homes, just 2,700 two-bedroom bungalows could be built at a conservative unit price of ₦5.0 million. With a housing deficit already of over 17.0 million units, this is clearly inadequate (Centre for Affordable Housing Finance in Africa 2014).

Table O.4 Housing Affordability Pyramid for Nigeria

Income range	Income US$/day	Percentage of all households	Maximum affordability HC:Y = 3	Monthly maximum rent levels affordable at R:Y of 10%
Very high	>4.00	5	>US$4,380	>US$12.17
High	2.00–4.00	15	US$4,380	US$12.17
Moderate	1.25–2.00	25 of households can afford housing costing from US$1,370 to US$2,190	US$2,190	US$6.08
Low	0–1.25	55 of households can afford housing costing US$1,370 or less	US$1,370	US$3.80

Source: Centre for Affordable Housing Finance in Africa 2014.

Yet increased budgetary allocations alone will not solve Nigeria's urban housing problems; rather, government efforts should focus on policies and reforms. These should be directed at land management, so as to reduce barriers to market-led housing development and increase housing costs. To reduce the cost of construction, the president launched an initiative, in 2014, to deliver affordable housing units. Under the initiative, land is given to developers for free, and negotiations with manufacturers of building materials take place to sell these materials to developers at factory prices. The government has also taken on the responsibility of negotiating with mortgage operators to increase the affordability of housing for low-income earners. More important, the land policy reforms discussed earlier will be an essential component of creating a policy environment that makes housing more affordable.

At the high end of the market, expanding mortgage financing will increase access to housing. Though growing fast—quadrupling from 2006 to 2011 and reaching US$1.42 billion—the mortgage sector is still small, even for Nigeria's level of development and urbanization (only about 0.5 percent of GDP in 2011). However, among the 3.8 million eligible contributors to Nigeria's Federal Mortgage Bank, only 12,000 mortgages have been provided.[19] Furthermore, interest rates are high, at about 20 percent, five times rates in France, Germany, and the United States (McKinsey 2014).

Upgrade Interregional Corridors to Reduce Market Fragmentation

Nigeria has an extensive transport network relative to other resource-rich African countries, but much of it is in poor condition. In 2013, federal government expenditure on maintenance, rehabilitation, and reconstruction for roads and bridges, rail, aviation, and inland waterways and maritime transport totaled US$3 billion (74 percent, 18 percent, 7 percent, and 2 percent, respectively).

International benchmarks suggest that the federal government should spend a minimum of 1.8 percent of GDP (US$9.1 billion) annually on transport infrastructure—a 204 percent increase over 2013's actual figure. About 1.2 percent of GDP (US$6.3 billion) should be allocated to roads (a 186 percent increase against 2013). Yet the reality is a backlog of federal road and bridge projects due to funding constraints of over 250 projects (new and maintenance). Beyond effects on connectivity and competitiveness, these delays have explicit additional costs of about US$18.8 billion (3.6 percent of GDP).

Invest in Urban Mass Transport to Lower Congestion Costs and Link People to Jobs

Investments to improve within-city connectivity will be important, as traffic congestion costs Nigerian cities an estimated 3–7 percent of local value added. Sprawl and low-density development exacerbate the congestion problem.

International experience suggests that investing in mass transit is better than expanding roads aimed at reducing congestion in cities, but Nigeria allocates very little to this. Integrated public transport systems, such as bus rapid transport and railway mass transit, have jump-started urban mobility in cities such as Curitiba, Brazil; Bogotá, Colombia; Istanbul, Turkey; and Ahmedabad, India. Not only do these systems help move many people affordably, they also have positive impacts on land values, urban growth, and road safety (Hidalgo and Gutiérrez 2013). Even so, successful high-capacity public transport systems such as bus rapid transport and railway mass transit are generally expensive to introduce, require coordination with land planning and existing bus or informal transport systems, and take years to come to fruition.

In all, the African Development Bank estimates that investments of US$40 billion in urban public transport infrastructure will be needed over 2011–20. This will be needed for repairing and rehabilitating roughly 30,000 km of urban and tertiary roads, paving and upgrading almost 15,000 km of urban and tertiary roads, and developing mass transit train and bus systems.

Improvements in connectivity also require coordination with policy and regulatory efforts. Colombia created the National Institute for Infrastructure in 2012, for instance, to manage and coordinate national projects. In Australia, the government brings industry and public agencies together through state logistical councils, funded by the government but made up of private and public actors (World Bank 2010).

Interventions to Reach the Most Vulnerable

Targeted interventions can respond to the needs of poor households, which are mainly in lagging regions and slums. For people in marginalized settlements and poor areas to move forward, a level playing field of regulations, protocols, and services can help jump-start gains in living conditions. Spatially blind policies can make services available to the same extent across a country. For example, several countries have used conditional transfer programs to poor families with solid results on education and health, such as Bolsa Familia in Brazil and Oportunidades in Mexico. Under Bolsa Familia, poor and vulnerable families receive cash transfers conditional on school attendance, regular health checkups, and more.

Enhance Regulations for Starting Businesses and Build Household Assets

Enhancing regulations and protocols can dramatically ease the way for Nigerians to start a business or build household assets. As a start, lowering the cost to formality imposed by land and planning regulations, such as the high transaction costs to exchange land, can help new businesses and families build assets and become mobile. Given Nigeria's variety of tenure types, freehold titling programs alone will not unlock capital (Durand-Lasserve and others 2007). Peru, for instance, now allows abandoned urban parcels to be formalized into community trusts by groups of long-term residents, and the intermediate rights recognized have allowed residents to leverage funding and grants to invest and improve their homes and neighborhoods.[20] This approach can remove the administrative roadblocks that prevent LGAs from partnering to invest in poor neighborhoods.

Protocols and processes for starting a business or moving goods should be streamlined so that ambitious businesses can operate across regions with fewer barriers, and businesses in slums can scale up and access formal markets. In Burundi, reforms created a one-stop shop that reduced business registration from 14 days to 1 day; in the following two years, the number of registered companies more than doubled from 700 to an estimated 1,500 (IFC 2013).

Operate in High-Need Areas

Investing in basic services in high-need areas can improve health and productivity. Such areas include already-built neighborhoods as well as those to be constructed. Planning institutions can use incentives to encourage new development to locate in areas where service networks and other infrastructure is already available or will be provided in the near future. Many informal neighborhoods that are already built and have stable systems of ad hoc land administration with local community leaders could unleash gains in productivity and health by extending the service network, and by encouraging coordination between these systems and formal LGAs.

New interventions will need funding, of course. Current sources for services are centralized, unpredictable, and lack mechanisms for cost recovery, impeding efficient operations and limiting large capital investments. Gathering funding for specific initiatives could be a first step in coordinating across scales. Targeted interventions for service provision and land protocols can overlap through focused locations. In Bogota, for example, living conditions improved for 650,000 of the neediest urban residents after a city program focused on 107 of the poorest informal neighborhoods to legalize plots, expand infrastructure, and add public spaces.

Place-blind investment in social services, such as education and health, can also increase opportunities for the poor and households in lagging regions, ideally with stable funding. National transfers to states, and the state funding system from oil, makes funding imbalanced, and often tips the scales toward better-off areas. Reforming these structures would give states and LGAs in lagging areas and neighborhoods the ability to start addressing their needs.

Semiautonomous funds can be another method of ensuring more regular funding for sectors, such as the structure of the National Health Insurance Scheme or the National Housing Fund. But these will need to be paired with strong oversight mechanisms to ensure that resources are prioritized for areas with high need.

Rewarding innovation and cross-sectoral collaboration in education and health can help good ideas spread. Promising policies are often piloted at a city level, but not necessarily shared. For example in Ibadan, water rates for homes reward higher-density and sustainable development. In low-density areas, each apartment or bungalow is charged ₦2,000 a month, in high-density areas, ₦1,000.

Land allocation systems and other housing subsidies can be streamlined to target the needy. Basing these subsidies on need can greatly increase their impact. Similarly, strategic realignment of the affordable housing and other housing assistance programs could multiply the power of government resources and channel them to address the housing shortage.

Targeted investments in social infrastructure, such as education and training, and health facilities, can also help raise productivity among firms, because healthier and more-skilled workers are more productive. Studies have shown that investments in physical infrastructure (roads, power, and so on) are more effective when combined with human capital interventions. Addressing these deficiencies is vital to economic development in Nigeria, because increased productivity raises demand for labor, simultaneously raising employment and wages.

The Way Forward: Start with Institutions

In the past decade, policy makers have focused their energies and creativity on targeted interventions. Programs that hone in on a specific place or population subgroup can generate impact and can pilot new ideas. Ambitious attempts at place- or people-based interventions in Nigeria have been developed over the past few years. New cities have been designed and constructed from scratch; these include Abuja and the new cities outside Port Harcourt. The new cities have required large investment of public resources, but they have not attracted economic activity, as initially expected. These setbacks do not necessarily indicate failure of the implementing actors as much as the lack of the right institutional and infrastructural context.

Within Nigerian cities, actions have targeted slum removal, but without success. National and local policy makers have invested time and money in thinking about how to address the growth of city slum areas. The focus of these efforts, however, has been to think about slums as areas that have to be cleared. Nigeria has a history of some of the largest slum clearance projects in the world, such as Makoko—an area of Lagos with an estimated half a million inhabitants in 1991 (Simon 1992).

While Nigerian policy makers have chosen to *start* with targeted interventions to address their challenges, international experience suggests that interventions should follow institutions and investment in infrastructure (World Bank 2009). When institutions to support investments and interventions are not in place, resources may be wasted.

Start with institutions. With strong institutions as a foundation, the resulting gains in funding and coordination facilitate the next step—effective investments in infrastructure. This then helps interventions have greater and longer-lasting impact. Three clusters of institutions can change daily lives for Nigerians:

Institutions that regulate land and planning can help cities bridge divisions for existing residents and businesses, and shape future urban growth to minimize congestion costs.

Reengineering the framework for basic service delivery could then deliver the critical ingredients—power, water, transport, affordable housing—for businesses to grow and households to thrive.

Reforms to the public finance system would allow states and local governments to have reliable sources of funds for public investments.

Then move to infrastructure investments. Nigeria requires large investments in infrastructure. Simply to address the backlog in maintenance on existing federal roads will cost an estimated US$18.8 billion (3.6 percent of GDP). Benchmarking analysis suggests that Nigeria will need to nearly triple its current yearly spending of 0.6 percent of GDP on transport infrastructure to just keep pace with the Russian Federation, Australasia, and Central and Eastern Europe. But successful implementation requires the right institutions.

Institutions and infrastructure strengthen interventions. For inclusiveness, Nigeria must extend basic infrastructure and services to all urban residents. Moving toward universal access will require large investments. But investments alone will not be enough, as Colombia's experience makes clear, where a focus on institutional foundations enabled a dramatic expansion in basic service coverage.

Targeted interventions can go a long way in addressing some of the immediate needs of a specific place or people. However, short-term interventions must be crafted to avoid depressing long-term growth. Similarly, interventions can be designed to increase the chances of generating economic returns that can support long-term operations. In Nigeria, given low labor mobility and concentrations of poverty, investments in the north are needed. But the only interventions that make sense are those that would generate competitiveness in cities. To take a recent example, a federal government initiative trained small manufacturers in Bauchi in a new technique, and provided them with bags of a material to help the process. But even if the producers in Bauchi improve output and volume, they will continue to face challenges selling their bags: namely, the high costs of trucking to Lagos.

Starting with institutions will not be easy. It will require a transition in which national and subnational authorities will need to recalibrate their priorities for public investment and design policies. But the life chances of millions of Nigerians depend on this transformation.

Annex: Matrix of Stakeholders and Recommendations

Policy area/intervention	Short term (as soon as possible)	Medium to long term (the next 5 years)	Relevant government institutions and agencies
To provide a transparent and efficient system for land management, service provision, and urban finance			
Clarifying land rights and management systems to facilitate investment and help cities plan	• Setting and enforcing land use rights and development standards, simplifying title registration and strengthening cadaster records, and guiding growth with strategic infrastructure investments • Development frameworks to guide urban growth and development or to respond effectively to the proliferation of informal urban expansion • Supporting capacity development, including professionalizing the Land Use and Allocation Committee and other land administration bodies	• Supporting the development of bridging (or hybridization) strategies between formal and informal urban land development sectors • Assisting in adapting the legal framework to encompass a broader spectrum of ownership types, such as use rights, grazing, or communal ownership, to enable marginalized groups to invest in assets • Assist in developing mechanisms for the delegation and decentralization of land management and administration responsibilities	Federal Ministry of Power, Works and Housing; relevant State House of Assembly Committees; State Ministries of Urban and Physical Planning; local government administrations (LGAs)
Creating organizations to improve urban management and service delivery	• Improving institutional capacity for service network extension and operations • Align responsibilities between agencies and improve coordination across jurisdictions	• Exploring institutional options for citywide and city-specific management and key service delivery functions	Relevant State House of Assembly Committees, State Ministries of Urban and Physical Planning, State Ministries of Works and Housing and Water Resources, LGAs
Improving systems of urban finance to provide resources for new investments and initiatives	• Coordinate between governments to mobilize resources and manage investments and services delivery • Provide earmarked finance for urban development • Improve state and local finance managerial skills • Promote public–private partnerships	• Strengthen own-source revenue collection and administration • Adjusting formulas and improving the oversight of the national transfer system	Federal Ministry of Finance, relevant State House of Assembly Committees, State Ministries of Urban and Physical Planning, State Ministries of Works and Housing and Water Resources, LGAs
To create an enabling and livable environment for businesses and households by addressing infrastructure needs in the cities			
Expand the utilities infrastructure for business development and urban livability	• Improving reliable access to electricity • Upgrading and improving urban water supply and sanitation, including in informal settlements	• Assist in improving the integration of local land	Federal Ministry of Power, Works and Housing; Federal Ministry of Water Resources; State Ministries of Urban

table continued next page

Annex: Matrix of Stakeholders and Recommendations *(continued)*

Policy area/intervention	Short term (as soon as possible)	Medium to long term (the next 5 years)	Relevant government institutions and agencies
	• Repairing, rehabilitating, and upgrading urban and tertiary roads • Targeted subsidies and support to community and private sector organizations for upgrading deficient areas	development and infrastructure provision	and Physical Planning; State Ministries of Works and Housing and Water Resources; LGAs
Make housing affordable to improve urban livability	• Establishing a housing market data observatory • Improving public and social housing production • Engage the informal housing sector • Support for renting along with affordable home loan alternatives (such as microfinance)	• Strengthening the formal finance sector by enabling banks to obtain longer term credit and greater levels of liquidity	Federal Housing Authority, Central Bank of Nigeria, Federal Ministry of Finance, relevant State House of Assembly Committees, State Ministries of Urban and Physical Planning
Upgrade interregional corridors to reduce market fragmentation	• Improve road conditions and enroute facilities across key trade corridors • Rehabilitation, renewal, and modernization of railways		Federal Ministry of Transport; Federal Ministry of Power, Works and Housing; Federal Roads Maintenance Agency; Nigerian Railway Corporation
Invest in urban mass transport to lower congestion costs and link people to jobs	• Support for the development of state mass transport policies and plans • Exploring and developing PPP options for urban infrastructure investments	• Investments in urban public transport infrastructure, including for developing mass transit train and bus systems	Relevant State House of Assembly Committees, State Ministries of Urban and Physical Planning, State Ministries of Works and Housing and Water Resources, LGAs

To support the most vulnerable through targeted interventions

Policy area/intervention	Short term (as soon as possible)	Medium to long term (the next 5 years)	Relevant government institutions and agencies
Enhance regulations for starting businesses and build household assets	• Streamline protocols and processes for starting a business or moving goods • Adapting the legal framework to encompass a broader spectrum of ownership types, such as use rights, grazing or communal ownership, to enable marginalized groups to invest in assets	• Streamline land allocation systems and other housing subsidies	Relevant State House of Assembly Committees, State Ministries of Urban and Physical Planning, LGAs
Operate in high-need areas	• Targeted investments in social infrastructure, such as education and training, and health facilities • Place-blind investment in social services such as education and health for the poor and households in lagging regions • Assist in the development of mechanisms to progressively introduce urban services to established informal developments which are without access to basic urban services	• Semiautonomous funds for ensuring more regular funding for sectors	Federal Ministry of Power, Works and Housing; Federal Ministry of Health; relevant State House of Assembly Committees; State Ministries of Urban and Physical Planning, LGAs

Notes

1. The recent GDP rebasing highlights some improvement in economic diversification (discussed below), but not enough to alter the conclusion that tradable sectors outside oil and gas have seen only limited development.

2. Esource curse refers to a paradox that economies abundant in natural resources have tended to grow slower than economies without substantial natural resources. Dutch disease models in economics demonstrate large natural sectors or booms in these sectors have impacts, often negative, on other sectors by pulling resources in and out of nontrable sectors. Source: Jeffrey D. Sachs and Andrew M. Warner. 1997. Natural Resource Abundance and Economic Growth. Harvard University, Cambridge MA. Available at: http://www.cid.harvard.edu/ciddata/warner_files/natresf5.pdf

3. This average refers to all countries during 1990–2013 with GDP per capita between $610 and $1,030 (both in purchasing power parity)—Nigeria's levels in 2003 and 2012, respectively.

4. In GDP per worker per sector; NBS data in McKinsey 2014.

5. Estimates for urbanization range between 48 percent and 52 percent. An urban settlement is defined as one with a population of 20,000 and above in Nigeria.

6. Nigeria Statistical Data Portal, National Bureau of Statistics; Haver Analytics DLX.

7. African Development Bank. 2013–17 Nigeria Country Partnership Strategy.

8. Despite its lackluster performance over the past several decades, manufacturing emerged as the largest contributor to economic growth in 2013, (22 percent) while a sharp decline in oil and gas (down 13.1 percent) brought down overall growth for the year. However, more time and research are needed before a resurgence in manufacturing can be declared.

9. These congestion costs are based on comparisons with free-flow speeds, which likely overestimate the costs. Additionally, cost estimates are based on aggregate "guestimates" of value of time, based on national wage rates. The use of more detailed figures based on stated preferences would be preferable; the World Bank is undertaking a study along these lines that should lead to more reliable estimates.

10. State-level employment data by industry offers a plausible proxy for the industrial composition of metropolitan regions. The analysis of industrial location was conducted excluding agriculture, and mining and quarrying (including oil and gas), as the location of these sectors is to a great extent driven by natural endowments.

11. A location quotient (LQ) is the industry share of state employment divided by the national industry employment share of total national employment. For example, an LQ=2 means that there is twice the proportion of that sector's employees in the state than the national economy.

12. NBS manufacturing employment data was altered by reducing the number of stated manufacturing workers in Katsina, as per informants' interviews. The data initially showed Katsina to be the largest manufacturing agglomeration, which is widely recognized as incorrect by industry experts and NBS professionals.

13. The authors' definition of middle class as those nonvulnerable (that is, having a less than 10 percent likelihood of falling into poverty) makes comparison with other middle-class definitions tenuous. For instance, using the definition of Kharas (2010), which includes those with $10–100 a day consumption, Nigeria's urban middle class is negligible.

14. A poverty line was calculated from the General Household Survey panel data based on the consumption of 3,000 calories per day as used for the official Nigerian definition of poverty. This generated a poverty line at ₦180 per capita per day in 2010. If an adjustment is made for purchasing power parity (PPP), the line becomes 1.4 dollars per capita per day, close to the 1.25 dollars PPP line used by the World Bank for international comparisons (World Bank 2014b).

15. Data in this section are drawn from travel demand surveys in the FCT/Abuja (2013), Kano (2012), and Lagos (2009, 2012) undertaken by the DFID-funded Nigeria Infrastructure Advisory Facility (NIAF), the largest travel demand survey programs undertaken in Nigeria.

16. Expanding sources of revenue and improving management at the local level is one side of the coin. The other is adjusting formulas and improving the oversight of the national transfer system.

17. Autonomy to State Water Agencies (SWAs), discussed in World Bank. 2000. "Nigeria Water Supply and Sanitation, Interim Strategy Note." November 2000.

18. Estimating up from the 2012 estimate of 17 million from the Federal Republic of Nigeria, National Housing Policy. The estimate is based on target goals of an occupancy rate of six people per house. If people per house were set at current household sizes, it would increase to 30 million units.

19. Keynote address of Nigeria's Minister of Finance, Dr Ngozi Okonjo-Iweala, to the 6th Global Housing Finance Conference at the World Bank, May 2014. http://urban-africa-china.angonet.org/content/unleashing-housing-sector-nigeria-and-africa-keynote-speech-6th-global-housing-finance.

20. Eficencia Legal Para la Inclusion Social (or Legal Efficiency for Social Inclusion) is a nonprofit global institution dedicated to generate and manage sustainable solutions against poverty and under-capitalization. Its mission is to promote the benefits of modernity in the poorer sectors, through the expansion of property rights and the fight against precarization. Eficencia Legal Para la Inclusion Social is located in Lima, Peru. http://www.ielis.org/index.php?fp_dis_abrir=526&fp_idioma=ENG.

References

Addison, D. 2007. "Managing Extreme Volatility for Long-Run Growth." In *Economic Policy Options for a Prosperous Nigeria*, edited by P. Collier, C. Soludo and C. Pattillo. London: Palgrave.

Adeniyi, P. O. 2011. *Improving Land Sector Governance in Nigeria - Implementation of the Land Governance Assessment Framework*. Abuja: World Bank.

AfDB (African Development Bank). 2013. *An Infrastructure Action Plan for Nigeria—Closing the Infrastructure Gap and Accelerating Economic Transformation*. Tunis: AfDB.

Akinwale O.P., A. K. Adeneye, A. Z. Musa, K. S. Oyedeji, M. A. Sulyman, J. O. Oyefara, P. E. Adejoh, and A. A. Adeneye. 2013. "Living Conditions and Public Health Status in Three Urban Slums of Lagos, Nigeria." *South East Asia Journal of Public Health* 3 (1): 36–41.

Arimah, C. B., and D. Adeagbo. 2000. "Compliance with Urban Development and Planning Regulations in Ibadan, Nigeria." *Habitat International* 24 (3): 279–294.

Birner, R. and A. Okumo. 2011. "Challenges of Land Governance in Nigeria: Insights from a Case Study in Ondo State." Nigeria Strategy Support Program Working Paper

No. 22, International Food Policy Research Institute, Washington, DC. http://ebrary .ifpri.org/cdm/ref/collection/p15738coll2/id/126875

Bloch, R., N. Makarem, M. Yunusa, N. Papachristodoulou, and M. Crighton. 2015b. *Economic Development in Urban Nigeria*. Research Report, Urbanisation Research Nigeria, ICF International, London.

Boex, J., and J. Alm. 2002. "An Overview of Intergovernmental Fiscal Relations and Subnational Public Finance in Nigeria." Working Paper 02-1, Andrew Young School of Policy Studies, Georgia State University, Atlanta.

Butler, Stephen B. 2009. "Improving Land Policy for Private Sector Development in Nigeria: Lessons and Challenges Ahead." Paper presented at the World Bank Conference on Land Governance in support of the MDGs, March 9–10, Washington, DC.

Centre for Affordable Housing Finance in Africa. 2014. "Housing Finance in Africa: A Review of Some of Africa's Housing Finance Markets." Parkview, South Africa: Centre for Affordable Housing Finance in Africa.

Corral, P., V. Molini, and G. Oseni. 2015. "No Condition is Permanent: Middle Class in Nigeria in the Last Decade." Policy Research Working Paper 7214, World Bank, Washington, DC.

Coste, Antoine. 2014. *Domestic obstacles to trade and transport in Nigeria and their impact on competitiveness*. Africa Trade Policy Notes No. 42, Washington, DC, World Bank.

Durand -Lasserve, Alain, Edesio Fernandes, Geoffrey Payne, and Carole Rakodi. 2007. "Social and Economic Impacts of Land Titling Programmes in Urban and Peri-Urban Areas: A Review of the Literature." http://www.birmingham.ac.uk/Documents /college-social-sciences/government-society/idd/research/social-economic-impacts /social-economic-impacts-literature-review.pdf.

Ebehikhalu, O. N., and D. P. Dawam. 2015. "A Review of Governmental Intervention on Sustainable Housing Provision for Urban Poor in Nigeria." *International Journal of Social Science Studies* 3 (6).

EMBARQ. 2012. "Transport in Cities: India Indicators." http://www.embarq.org/sites /default/files/12-Indian-Cities-Transport-Indicators-Database.xls.

Foster, V., and N. Puschak. 2011. "Nigeria's Infrastructure: A Continental Perspective." World Bank Policy Research Working Paper 5686, World Bank, Washington, DC.

Gajigo, Ousman, and Mary Hallward-Driemeier. 2012. "Why Do Some Firms Abandon Formality for Formality? Evidence from African Countries." Working Paper Series No. 159, African Development Bank, Tunis, Tunisia.

Hidalgo, Darío, and Luis Gutiérrez. 2013. "BRT and BHLS around the World: Explosive Growth, Large Positive Impacts and Many Issues Outstanding." *Research in Transportation Economics* 39 (1): 8–13.

Iarossi G., P. Mousley and I. Radwan. 2009. *An Assessment of the Investment Climate in Nigeria*. Washington, DC: World Bank. http://elibrary.worldbank.org/doi/abs /10.1596/978-0-8213-7797-0

IFC (International Finance Corporation). 2013. "Business Reforms in Burundi are Lowering Barriers for Small Businesses." Fragile and Conflict-Affected Areas, Stories of Impact, IFC, Washington, DC. http://www.ifc.org/wps/wcm/connect/d2403e8040 7f5639853f95cdd0ee9c33/ready+for+pdf.stories+of+impact.burundi+investment +climate.pdf?MOD=AJPERES

Kenworthy, J., and F. Laube. 1999. "Patterns of Automobile Dependence in Cities: An International Overview of Key Physical and Economic Dimensions with Some

Implications for Urban Policy." *Transportation Research Part A* 33. 691–723. http://www.sciencedirect.com/science/article/pii/S0965856499000063.

Kharas, H. 2010. "The Emerging Middle Class in Developing Countries." OECD Development Centre Working Paper No. 285. http://www.oecd.org/dev/44457738.pdf.

Khemani, S. 2001. "Fiscal Federalism and Service Delivery in Nigeria: The Role of States and Local Governments." Paper prepared for the Nigerian PER Steering Committee.

Meagher, K. 2010. *Identity Economics: Social Networks and the Informal Economy in Nigeria.* Woodbridge, Suffolk: James Currey. ISBN 978-1-84701-016-2.

Miles, N. 2013. "An Economic Analysis of Kano City and its Immediate Region." Nigeria Infrastructure Advisory Facility, Background study.

National Bureau of Statistics. 2011. General Household Survey (GHS) 2010–11. Abuja.

OECD (Organisation for Economic Co-operation and Statistics). 2006. "Food Security and Cross-border Trade in the Kano–Katsina–Maradi K²M Corridor." Joint Mission Report, Sahel and West Africa Club Secretariat/OECD, Paris.

Okojie, Christiana. 2009. "Decentralization and Public Service Delivery in Nigeria." Background Paper NSSP 004, International Food Policy Research Institute, Nigeria Strategy Support Program, Benin City, Nigeria.

Oseni, Gbemisola, Paul Corral, Markus Goldstein and Paul Winters. 2014. "Explaining Gender Differentials in Agricultural Production in Nigeria." Policy research working paper WPS 6809, Washington, DC, World Bank. http://documents.worldbank.org/curated/en/2014/03/19269811/explaining-gender-differentials-agricultural-production-nigeria.

Oviedo, Ana Maria, Mark R. Thomas, and Kamer Karakurum-Ozdemir. 2009. "Economic Informality: Causes, Costs, and Policies—A Literature Survey." Working paper 167, Washington, DC, World Bank.

Oyelaran-Oyeyinka, Oyebanke. 2014. "Industrial Clusters, Institutions and Multidimensional Poverty in Nigeria." Submission to the first Annual Bank Conference on Africa: "Harnessing Africa's Growth for Faster Poverty Reduction", Paris School of Economics and World Bank, June 23–24.

United Nations. 2014. *World Urbanization Prospects: The 2014 Revision.* Department for Economic and Social Affairs. New York: United Nations.

UITP (International Association of Public Transport). 2006. "Better Mobility for People Worldwide." Mobility in Cities database.

USAID (United States Agency for International Development). 2013. "Lagos-Kano-Jibiya (LAKAJI) Corridor Performance: Baseline Assessment Report on the Time and Cost to Transport Goods." Executive Summary, USAID. http://www.carana.com/images/summary_of_findings.pdf.

World Bank. 2009. *World Development Report 2009: Reshaping Economic Geography.* Washington, DC: World Bank.

———. 2010. *How to Decrease Freight Logistics Costs in Brazil.* Washington, DC: World Bank.

———. 2011. "Nigeria 2011: An Assessment of the Investment Climate in 26 States." Report edited by Giuseppe Iarossi and George R. G. Clarke. http://www-wds.worldbank.

org/external/default/WDSContentServer/WDSP/IB/2012/08/17/000386194
_20120817041046/Rendered/PDF/718910WP0Box370Climate0in0260States.pdf.

———. 2013a. *Planning Connecting and Financing Cities: Now.* Washington, DC: World Bank.

———. 2013b. *Nigeria Economic Report No.1.* Washington, DC: World Bank.

———. 2014a. "Tunisia Urbanization Review. Reclaiming the Glory of Carthage." Washington, DC, World Bank.

———. 2014b. *Nigeria Economic Report No. 2.* July. Washington, DC: World Bank.

———. 2014c. Project Appraisal Document: Third National Urban Water Sector Reform Project (P123513). http://www-wds.worldbank.org/external/default/WDSContent Server/WDSP/IB/2014/07/23/000470435_20140723133415/Rendered/PDF/89630 0WP0Niger0Box0385289B00PUBLIC0.pdf.

———. 2016. "More, and More Productive, Jobs for Nigeria: A Profile of Work and Workers." World Bank, Washington, DC. http://documents.worldbank.org/curated /en/2016/03/26066141/more-more-productive-jobs-nigeria-profile-work-workers.

CHAPTER 1

Urbanization in Nigeria

Introduction[1]

Nigeria has a long history of urbanization and urban development that distinguishes it from other Sub-Saharan African countries—and influences the form and trajectory of its contemporary urban transition, as box 1.1 illustrates.

Urbanization, alongside high economic growth, appears in recent years to have reduced high levels of poverty in cities and towns, although the reduction has been limited. The promise of urbanization has not yet been realized. Greater urbanization would help increase per capita incomes, urban employment, and competitiveness and productivity, and improve living conditions. It would also better integrate the national economy in this populous and diverse country (map 1.1) marked by significant and enduring social and economic divisions.

Urbanization and the accompanying physical development in Nigeria is often understandably portrayed as poorly managed, inequitable, exclusionary, and fragmented. Real opportunities and an overriding necessity nonetheless exist for urban reforms in Nigeria that can enable more inclusive, productive, and integrated metropolitan areas, cities, towns, and regions.

This chapter analyzes the key dynamics and trends of Nigeria's rapid, massively scaled and spatially expansive urbanization. It covers urbanization and its drivers, urban expansion, and urban poverty and living conditions.

Rapid Urbanization on a Massive Scale

An estimated 85 million Nigerians now live in urban settlements—about half the total population and about double the 42.8 million at the turn of the century (figure 1.1).[2] Moreover, Nigeria's urban population is still growing rapidly, 4.8 percent a year from 2000 to 2013 on average. The urbanization level rose from 35 percent to 47 percent during this period, higher than the average urban population share of 37 percent of Sub-Saharan Africa. Cities with a population of more than 300,000 doubled, from 21 to 42.

Box 1.1 A Brief History of Urbanization in Nigeria

In contrast to many other Sub-Saharan African countries, Nigeria has been urbanizing since precolonial times, with large urban centers and many small towns and villages. This has created complex urban subsystems that have developed over hundreds of years. More understanding is needed of how these subsystems function in the present and how to harness them to promote economic growth and reduce poverty.

Prior to the entry of European powers in the second half of the nineteenth and the early twentieth centuries, a complex system of urban trading economies existed. This system of towns and cities had been developing since the early medieval period (circa the seventh century) and was particularly evident in the north, where cities such as Kano, Katsina, and Sokoto developed to support Saharan and trans-Saharan trade routes, often bringing together a large number of Hausa and Fulani traders and migrants from adjacent areas. Urban settlements also developed about the same time in the Yoruba part of the country, in the southwest—initially as a consequence of Yoruba colonization—which soon became trading centers themselves.

With the arrival of European explorers during the late fifteenth century, the flow of trade began to orient more toward the coast and harbors, increasing the importance of the Niger and other rivers for transporting slaves and commodities from the heart of the territory. Consequently, new settlements developed in the Niger Delta, including Calabar and Bonny.

The colonial period fostered the development of the Nigerian urban system. Through the 1917 Township Ordinance, three classes of cities (first, second, and third) emerged, contributing to the emergence of urban centers as administrative headquarters (Kaduna and Nsukka) or industrial hubs (Jos and Enugu). The previously rural southeastern part of the country also urbanized. Four core cities in the area—Port Harcourt, Aba, Enugu, and Owerri—were established to support processing and export of raw materials.

Nigeria urbanized rapidly in the period before and after independence in 1960, with the urban population rising from 3.9 million in 1950 to 7.4 million by 1960 and 16.2 million by 1975. City dwellers numbered 34.4 million by 1990.

This significant transformation is closely related to changes in administrative structure: the number of states and Geopolitical Zones increased, establishing newly created state capitals as growth centers, attracting new inhabitants, and hosting a wide array of emerging economic activities, including administrative functions; manufacturing firms in the textile, steel, and automotive sectors; and small business enterprises.

In this phase, and notably from the 1970s, the country used oil revenues to develop urban and transportation infrastructure (highways, bridges, water supply systems) and to promote industrialization, fueling urbanization.

During structural adjustment in the 1980s and 1990s, Nigerian cities simultaneously grew and physically deteriorated: even as they absorbed newcomers, they often lacked the resources to provide appropriate infrastructure and services to burgeoning populations. This decline was closely linked to the collapse of oil prices, which meant a shortage of resources for housing, water supply, security, or waste management. Informal settlements appeared and became a component of Nigerian urban structure at this time.

Source: Bloch, Fox, and others 2015.

Map 1.1 Nigeria: Geopolitical Zones, States, and Capitals

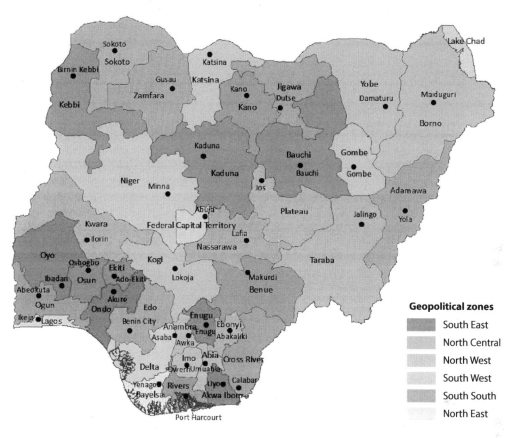

Source: Bloch, Fox, and others 2015.

Figure 1.1 Urban Population as a Share of the Nigerian Total

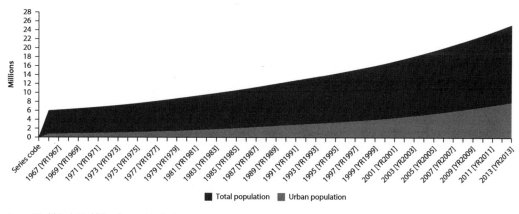

Source: World Bank, World Development Indicators.

Box 1.2 Key Terms

Urbanization: The increase in the proportion of a country's population residing in urban areas.

Urbanization level: The percentage of a country's total population residing in urban areas.

Urbanization rate: The projected average rate of change of the size of the urban population over a given period of time.

Urban population: The total number of people residing in urban areas.

Urban population growth: The increase in the absolute size of a country's urban population.

The urban population is expected to double again within the next 20 years—another 85 million people in already crowded towns and cities, and could surge to 295 million by 2050.

Population growth driven by declining mortality and persistently high fertility are the underlying causes of rapid urbanization in Nigeria (Bloch, Fox, and others 2015). From 1990 to 2013, total under-five mortality declined by 24.6 percentage points, and total fertility declined by just 8.3 percentage points. The resultant population boom is driving urbanization through natural population increase in existing urban areas; in addition, growing population density in rural areas is resulting in the reclassification of what were rural settlements.

Rural-urban migration is a third driver of Nigeria's rapid urbanization and is itself driven by several factors. These include demographic pressure on natural resources in rural areas, (perceived) higher potential incomes and economic opportunities in urban areas, and, particularly in the northeast, conflict in more remote rural areas.[3] Of the three drivers, recent studies have tended to overestimate the importance of rural-urban migration, while understating the importance of declining mortality and persistently high fertility.

In the following discussion of the three drivers, it is important to distinguish between urbanization and urban population growth, which are sometimes used synonymously in the literature, to some confusion (box 1.2). The generally accepted definition of urbanization is that it is the increase in the *proportion* of a country's population residing in urban areas, and urban population growth is the increase in the *number* of people residing in urban areas. Urbanization measures the urban population relative to the rural population; urban population growth measures it in absolute terms.

Natural urban population increase plays an often underestimated role in driving urban population growth. Nigeria's population is booming, leading to rapid population growth in both rural and urban areas. Although fertility rates tend to be lower in urban areas than in rural areas generally, in Nigeria urban fertility rates have remained high at 4.7 and did not change during 2008–13 (Bloch, Fox, and others 2015).

Additionally, the percentage of young adults in urban areas is higher than in rural ones, which may somewhat offset the lower fertility rates in cities. In the 1991 census, 42 percent of the urban population was of the ages 15–39, and 37 percent of the rural population was in that age group. "Natural" population increase therefore likely drove much of Nigeria's urban population growth.

Population growth in rural settlements contributes to urbanization through the reclassification of rural settlements as urban as their populations increase, effectively creating "new" towns. Often overlooked, this is a significant driver of both urbanization and urban population growth, as population is immediately shifted from rural to urban when a settlement reaches a population of 20,000 and above, a threshold in Nigeria for an urban settlement.

Despite common perceptions to the contrary, rural-urban migration is not the main contributor to urban population growth in Nigeria, though its exact contribution is difficult to estimate due to lack of data, and varies considerably across states and cities. No data exist on the absolute volume of migrant flows, but the 2010 Internal Migration Survey indicates that migration to urban areas accounted for 60 percent of flows, compared with 40 percent for migration to rural areas. Thus, the net impact of migration is undoubtedly adding to urbanization and city population growth, though the extent is unknown.

Reflecting the variability noted above, migration caused by conflict in recent years has increased urbanization in the North East Geopolitical Zone, as box 1.3 describes.

In summary, urbanization in Nigeria is often presented as the story of rural-urban migration. This creates the misconception that migration is driving urban population growth when natural population increase is likely the *actual* main driver.

Box 1.3 The Impact of Conflict on Urbanization

Since 2009 an insurgency by the Islamist militant group Boko Haram has displaced more than 1.5 million people in the North East Zone states of Borno, Yobe, and Adamawa, more than half of them from Borno State (*Economist* 2015). Although some of these internally displaced people are now living in camps, many have fled their villages in the countryside, where Boko Haram has more influence, and migrated to the towns and cities in the region.

The dynamics of the displacement vary considerably. Rural inhabitants are fleeing their villages and seeking refuge in the surrounding capitals of the local government areas and in the state capitals Yola, Maiduguri (where some 65 percent of Borno State's internally displaced are now located), and Damaturu. Urban dwellers are seeking safety in Abuja Federal Capital Territory and other state capitals. Conflict has undoubtedly accelerated urbanization in the country's northeast and center. Although accurate estimation is difficult to come by, it is thought that Maiduguri's population may have more than doubled to 2 million due to the influx of internally displaced people (*Economist* 2015). This is adding to pressure on existing urban infrastructure and services.

The Nigerian Urban System

Urbanization is traditionally associated with economic structural transformation toward manufacturing and services and away from agriculture, but cities are also central to greater agricultural output. The efficiency of agricultural production is tied to the urban system, and small cities, in particular, are needed to connect farmers to input and output markets by performing a market-aggregation function. Medium-sized cities, in turn, must be effective logistic hubs for transport of goods, and also to house larger local markets. Finally, large cities, such as Lagos, play an important role in connecting the economy to the world. Because of the agglomeration economies they provide, they also have the potential to become nodes for high-value services.

In short, cities can support and facilitate greater efficiency and thus productivity in Nigeria's economy, both in a transition to more productive agriculture and in economic diversification toward higher value activities.

The Nigerian urban system is composed of one megacity (Lagos),[4] seven metropolitan areas with a population of greater than 1 million, 15 large cities with populations from 500,000 to 1 million, 19 medium-sized cities with populations from 300,000 to 500,000, and a network of hundreds of smaller towns beneath this.

Urban population increase in Nigeria is occurring at all levels: from Lagos and the other metropolitan cities of Kano, Abuja, and Ibadan to other state capitals and smaller secondary and tertiary cities. By 2020, another three cities—Uyo, Nnewi, and Aba—are projected to reach metropolitan size, and by 2030 the number of cities with more than 1 million inhabitants will be 23—just 41 such cities exist in all of Sub-Saharan Africa today.

As table 1.1 shows, cities in all size classes in Nigeria are projected to grow at about 4.5 percent over the next five years. Map 1.2 locates all cities with a population of 300,000 or more in 2015, with a projection to 2020.

Contrary to common perception, Nigeria does not show a high degree of urban primacy, and Lagos is not "too large" in relation to the rest of the urban system. In fact, Nigeria conforms to Zipf's law: a regularity found in most countries which suggests that the relationship between population size and city-size rank is generally close to −1 (figure 1.2).

Population in Nigeria now concentrates in four city clusters (map 1.3): centered on Kano in the north; in the Lagos to Ibadan corridor and surrounding area in the southwest; in the southeast around and to the north and west of Port Harcourt; and on a new corridor developing from the capital Abuja to Jos. Even though it is relatively well-balanced across city-size classes, the degree and pace of urbanization is not uniform across the country, and spatial analysis indicates this trend will continue.

Concentration of population in these four areas could lead to the development of four Nigerian mega-regions—clusters of cities connected by physical infrastructure and linked economically with well-functioning markets—which could reshape the country's urban and regional landscape.

Table 1.1 Urban Population Growth Trends by Settlement-Size Class, 2015–20

City-size class	2015 population (millions)	2020 population (millions)	Average growth rate, 2015–20	Number of cities	Names of cities
5 million or more	13.12	16.17	4.65	1	Lagos
1 million–5 million	15.18	18.45	4.31	7	Abuja
					Benin City
					Ibadan
					Kaduna
					Kano
					Onitsha
					Port Harcourt
500,000–1 million	10.76	13.10	4.35	15	Aba
					Akure
					Enugu
					Ikorodu
					Ilorin
					Jos
					Maiduguri
					Nnewi
					Oshogbo
					Owerri
					Sokoto
					Umuahia
					Uyo
					Warri
					Zaria
300,000–500,000	7.69	9.41	4.47	19	Abakaliki
					Abeokuta
					Ado-Ekiti
					Bauchi
					Calabar
					Effon Alaiye
					Gboko
					Gombe
					Ife
					Igbidu
					Katsina
					Lokoja
					Makurdi
					Minna
					Ogbomosho
					Okene
					Okpogho
					Ondo
					Oyo

Source: UN DESA 2014.

From Oil to Cities • http://dx.doi.org/10.1596/978-1-4648-0792-3

Map 1.2 Cities in Nigeria with Populations of 300,000 or More in 2015

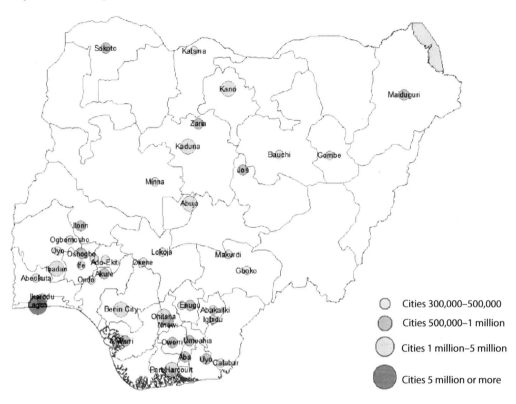

Cities 300,000–500,000

Cities 500,000–1 million

Cities 1 million–5 million

Cities 5 million or more

Source: World Bank staff mapping with data from UN DESA 2014.

Figure 1.2 Nigeria's Urban Size Distribution Conforms to International Standards

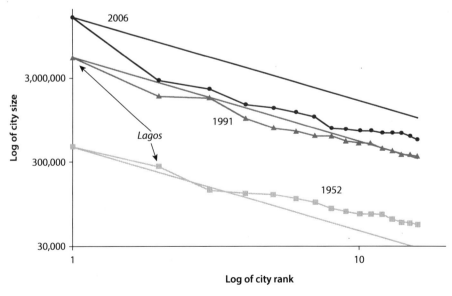

Source: Bloch, Fox, and others 2015.

Map 1.3 People per Square Kilometer per Local Government Area in 2014

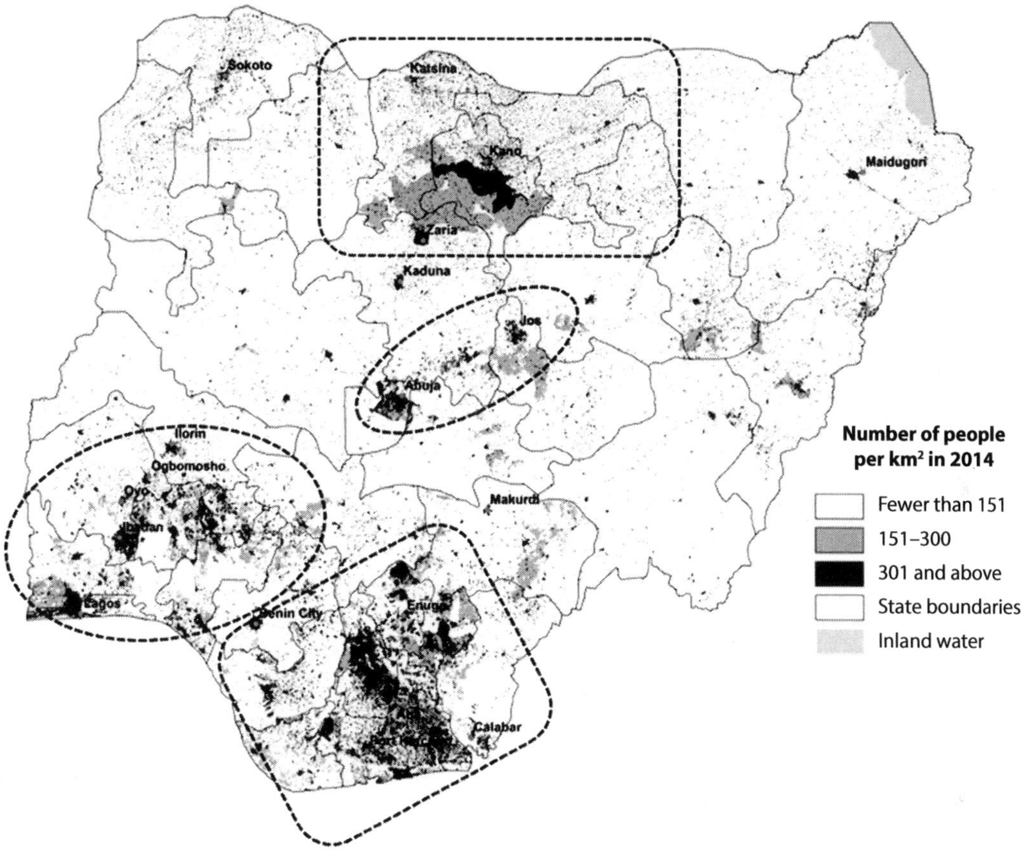

Number of people per km² in 2014

	Fewer than 151
	151–300
	301 and above
	State boundaries
	Inland water

Source: Bloch, Fox, and others 2015.

Note: km² = square kilometers. Population distribution in Nigeria is remarkably dense, with only small states such as Burundi, Rwanda, and the Seychelles denser. Globally, Nigeria is 50 percent denser than other large developing countries such as Indonesia and Thailand, and approaches similar density as Germany, Italy, and Pakistan.

Cities in Nigeria such as Lagos, Kano, and Port Harcourt are considerably denser than other urban areas of similar population size, such as London, Nairobi, and Dar es Salaam, as shown in figure 1.3.

Physical Development and Spatial Expansion

Present-day urbanization in Nigeria is marked by a heightened and accelerated spatial expansion, which is driven by urban population growth and is expected to continue with urban land cover expected to double by 2030. The actual rate of increase will depend on whether the population in Nigerian cities remains at current, relatively dense levels. In general, rates of urban spatial expansion have exceeded rates of population growth in West Africa (Angel 2012). If this trend is maintained in Nigeria, then urban land cover could treble or even quadruple

Figure 1.3 Nigerian City Density Relative to Other African Cities and to World Averages

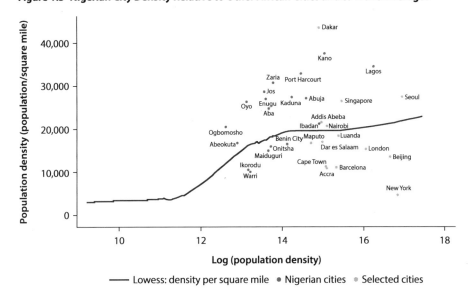

Source: Demographia 2013; World Bank staff elaborations.

from 2000 to 2030 (see table 1.2). Urban population growth and rising incomes are also involved in this trend, as box 1.4 shows.

The growth of Nigeria's urban population has been accompanied by both the intensification of development in built-up areas, and by the appearance of new suburban developments and the progressive absorption of adjacent, formerly peri-urban settlements, on the urban periphery.

Peripheral expansion and the associated increase in urban land cover have important implications for the efficiency of Nigerian cities in infrastructure and service provision, as well as environmental implications. Although new housing can be provided on cheaper land, dispersed settlement and land use patterns can increase both the cost of travel for individual households and businesses as well as the cost of developing complimentary transport infrastructure, and tends to encourage private car usage, increasing annual vehicle kilometers travelled and annual transport related greenhouse gas and particulate emissions. Unless planned in relation to the location of employment centers, dispersed settlement patterns can also increase travel time, reduce the productivity of workers and businesses, and hinder the growth of the wider urban economy.

In Nigeria, contemporary spatial expansion is concentrating on the periphery of existing settlements. The urban edge is constantly redefined by further developments as cities and towns grow. This generalized pattern has been framed in Nigeria, as elsewhere in Sub-Saharan Africa (and globally), as "sprawl," but this term is far too limited and descriptive to properly encapsulate the variety and complexity of spatial expansion.

Table 1.2 Urban Land Cover Estimates and Projections, 2000–30

Urban land cover in 2000 (hectares)	Assumed annual density decline (%)	Projected urban land cover in 2030 (hectares)	Percentage change, 2000–2030
464,192	0	1,262,215	172
	1	1,703,812	267
	2	2,299,905	395

Source: Angel 2012.

Box 1.4 The Relationship between Income and Land Consumption per Capita

As Nigerian income status rises, one would expect per capita land consumption to increase. Global evidence suggests that growing urban populations and rising incomes are likely to lead to an expansion in urban land consumption. Cities in countries with higher incomes tend to have lower densities, and a doubling of income per capita is associated with a 40 percent decline in average density (figure B1.4.1).

Figure B1.4.1 Density Change as a Function of Initial Density and Income Change in a Subsample of 20 Cities, 1990–2000

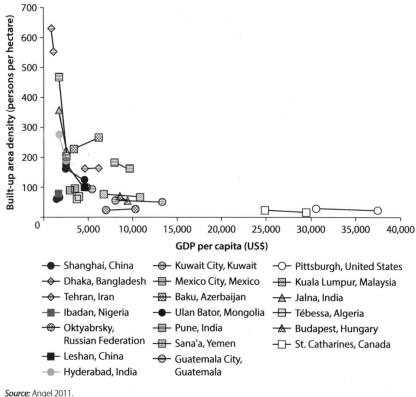

●— Shanghai, China	⊕— Kuwait City, Kuwait	○— Pittsburgh, United States
◆— Dhaka, Bangladesh	▤— Mexico City, Mexico	▨— Kuala Lumpur, Malaysia
◇— Tehran, Iran	▨— Baku, Azerbaijan	△— Jalna, India
■— Ibadan, Nigeria	●— Ulan Bator, Mongolia	▥— Tébessa, Algeria
◉— Oktyabrsky, Russian Federation	▤— Pune, India	▲— Budapest, Hungary
■— Leshan, China	▦— Sana'a, Yemen	□— St. Catharines, Canada
●— Hyderabad, India	⊖— Guatemala City, Guatemala	

Source: Angel 2011.
Note: GDP = gross domestic product.

Land in Nigeria has traditionally been supplied—and converted to urban uses—in disregard of formal state regulatory instruments. Its cities have historically lacked the appropriate physical planning mechanisms to address urban expansion. Metropolitan-level or city-wide masterplans, when present, have traditionally been poorly implemented due to financial and technical constraints. In a context of a largely unregulated land market, this has resulted in the emergence of unplanned, unguided, and scattered urban development.

Decentralization of both population and economic activity, increasingly marked by a low-density pattern can thus be observed. This is notable on the urban periphery, potentially reducing the high urban densities referred to above. The tremendous and diverse suburban development on the outskirts of cities throughout Nigeria in the last decade is manifested in residential, industrial, and commercial urban typologies: residential estates geared for the emerging urban middle class are frequently located alongside unplanned informal settlements; and industrial and commercial uses, formal and informal, coexist with these planned and unplanned residential areas.

Simultaneously, residential, industrial, and commercial formats are interpenetrated by a diversified network of open spaces of different kinds—encompassing unused land, natural features and formal recreation areas—as well as particular land use specializations. These can incorporate formal and informal markets, government and educational facilities, and mixed-use retail and commercial structures.

In Abuja, for instance, mixed-use commercial and retail facilities have emerged along road networks in the vicinity of newly developed suburban areas. An example is the Abuja Mall, opened in 2012 adjoining the Murtala Mohammed Expressway, to the east of the city. The structure is anchored by the large supermarket, Shoprite, and also includes diverse retail activities. Shopping centers of this type located along transport corridors complement adjacent residential areas, and thus become stronger nodes of economic activity.

With their development, Nigerian cities are developing in a more polycentric pattern. Metropolitan Lagos, for example, now encompasses a wide array of urban districts. These include the island of Lagos, Ikoyi (the seat of traditional administration in Lagos State) and areas planned in the past such as Apapa, Ebute-Metta, Yaba, Ilupeju, Surulere, and Ikeja and now marked by increased commercial activities and industry. It also includes newly planned towns and estates including Festac Town, Satellite Town, Gowon Estate, Ipaja, Amuwo-Odofin and Anthony Village, Mushin, Iwaya, Iponri, Maroko, and Ajegunle and older local villages absorbed and incorporated into the urban fabric as the city expanded. These urban centers provide different functions, and their polycentric structure is emerging in many metropolitan or larger-sized Nigerian cities such as Abuja, Kaduna, Kano, Enugu, Ibadan, and Port Harcourt.

Contemporary Nigerian cities are thus complex, multifaceted, and dynamic. They are characterized by the—frequently unplanned and disorganized—juxtaposition of the traditional core city and its attached residential, commercial, and industrial areas with a diverse array of new suburban or peripheral areas.

From Oil to Cities • http://dx.doi.org/10.1596/978-1-4648-0792-3

The development of a more polycentric urban pattern can help alleviate some of the infrastructural, service provision, and environmental challenges associated with urban spatial expansion. The length of trips within an urban agglomeration is a direct reflection of the urban structure, in particular, the relative spatial distribution of residential, employment, retail, leisure, and commercial land uses. In mixed land use areas, average trip lengths are significantly shorter than corresponding trip lengths in regions subject to haphazard uncontrolled development or more rigid land use zoning policies where residential and nonresidential land use functions tend to be strictly segregated—that is, a monocentric form with a single central business district.

Cities are also developing beyond their designated borders to form extensive urban corridors and conurbations. As Lagos has expanded, it has grown well beyond the borders of Lagos State, forming an extensive urban corridor reaching to and beyond Ibadan to its east—and anchoring the southwestern conurbation discussed above.

Similar formations are emerging elsewhere in the country, centered on Kano, Abuja, and Port Harcourt. Abuja is developing a polycentric metropolitan structure due to the economic and residential linkages between the city with its satellite towns, as well as towns to the east in adjoining Nasarawa State. An urban transborder corridor has also emerged in the north of the country connecting Maradi, Katsina, and Kano, and linking Nigeria and Niger (West African Borders and Integration 2006). The K^{2}M area, as it is known, concentrates a population of about 19 million, with a density of about 200 inhabitants per square kilometer, and is regarded as one of the most densely populated areas in West Africa.

Urban expansion has fostered the emergence of metropolitan areas increasingly characterized by overall lower levels of density. At the same time, the constant redefinition of urban boundaries is leading to an unprecedented scale of urbanization in the complex form just discussed.

Urban Poverty and Living Conditions

Measuring the incidence of poverty in urban and rural areas in Nigeria poses great difficulties. This section therefore focuses not only on absolute income and consumption measurements of poverty, but also on the more measurable aspects of urban living standards and conditions. Limited improvements in living conditions resulted from limited access to basic services, including health care and education, expensive urban transport that keeps people from jobs, and deteriorating environmental conditions.

Poverty: Regional, Urban, and Rural Disparities

Despite remarkable economic growth in recent years, poverty remains prevalent in much of the country. The 2009/10 Nigeria Harmonized Living Standard Survey indicates only a slight decrease in poverty compared to 2002/03. The poverty rate using the adult equivalent approach was 46 percent in 2009/10 compared to 48 percent in 2002/03.

From Oil to Cities • http://dx.doi.org/10.1596/978-1-4648-0792-3

In per capita terms, the poverty rate was 62 percent and 64 percent respectively for the same period (World Bank 2014a). But some evidence suggests that consumption was underestimated in the Nigeria Harmonized Living Standard Survey, and more recent estimates from the General Household Survey (GHS) support the hypothesis that poverty rates in Nigeria could be significantly lower than estimates based on the 2009/10 survey (World Bank 2013). Per capita poverty based on the GHS was estimated at 35 percent in 2009/10 and 33 percent in 2012/13. Nonetheless, although per capita national poverty rates indicate progress in poverty reduction from 2010/11 to 2012/13, in absolute terms about 58 million remained poor.

Data suggest a continued and even growing divide between the north and south of Nigeria in poverty and poverty reduction.[5] About two-thirds of the poor reside in the north of the country (table 1.3). The poverty rate in the South West Geopolitical Zone was only 16 percent in 2012/13, compared to 50 percent in the North East Zone. The North Central Zone had the lowest poverty rate among northern areas, with 30 percent, still higher compared to all southern parts of the country. Progress in poverty reduction is observed in all three southern zones and in the North Central Zone from 2009/10 to 2012/13. But the North West Zone has witnessed little change, and poverty in the North East Zone has actually increased. The observed spatial distribution of the poor exhibits deepening regional disparities.

Regional disparities are also reflected in state poverty rates (map 1.4). State data, using National Bureau of Statistics (NBS) data in 2004 and 2010, suggest no clear pattern of variation in poverty reduction, implying that reductions may be due to conditions in the individual states, rather than to nationwide factors. For example, poverty in Lagos State in the southwest of the country declined to

Table 1.3 Nigeria's Poverty Rates Per Capita (% of Population)

Region	Poverty headcount			Poverty gap		Poverty severity		Poverty headcount
	GHS 2010–11	GHS 2012–13	Diff.	GHS 2010–11	GHS 2012–13	GHS 2010–11	GHS 2012–13	HNLSS 2009–10[a]
National	35.2	33.1	−2.1	9.2	9.6	3.7	3.9	62.6
Rural	46.3	44.9	−1.4	12.9	13.1	5.2	5.3	69.1
Urban	15.8	12.6	−3.2	2.8	3.6	1.0	1.3	51.2
North Central	33.4	31.1	−2.3	8.9	8.9	4.0	3.5	65.8
North East	47.1	50.2	3.1	15.9	13.0	6.9	5.2	75.4
North West	46.9	45.9	−1.0	12.4	12.4	4.6	4.8	74.2
South East	31.7	28.8	−2.9	8.1	10.3	3.2	4.7	54.9
South South	27.7	24.4	−3.3	6.7	7.7	2.7	3.2	53.3
South West	21.2	16.0	−5.2	3.6	5.4	1.3	2.0	47.9

Source: World Bank 2014a.
Note: Diff = difference; GHS = General Household Survey; HNLSS = Harmonized Nigeria Living Standard Survey.
a. Data are not directly comparable to GHS results. They are presented just for illustrative purposes.

Map 1.4 Poverty Headcount by State, 2004 and 2010

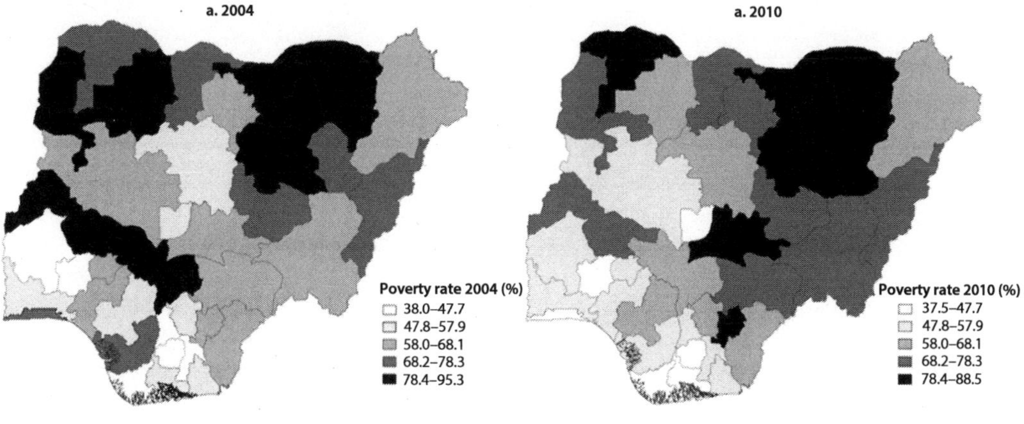

a. 2004

a. 2010

Poverty rate 2004 (%)
- 38.0–47.7
- 47.8–57.9
- 58.0–68.1
- 68.2–78.3
- 78.4–95.3

Poverty rate 2010 (%)
- 37.5–47.7
- 47.8–57.9
- 58.0–68.1
- 68.2–78.3
- 78.4–88.5

Source: Bloch, Makarem, and others 2015.
Note: Data are not directly comparable to General Household Survey results. They are presented just for illustrative purposes.

40 percent in 2010 from 69 percent in 2004; in Ebonyi State in the southeast, it increased to 83 percent from 63 percent.

Poverty incidence is lower on average in urban areas than in rural areas in Nigeria. GHS estimates indicate that, on aggregate, poverty in rural areas was 46 percent in 2010/11 and 45 percent in 2012/13, compared to only 16 percent and 13 percent for urban areas, respectively. But the urban-rural classifications informing these estimates have not been updated since 1991, and therefore a substantial number of people living on the urban periphery could be categorized as rural poor, making it difficult to compare poverty rates in rural and urban areas.

Moreover, evidence from other developing countries suggests that the proportion of the urban population "living in poverty" substantially exceeds the proportion defined as poor in official statistics based on poverty lines (Satterthwaite 2014). This is because measurements do not account for other costs, such as housing and other basic services—electricity and water, transport, health and education—which all tend to be higher in urban areas.

Inequality has increased in Nigeria, as measured by the Gini index (table 1.4),[6] and is the highest in West Africa. The national Gini coefficient increased from 0.33 in 2010/11 to 0.34 in 2012/13 (World Bank 2014a). Inequality is highest in the South East (0.36) and South (0.35), but lowest in the South West region (0.29). Inequality in the three northern states is fairly constant (World Bank 2014b). Increasing concentration of incomes at both the highest and lowest deciles and a "hollowing out" of the middle is also evident. In addition, the country is undergoing increasing polarization—the combination of divergence from global and convergence on local mean incomes (Clementi and others 2014). This appears to be somewhat at odds with the emerging narrative on Sub-Saharan Africa that tells a story of a rapidly growing consumer middle class (AfDB 2011).

Table 1.4 Inequality and Mean Consumption

Region	Gini		Mean consumption pc	
	GHS 2010–11	GHS 2012–13	GHS 2010–11	GHS 2012–13
National	0.33	0.34	100,824	103,817
Rural	0.30	0.32	82,806	85,494
Urban	0.31	0.32	132,390	135,731
North Central	0.30	0.30	97,189	98,778
North East	0.30	0.31	83,904	76,254
North West	0.31	0.32	85,047	85,365
South East	0.36	0.36	110,597	119,948
South South	0.34	0.35	114,899	126,817
South West	0.30	0.29	118,690	122,467

Source: World Bank 2014a; GHS 2010/11–2012/13: post-planting and post-harvesting visits.
Note: GHS = General Household Survey.

The pattern of distributional change, however, is not entirely homogeneous within Nigeria. From 2003/04 to 2012/13, households living in the north of the country increasingly moved from the center toward the bottom of the consumption distribution, and southern households increasingly moved upwards (Clementi and others 2014). This has accentuated the North-South divide.

Moreover, vulnerability to poverty is more widespread than poverty itself: 58 percent of the population lives at a level less than 40 percent of the poverty line (figure 1.4). In rural areas, this number reaches almost 70 percent of people, compared to 30 percent for urban areas in 2012/2013 (World Bank 2014b). Sources of vulnerability include, but are not limited to, economic shocks and crises such as unemployment, uncertain land tenure, illness, natural disaster, or conflict.

Even though the impoverished and vulnerable share of the population has declined, it appears that perceptions of poverty have actually worsened, as few citizens have entered the global middle class. From 2003 to 2013, Nigeria's "middle-class" or nonvulnerable population, calculated as a less than 10 percent chance of falling into poverty, increased from 13 percent of the population to 19 percent (Rodas and others 2015). Yet, Nigeria still did not develop a global consuming middle class over this period, defined as US$10–US$100 daily consumption (Kharas 2010).

Improvements in average incomes on aggregate mask what has been a less impressive improvement in urban living standards. Indeed, perhaps a more telling indicator of limited poverty reduction is that from 2004 to 2010, Nigerians who defined themselves as poor rose from 76 percent to 94 percent. Given this greater inequality, income polarization, and continued vulnerability, a broader assessment of poverty conditions in Nigeria is required.

Urban Living Conditions
Informality is the norm in housing markets, and most urban Nigerians live in informal settlements. Although slums, conventionally understood as shanty towns, are

Figure 1.4 Distance from Poverty Line

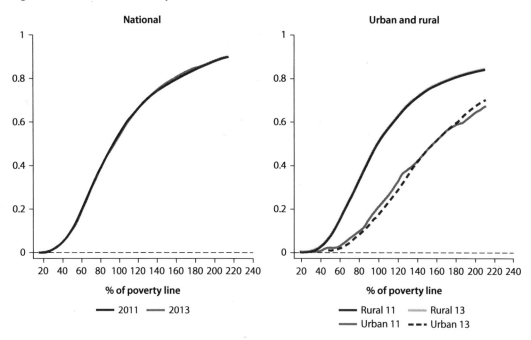

Source: World Bank 2010.

actually quite rare in the country, the word is often used to describe the unplanned, generally substandard housing where the majority of the population lives.

The government, using the UN-Habitat definition of slums, estimates that the overall slum population declined from 73 percent in 1990 to 60 percent in 2009; but other estimates place the number as high as 80 percent. Formal housing is expensive to build and thus unaffordable to most; informal housing is both easy to produce and affordable, but lacks access to basic services.

Expansion of informal settlements, which concentrates the poorest residents, increases risks of marginalization and exclusion. Poor and informal living conditions limit social and economic opportunities. Living in slums or slum-like conditions not only carries high risk of exposure to disease, violence, and insecurity, but is also associated with lower educational outcomes and life opportunities.

It is notable that Nigerian children living in slums are 35 percent less likely to attend school. The school dropout rate for women living in slums is also considerably higher, with 27 percent leaving school early as a result of pregnancy/early marriage (ages 15–24) compared to 16 percent for non-slum dwellers (UN-Habitat 2010).

The trend in access to and quality of education is regionally fragmented. Nigerian literacy is relatively low at 66 percent, below the Sub-Saharan African average of 76 percent (World Bank 2014d). And the country has one of the lowest rates of primary school enrollment in the world, with significant gender imbalances in some regions (Agunwamba and others 2009). Map 1.5 illustrates a clear North-South divide in adult literacy rates by state in 2010, and therefore in educational attainment.

Even though Nigeria is making progress with basic primary education enrollment, other studies (Oruwari 2006) show that returns on education are falling, as school achievement does not guarantee employment. Urban dwellers are ostensibly more able to access education than their rural counterparts and literacy rates for children are higher in urban areas (45 percent) than rural areas (19 percent), and for urban women (87 percent) than rural women (57 percent) (Agunwamba and others 2009). But marked discrepancies in school enrollment rates between sexes still exist: gross enrollment ratios nationally have been consistently over 10 percent higher for boys than for girls (Hagen-Zanker and Holmes 2012).

In urban areas, quality of education is a particular challenge, as significant population pressure results in class sizes that can exceed 100 students. This affects educational outcomes, and, according to UNICEF (United Nations Children's Fund) data, 30 percent of pupils drop out of primary school and only 54 percent transit to junior secondary schools. And quality of education remains very weak: 44 percent of students completing grade 6 cannot read a complete sentence (World Bank 2014c). Sharp differences in services in the country motivates families to leave the less-developed regions. In a 2005

Map 1.5 Adult Literacy Rate by State, 2010

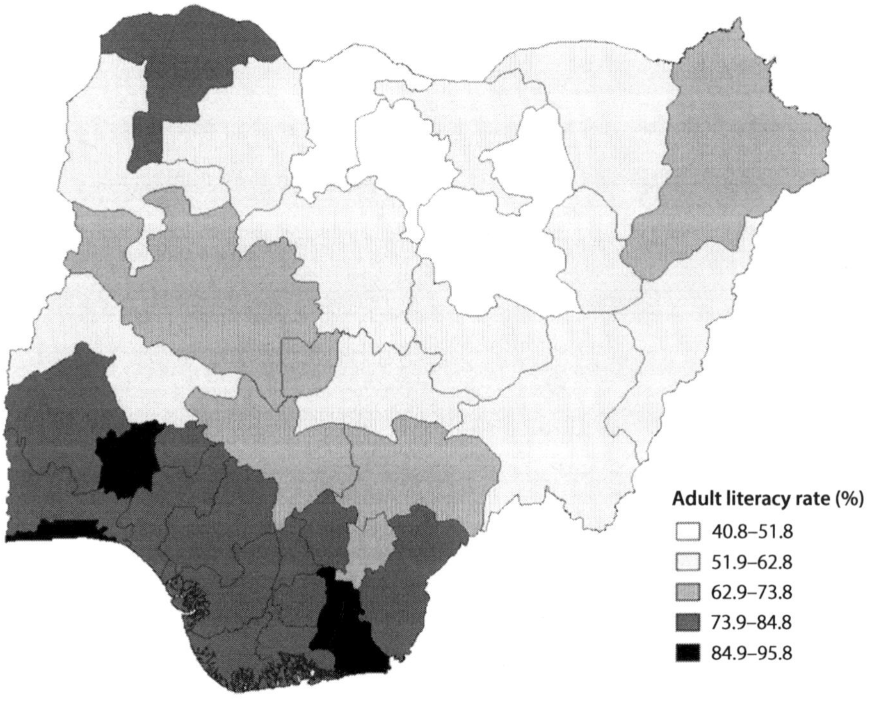

Adult literacy rate (%)
☐ 40.8–51.8
☐ 51.9–62.8
▨ 62.9–73.8
▨ 73.9–84.8
■ 84.9–95.8

Source: Bloch, Makarem, and others 2015.

study, 16 percent of migrants leaving the South East cited education as their primary reason for leaving.

Evidence exists of intergenerational immobility for people living in informal conditions. In Lagos, up to 50 percent of the population lives in informal conditions across some 200 informal settlements spread across the city (Amao 2012; Agunwamba and others 2009).

A recent survey in three slums in the city reveals the appalling conditions of slum dwellers. Some 22 percent and 35 percent of the respective respondents in the Makoko and Ajegunle areas have been living in the slum from 5 to 10 years; in Ijora Oloye, 45 percent of the respondents lived there for more than 15 years. That such a large percentage of the respondents have lived in the slum for a long period and that over 50 percent were even born there, suggests that slums are poverty traps rather than temporary living quarters for migrants incorporating into the urban economy.

Informal settlements are in general also not connected to trunk infrastructure. As a consequence, the majority of urban households in Nigeria lack access to basic services. Informal settlements are not on the service "grid" and so residents must pay other providers. These alternatives are almost always more expensive. In Lagos State, buying informal water and garbage pickup costs 1.3–3.0 times greater than the tariffs charged by the state.

A quarter of the population has no access to improved water sources. According to the 2013 Nigeria Demographic and Health Survey, 76 percent of urban households had access to an "improved" source of drinking water, compared with 49 percent in rural areas. But just 5.5 percent of urban households had piped water to the dwelling, and a further 9 percent had access to piped water in the yard or a shared public standpipe.

The vast majority then are not connected to the water supply grid and must use other sources, such as boreholes, protected wells, or water tankers to access water. These statistics further mask the considerable variation in quality of water accessed, as the definition of improved water includes sources of water that are still associated with relatively high incidence of waterborne diseases, such as tube wells or boreholes, protected dug wells and springs, as well as rainwater collection.

Two-thirds of urban households have no access to improved sanitation. Just 35 percent of urban households have access to improved sanitation, compared with 27 percent in rural areas. Moreover, only Lagos and Abuja have sewerage systems, and even in these two cities the majority of households are not connected, which means that just 6 percent of urban households have a pour/flush toilet connected to a piped sewer system (World Bank 2005).

Although the proportion of households with no toilet in 2011 is relatively low (about 15 percent of all households and less than 10 percent of households in urban areas), there is a strong reliance on pit latrines, with 62 percent of all households and 47 percent of urban households (European Commission 2006).

Regions differ strongly in access to basic services. Access to improved water in the northern states is considerably lower than in the southern states (figure 1.5).

Figure 1.5 Access to Improved Water Source across Geopolitical Zones in Nigeria

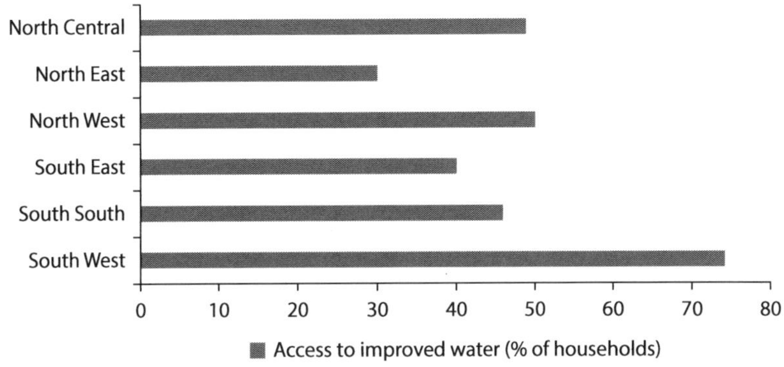

Source: Osabuohien and others 2012, using data from National Bureau of Statistics.

This disparity is clearest in the northeast, where access to improved water is estimated at 30 percent of the population. Disparities in access to basic services are confirmed by evidence from the GHS 2011. Over 62 percent of urban households in Sokoto have access to piped water in their homes, but only 17 percent in Anambra, 19 percent in Ekiti, and less than 12 percent in Katsina do (General Household Survey 2011). Access to services in urban areas also vary considerably within each region.

A lack of sanitary landfills and waste collection services is also common in many cities. The majority of solid waste in urban settlements is disposed of or recycled informally, lacks public oversight, and generates health hazards. State-managed waste collection services are often tied to land formality, excluding the majority of households living in informal settlements; and even where formal collection is available, it is expensive.

Many households and businesses instead rely on informal area dumps or collection by cart pushers. Recyclables are collected by waste-pickers and scavengers or sold directly to local merchants and a wide range of micro- to medium-sized separation and recycling enterprises. These sanitation conditions create health hazards and increase household burdens, particularly for women, who tend to take responsibility for health care in the household. Increased household expenditure can also result from the need to access sanitation and health services privately.

Inadequate water supply and sanitation lead to a high incidence of diarrhea, cholera, and other diseases. Because of improperly disposed of commercial and domestic wastes, large volumes of rubbish litter streets and accumulate in open dumps, allowing flies, other disease carrying insects, and rodents to proliferate. Open drains are often clogged, exacerbating already high urban flood risk, a key climate-related hazard risk.

Potholes in the streets, pools of stagnant water, and wastewater gushing from bathrooms and kitchens are breeding sites for malarial mosquitoes and other disease vectors. Food contamination and poisoning, especially in the rapidly growing street foods and catering industry, pose a serious threat to public health; and air pollution, especially toxic fumes from open cooking fires and stoves in poorly ventilated homes, causes a wide variety of respiratory infections among women and children.

Nigeria's health status indicators have improved, but they are still poor. Child and maternal mortality rates are among the highest in the world and, with a population of 3.5 million living with HIV, Nigeria has the second-highest incidence in the region. Life expectancy of 51 years is well below the lower-middle-income average of 66 years (World Bank 2014d). Health care statistics for both urban and rural areas remain poor, and there is little evidence to suggest that urban areas are considerably better at delivering health services. For example, the prevalence of stunting in urban areas was high at 29 percent, compared to 43 percent in rural areas in 2003.

In the same year, the proportion of births attended by health care workers in urban areas was 59 percent, compared to 27 percent in rural areas. HIV/AIDS rates are higher in urban areas than rural areas in all zones of the country, but important regional disparities persist. Prevalence in the South and North Central Zones is 8 percent, but only 5 percent average in urban areas. Health care workers per capita is insufficient,[7] and primary health facilities suffer from decaying infrastructure.[8]

Strong regional and income inequalities exist in access to health services; health care workers are more concentrated in the southwest, mostly in Lagos (AHWO 2008). Research in 2005 found that child mortality rates in northern states were among the worst in the world, at 260 deaths per 1,000 population, and those in southern states were comparable to countries such as Kenya and Ethiopia at 180 per 1,000 inhabitants. This research also indicates that Nigeria has the highest rich-poor difference in child mortality rates, immunization rates, and malnutrition in Sub-Saharan Africa (World Bank 2005). Little evidence exists to suggest significant improvements in these trends in recent years.

The share of the urban population with access to electricity is relatively high at 84 percent compared to 34 percent in rural areas. But poor reliability and incessant power outages mean that connection to the grid does not guarantee supply of electricity. Consequently, many homes and businesses must rely on a generator for the majority of their electricity needs.

Transport costs and congestion deepen urban divisions (figures 1.6 and 1.7). The poor spend up to half of their income on transportation, and lack high-quality, high-capacity public transport that links homes with workplaces (figure 1.6). According to a series of comprehensive travel demand surveys[9] undertaken in recent years in the Federal Capital Territory (FCT)/Abuja (2013), Kano (2012) and Lagos (2009, 2012), low-income households spend 49 percent, 40 percent, and 33 percent of household income on public transport, compared with 18 percent, 19 percent, and 10 percent for middle and upper-income households. The average percentage of household expenditure on

Figure 1.6 Household Public Transport Expenditure by Household Income, Three Nigerian Agglomerations

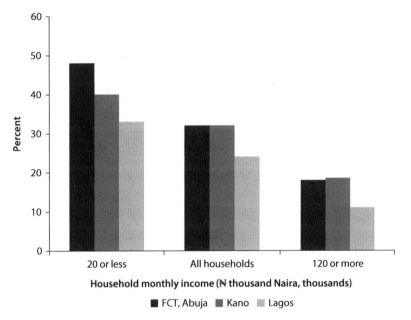

Source: FCT 2013 Travel Demand Survey; Kano 2012 Travel Demand Survey; Lagos 2012 Travel Demand Survey.
Note: FCT = Federal Capital Territory.

Figure 1.7 Average Trip Length for Passengers on Public Transport, Selected Cities across the World

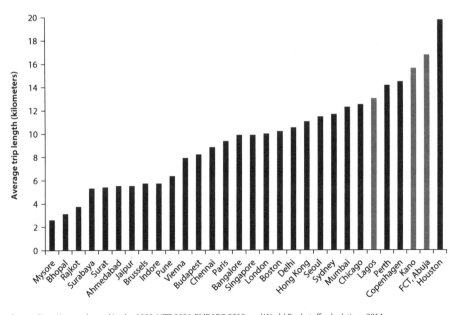

Source: Data, Kenworthy and Laube 1999; UITP 2006; EMBARQ 2012; and World Bank staff calculations 2014.
Note: FCT = Federal Capital Territory.

public transport in FCT/Abuja, Kano, and Lagos is 31 percent, 32 percent, and 24 percent, respectively.[10] The urban poor experience greater congestion, have a poorer work–life balance (by spending longer traveling), and are thus more likely to suffer from sleep deprivation. The cost of transport leads most urban residents to walk to work, limiting access to jobs.

The characteristics of the mode of choice highlight important transport-related welfare and inclusivity challenges. The informal transport sector plays an important role in the provision of personal mobility within the three urban agglomerations, helping to bridge the significant public transport deficit.[11] The findings highlight the immense importance of a high-quality, sustainable, integrated, and regulated public-transport system encompassing high-capacity mass transit services that responds to the opportunities highlighted by the informal transport sector.

Car availability rates steadily increase as household income increases, and increasing among the middle and upper income groups in all three urban agglomerations, reaching twice the metropolitan average and some 3–7 times the lower-income band rate for higher-income bands. This is consistent with international experience (figure 1.8). Car availability averages 60–197 per 1,000 people[12]

Figure 1.8 Car Ownership as a Function of Gross National Income

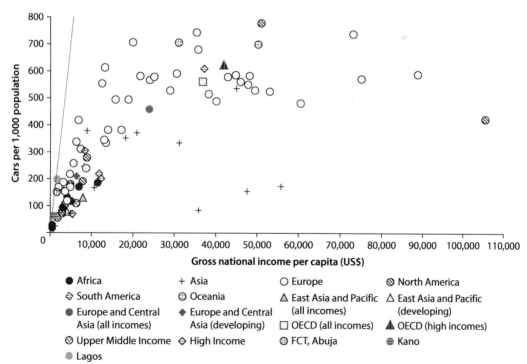

Source: Based on World Bank, World Development Indicators; World Bank.
Note: FCT = Federal Capital Territory.

From Oil to Cities • http://dx.doi.org/10.1596/978-1-4648-0792-3

and 105–332 per 1,000 adults in the three urban agglomerations and is growing appreciably, although lower than in wealthier countries.

Transport affordability is important to welfare considerations, which recognize an individual's fundamental right to access and mobility. Transport must be affordable for the vast majority of urban dwellers, and, where it is not, they must have a realistic alternative, such as nonmotorized transport to access essential activities, facilities, and services. Households within the three urban agglomerations spend an inequitably large proportion of household income on public transport fares and on fuel for the operation of household vehicles.

Poorer households can in fact spend upwards of 30 percent and as much as 60 percent or more of household income on public transport services, accordingly to travel demand surveys in the FCT/Abuja (2013), Kano (2012), and Lagos (2009, 2012), undertaken by the Nigeria Infrastructure Advisory Facility (NIAF) and funded by the U.K. Department for International Development (DFID). These findings appear to differ from some international research (Kauppila 2011), which shows that in the European Union, for example, more affluent households spend a greater proportion of household income on transport services and on the operation of motor vehicles than poorer households. But other international research (Sumich 2010; World Bank 2005) indicates that poorer households in urban agglomerations in Argentina, Brazil, India, Malaysia, Mexico, Mozambique, Nigeria, the Philippines, and South Africa spend a greater proportion of household income on public transport services than the more affluent households.

It is clear that because Nigeria is failing to provide high-quality mass transit services and a safe and accessible nonmotorized transport network as its urban agglomerations expand, the urban poor suffer disproportionally more than the more affluent.[13] This effectively excludes the poorest households from a wider choice of employment, educational, health, and social services, reducing their life chances and opportunities for social mobility.

Notes

1. Chapters 1 and 2 of this report include extracts from research reports produced by the Urbanisation Research Nigeria program. The report *Urbanisation and Urban Expansion in Nigeria* by Robin Bloch, Sean Fox, Jose Monroy, and Adegbola Ojo was drawn upon for the analysis in this chapter on the dynamics and drivers of urban population growth and the spatial expansion and physical configuration—or urban structure—of Nigerian cities.

2. Estimates for the level of urbanization range from 48 percent to 52 percent. An urban settlement is defined as one with a population of 20,000 and above in Nigeria. As seen in figure 1.1, the territory of Nigeria is made up of six geopolitical zones, 36 states, the Federal Capital Territory, for which Abuja is used as a shorthand, and 774 Local Government Areas. Municipal (city or town) administrations or governments do not exist in Nigeria, only local government areas, both urban and rural, which are administered by local government councils. Statistics are typically not collected at city or town level.

3. The Boko Haram insurgency is estimated to have displaced 1,500,000 people in the past five years.

4. As is well known, estimations of the Lagos population vary from 12 million to 20 million.

5. The north here is defined broadly as the North West, North Central, and North East Geopolitical Zones. A narrower definition would exclude the North Central zone.

6. The Gini index is a measure of the inequality of income or consumption expenditure among individuals or households within an economy.

7. Nigeria has one of the largest stocks of human resources for health in Africa. However, with 1.95 nurses, midwives, and doctors per 1,000 people, the density of health workers is nonetheless too low to effectively deliver services (AHWO 2008).

8. Research conducted in Primary Health Care facilities in four states found that three out of four facilities did not have waste disposals, electricity, a refrigerator or icebox, or toilets (Bonilla and others 2010).

9. A series of comprehensive travel demand surveys have been undertaken in recent years within FCT/Abuja, and Kano and Lagos states to support ongoing and future evidence-based planning activities. The mode choice of travelers within the three cities is influenced by a variety of factors including the availability, affordability, and acceptability of public transport services; household car availability; the accessibility of activities, services, and homes by a variety of modes; the spatial distribution of land uses and the nature of the urban form; the affordability of housing; and the extent of the integration of land use development and transport investment.

10. Data in this section are drawn from travel demand surveys undertaken in FCT/Abuja (2013), Kano (2012) and Lagos (2009, 2012).

11. The informal transport sector, however, is characterized by lack or absence of route and service licensing and regulation; absence of a corporatized organizational structure; limited number of operational vehicles per "operator"; presence of unregistered vehicles and/or drivers; presence of nonskilled vehicle drivers; absence of externally regulated service tariff structure; the pickup and drop-off of passengers at undesignated locations; failure to abide by road traffic laws; and limited regard for vehicle roadworthiness and the safety of passengers and other road users. These factors serve to lower the cost of operations for the informal transport sector, making services more flexible to changes in demand and potentially more affordable by poorer travelers.

12. The estimated 2013 Nigerian national car availability rate is 43 cars per 1,000 people.

13. Low incomes and high housing and transport expenditure confines the urban poor to a cycle of subsistence living.

References

AfDB (African Development Bank). 2011. "The Middle of the Pyramid: Dynamics of the Middle Class in Africa." Market brief, African Development Bank.

Agunwamba A., D. Bloom, A. Friedman, M. Ozolins, L. Rosenberg, and others. 2009. "Nigeria: The Next Generation—Literature Review." Nigeria: The Next Generation project, British Council Nigeria.

AHWO (Africa Health Workforce Observatory). 2008. *Human Resources for Health, Country Profile Nigeria.* Brazzaville, Republic of Congo: AHWO.

Amao, F. L. 2012. "Housing Quality in Informal Settlements and Urban Upgrading in Ibadan, Nigeria." *Developing Country Studies* 2 (10): 68–80.

Angel, S. 2011. "Making Room for a Planet of Cities." Policy Focus Report. Cambridge, MA: Lincoln Institute of Land Policy.

———. 2012. *Planet of Cities*. Cambridge, MA: Lincoln Institute of Land Policy.

Bloch, R., S. Fox, J. Monroy, and A. Ojo. 2015. *Urbanisation and Urban Expansion in Nigeria*. Research report, Urbanisation Research Nigeria, ICF International, London.

Bloch, R., N. Makarem, M. Yunusa, N. Papachristodoulou, and M. Crighton. 2015. *Economic Development in Urban Nigeria*. Research report, Urbanisation Research Nigeria, ICF International, London.

Bonilla Chacin, M. E., A. Okigbo, N. Malife, L. Sherburne Benz, and O. Ruhl. 2010. "Improving Primary Health Care Delivery in Nigeria: Evidence from Four States." Working Paper 187, Africa Human Development Series, World Bank, Washington, DC.

Clementi, F., A. L. Dabalen, V. Molini, and F. Schettino. 2014. "The Centre Cannot Hold: Patterns of Polarization in Nigeria." Working Paper 2014/149, UNU-WIDER, Helsinki.

Demographia. 2013. *World Urban Areas*. 9th Annual Edition. http://demographia.com/.

Economist. 2015. "Special Report: Nigeria." June 20.

European Commission. 2006. "Nigeria: Support to the Federal Ministry of Water Resources." Water Resources Management and Policy.

Federal Republic of Nigeria. 2010. *Nigeria Millennium Development Goals. Report 2010*. Abuja: Government of the Federal Republic of Nigeria.

Hagen-Zanker, J., and R. Holmes. 2012. "Social Protection in Nigeria: Synthesis Report." Overseas Development Institute, London.

Kauppila, J. 2011. "Ten Stylised Facts about Household Spending on Transport." Statistical Paper No. 1/2011, Joint Transport Research Centre of the OECD and the International Transport Forum.

Kharas, H. 2010. "The Emerging Middle Class in Developing Countries." Working Paper 285, Development Centre, Organisation for Economic Co-operation and Development, Paris.

Oruwari, Y. 2006. "Youth in Urban Violence in Nigeria: A Case Study of Urban Gangs in Port Harcourt." Working Paper 14, Niger Delta Economies of Violence, Port Harcourt, Nigeria.

Osabuohien, E. S., U. Efobi, and C. M. W. Gitau. 2012. "Environmental Challenge and Water Access in Africa: Empirical Evidences Based on Nigeria's Households Survey." Revised Conference Paper of the 2012 Berlin Conference of the Human Dimensions of Global Environmental Change on Evidence for Sustainable Development. Berlin, Germany, October 5–6.

Rodas, C., P. Andres, V. Molini, and G. Oseni. 2015. "No Condition Is Permanent: Middle Class in Nigeria in the Last Decade." Policy Research Working Paper Series 7214, World Bank, Washington, DC.

Satterthwaite, D. 2014. "If We Don't Count the Poor, the Poor Don't Count." International Institute for Environment and Development (blog), June 12. http://www.iied.org/if-we-dont-count-poor-poor-dont-count.

Shultze-Kraft, M. 2013. "Nigeria's Post-1999 Political Settlement and Violence Mitigation in the Niger Delta." Evidence Report 5, Institute for Development Studies, Brighton, U.K.

Sumich, J. 2010. "Nationalism, Urban Poverty and Identity in Maputo." Working Paper 68, Crisis States Working Papers Series 2, London School of Economics and Political Science, London.

UN DESA (United Nations Department of Economic and Social Affairs). 2014. *World Urbanization Prospects.* 2014 Revision. New York: UN.

UN-Habitat (United Nations Human Settlements Programme). 2010. *The State of African Cities: Governance, Inequality and Urban Land Markets.* Nairobi UN-Habitat.

Usman, L. M. 2010. "Street Hawking and Socio-Economic Dynamics of Nomadic Girls of Northern Nigeria." *International Journal of Social Economics* 37 (9): 717–34.

West African Borders and Integration. 2006. "Food Security and Cross-Border Trade in the Kano-Katsina-Maradi (K2M) Corridor." https://www.oecd.org/swac/events/38490617 .pdf.

World Bank. 2005. "Affordability of Public Transport in Developing Countries." Transport Paper 3, World Bank, Washington, DC.

———. 2013. "Nigeria, Where Has All the Growth Gone? Policy Note, World Bank, Washington, DC.

———. 2014a. *Nigeria Economic Report.* Report No. 2, World Bank, Washington, DC.

———. 2014b. "Local Service Delivery in Nepal." Working Paper 87922-NP, World Bank, Washington, DC.

———. 2014c. "First Lagos State Development Policy Operation." Implementation Completion and Results Report. Report No. ICR00003101. World Bank, Washington, DC.

———. 2014d. *World Development Indicators.* Washington, DC: World Bank.

CHAPTER 2

Nigeria's Spatial Economy

Introduction[1]

Urbanization generally coincides with structural transformation and poverty reduction, but these relationships have not held in Nigeria (figure 2.1) Strong economic growth over the last decade has not translated into meaningful improvements in living standards for the majority of Nigerians. A key reason for this outcome is that the urban economy has not created sufficient jobs. The limited growth of job opportunities is attributable to several interrelated factors:

- *The sectoral distribution of jobs.* Fast-growing sectors are capital-intensive and use little labor, and labor-intensive industries feature low productivity and slow growth.
- *Informal firms struggling to enhance productivity.* Informal firms are less likely to grow and to take advantage of urban economies of scale and specialization. Limited property rights and access to land and the formal legal system reduce incentives to invest in physical and human capital, reducing productivity and slowing growth.
- *A poor business environment.* Businesses face unreliable electricity supplies, poor transportation, and congestion due to insufficient road maintenance, high interest rates, precarious availability of finance, and red tape. These barriers hurt business development across sectors, but they have particularly pernicious effects on manufacturing firms.
- *Market fragmentation.* "Thick" borders between cities increase production costs in the tradable sector and prevent firms from expanding beyond local markets, reducing the potential for firm clustering and having agglomeration and localization effects.

Growth and Employment in the National Economy

After two decades of economic stagnation, Nigeria in the past 10 years has been one of the fastest growing countries in Sub-Saharan Africa, with gross domestic product (GDP) growth exceeding 7 percent per year. A recent revision in the

Figure 2.1 Urbanization, Structural Transformation, and Poverty Reduction

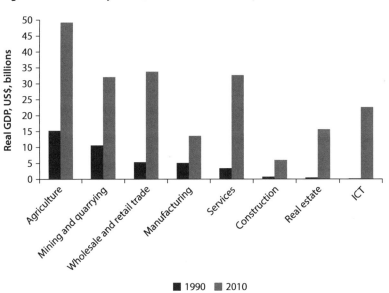

a. Industrial employment versus urbanization

b. Poverty versus urbanization

● All countries   ——— Nigeria, 1983–2004

● All countries   ——— Nigeria, 1986–2010

Sources: World Bank, World Development Indicators; World Bank staff calculations.
Note: PPP = purchasing power parity.

Figure 2.2 Real GDP by Sector, 1990–2010

■ 1990   ■ 2010

Source: National Bureau of Statistics data, various years.
Note: GDP = gross domestic product; ICT = information and communication technology.

calculation of Nigeria's GDP shows that, with a gross national product of US$509 billion in 2013, the country has the largest economy in Africa and the 26th largest in the world.

Nigeria's economy has also diversified over the past two decades (figure 2.2). All sectors of the economy have grown in real terms since 1990, and many have emerged from negligible levels, namely information and communication technology (ICT), real estate, construction, and services—all predominantly urban sectors of the economy. As a result of this rebalancing, the share of the agriculture and oil and gas sectors fell from 60 percent of GDP in 1990 to 40 percent in 2010. This development is good news because it reflects initial moves away from commodity dependency.

GDP growth over the past two decades was not as dominated by primary products and resources as before, and this again shows signs the economy is moving away from commodity dependence. Over one-third of GDP growth during 1990–2010 was driven by services growth (18 percent); wholesale and retail trade sectors (17 percent); and 26 percent by the ICT, real estate, and construction sectors (14, 9, and 3 percent, respectively) (figure 2.3). The growth of these noncommodity sectors is testament to the ability of predominantly urban entrepreneurs, investors, and workers to overcome endemic urban inefficiencies and governance failures by starting and growing business in cities.

Nigeria's industrial structure has experienced some rebalancing following a significant reduction in dependence on natural resources over the past two decades. Although the agriculture and mining and quarrying (mainly oil and gas) sectors still contributed 40 percent of GDP in 2010, their share has shrunk considerably from 37 percent in 1990 to 24 percent in 2010 for agriculture, and from 26 percent to 16 percent for oil and gas (figure 2.4).

High-end services related to the oil and gas sector and their multiplier effects drove a substantial share of growth. Just over 6 percent of the growth

Figure 2.3 Sectoral Contribution to GDP Growth, 1990–2010

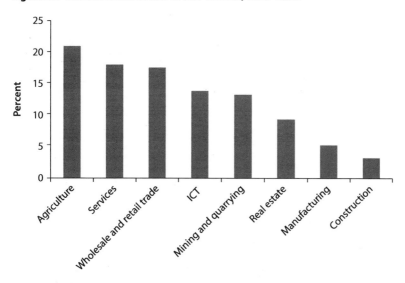

Sources: National Bureau of Statistics data, various years; World Bank staff calculations.
Note: GDP = gross domestic product; ICT = information and communication technology.

Figure 2.4 Sectoral Breakdown of GDP by Broad Industries, 1990 and 2010

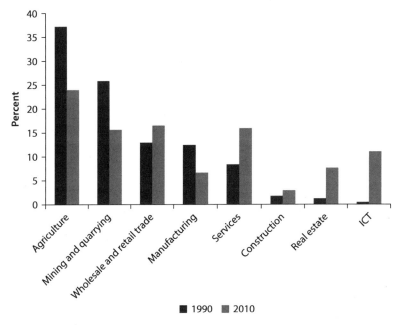

Sources: National Bureau of Statistics, various years; World Bank staff calculations.
Note: GDP = gross domestic product; ICT = information and communication technology.

in output from 1990 to 2010 was driven by the highly productive (a) finance and insurance and (b) professional, scientific, and technical services industries, which to a significant extent offer business services to the oil and gas sector. Multiplier effects, while difficult to measure precisely, are evident in the robust growth of the real estate and construction sectors, and the related impact of the spending of the consuming urban middle class with further multiplier effects in wholesale and retail, ICT, and other services subsectors.

The greater share of growth, however, was driven by non-oil-related sectors of the economy. The impact of the oil and gas sector, while encouraging with its diversification into business services, should not be exaggerated. This is because economic growth over the past two decades was predominantly driven by non-oil related sectors, such as ICT, agriculture, wholesale and retail, and services other than (a) professional, scientific, and technical and (b) finance and insurance. These no doubt have also had positive multiplier effects on the real estate and construction sectors.

The manufacturing sector has made a negligible contribution to growth, contributing just 5 percent to GDP growth from 1990 to 2010, little more than one-third of that of the oil and gas sector and less than one-quarter of that of agriculture. Moreover, manufacturing's share of output declined from 12 percent in 1990 to 7 percent in 2010.

Despite impressive growth and diversification, Nigeria's economy has failed to translate the growth in output into a reduction in unemployment in the form of an increase in formal employment, and this failure has resulted in significant underemployment. According to National Bureau of Statistics data, unemployment rose from 8 percent in 1999 to 21 percent in 2010 (figure 2.5). Nigeria's actual unemployment rate according to the International Labour Organization definition, however, is likely to be significantly lower than the official estimate, which requires 40 or more hours of work a week to be considered employed. The *Nigeria Jobs Report* (World Bank 2015) estimates unemployment at 6 percent, with a definition of the unemployment rate as the share of the active population that is not employed and is looking for work. The problem then is best interpreted as underemployment, particularly for those working in the informal sector engaged in low-productivity and low-paying occupations.

Not surprisingly, jobs are a central issue in the public debate in Nigeria, particularly for youth (see box 2.1). Nigeria is an outlier in its failure to translate per capita GDP growth into a reduction in unemployment (figure 2.6). When asked to rank the main problems facing the country, more than twice as many people cite unemployment than other issues, which include poverty, electricity, crime, education, infrastructure, and corruption (figure 2.7).

Despite recent improvements, labor productivity in Nigeria also lags behind many of its competitors. Labor productivity did grow by 3.4 percent per year from 2010 to 2013 and now contributes 55 percent of GDP growth. However, in 2013, output per worker was still just US$10,300 per year—57 percent less than the average of seven large developing economies (Leke and others 2014). Nigeria's low productivity is reflected in low wages; figure 2.8 shows the median wage across various sectors.

Figure 2.5 Unemployment in Nigeria, 1999–2010

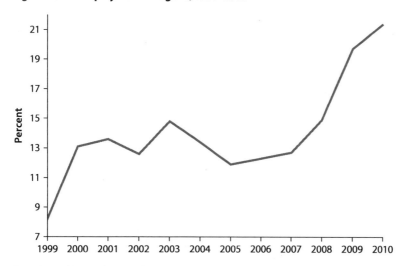

Source: National Bureau of Statistics data, various years.

Box 2.1 Youth Unemployment in Nigeria

Nigeria's population, like in much of Sub-Saharan Africa, is exceptionally young. Overall, out of 100 Nigerians, 55 are under age 20, and 28 are between ages 20 and 40. This abundant supply of labor is a good demographic opportunity and, if fertility rates are reduced, the country will also benefit from an increase in the proportion of working-age adults to young dependents. But creating enough jobs for this youthful population also presents a significant challenge.

The youth unemployment rate was 14 percent in 2011[a]—which means that some 8 million people ages 15–24 were not working or studying. Youth are less likely to be employed than older workers, and this is reflected in the finding that youth are more likely to consider unemployment the most pressing concern facing Nigeria than older workers (see figure 2.7).

The problem is not just one of youth unemployment, but also underemployment and a lack of productive opportunities for young workers. Although younger generations have greater access to primary levels of education than their predecessors had, their employment opportunities have not improved. Worryingly, youth with more than primary education are more likely to be unemployed than those with primary education or below, with those with tertiary education the most likely group to be unemployed.

The share of those ages 15–24 working in agriculture was almost 20 percent higher than those ages 25–64 in 2011. For men ages 15–24 the share has remained around 70 percent since 1999, while for women ages 15–24 it has risen from 45 to 58 percent. Perhaps most tellingly, the share of youth with more than primary education working in agriculture has risen dramatically since 1999, from 25 percent to 55 percent for women and from 42 to 62 percent for men. Moreover, there is no guarantee of a transition into more productive work.

The challenge is not just to create sufficient jobs for the growing working-age population, but to create jobs that offer real productive opportunities for Nigeria's youth. The economy needs to create 40 million–50 million jobs from 2010 to 2030, or over 2 million jobs a year. Furthermore, these jobs need to offer better opportunity to make a living than is currently the case.

Source: World Bank 2015.
a. Using the estimate from World Bank 2015, above overall unemployment at 6 percent.

The Nigerian economy is bifurcated into highly productive industries employing an insignificant share of formal sector workers, and very low-productivity sectors employing the bulk of workers. The three sectors employing the largest share of workers are services (31 percent), wholesale and retail trade (23 percent), and agriculture (30 percent). Together they account for less than 85 percent of employment, but only 56 percent of output. The productivity of workers in these sectors is very low, ranging from US$4,000 to US$6,000.

The three most productive sectors in 2010 were mining and quarrying (predominantly oil and gas), real estate, and ICT (see table 2.1). These sectors contributed over one-third of 1990–2010 GDP growth, but together accounted for a mere 1.5 percent of formal 2010 employment.

Figure 2.6 Changes in Unemployment versus Economic Growth

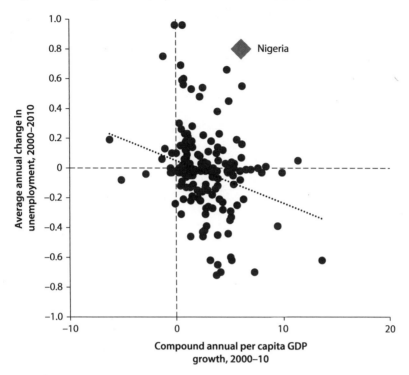

Source: World Bank, World Development Indicators.
Note: GDP = gross domestic product.

Figure 2.7 Most Pressing Problems Facing Nigeria

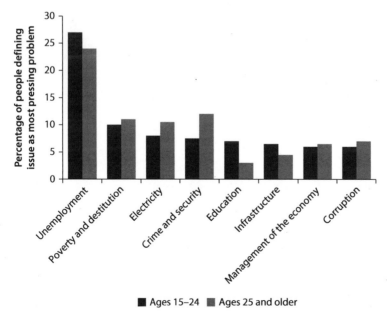

■ Ages 15–24   ■ Ages 25 and older

Source: World Bank 2014.

Figure 2.8 Wages by Sector in 2013 (median wage per month, US$)

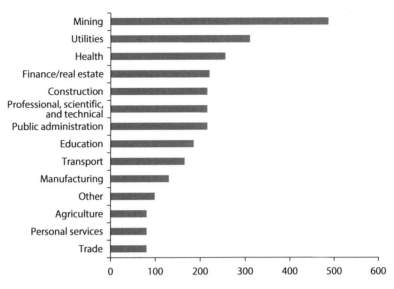

Source: World Bank 2014; estimates based on General Household Survey (GHS), Panel 2012–13, Wave 2.

Table 2.1 Share of Employment and Productivity by Broad Sector, 2010

Industry	Employees	Share (%)	Productivity (US$)
Real estate	68,697	0.14	399,799
Mining and quarrying	146,485	0.30	384,007
ICT	469,513	0.97	84,471
Construction	1,142,569	2.36	9,148
Agriculture	14,737,693	30.39	5,864
Wholesale and retail trade	11,363,603	23.43	5,217
Manufacturing	5,335,898	11.00	4,462
Services	15,234,466	31.41	3,761
Total	**48,498,924**		**7,436**

Source: World Bank staff calculations using National Bureau of Statistics data.
Note: ICT = information and communication technology. The total productivity figure is national productivity calculated as total gross domestic product (US$360.6 billion) divided by total number of workers in 2010.

Manufacturing productivity is lower than in the agricultural sector, at US$4,462 in 2010, compared with US$5,864 for agriculture. Manufacturing productivity is also substantially lower than in comparable countries. A 2009 United Nations Industrial Development Organization study showed the manufacturing productivity of Nigerian workers was 10 percent of workers in Botswana and 50 percent in Ghana and Kenya. South Africa's manufacturing productivity was US$27,000 in 2013 (Leke and others 2014).

Recent GDP data, however, show that Nigerian manufacturing might be on the uptrend, with the sector growing 4.4 percent[2] from 2010 to 2013 (inflation-adjusted compound growth), contributing 14 percent to overall GDP growth over the period. The food, beverage, and tobacco subsector predominantly drove this growth contributing 11 percent to the growth in output. It has yet to be seen whether this trend develops into sustained growth; if it does, it would offer significant opportunity for smaller cities and towns to play a stronger integrative role in connecting farmers to both agricultural input and output markets, including food processing facilities.

Of the 13 manufacturing subsectors, 10 showed real (inflation-adjusted) compound growth rates above 10 percent from 2010 to 2013. The plastic and rubber products industry grew by an average of 23 percent per year over this period, basic metal, iron, and steel by 20 percent, and food, beverage, and tobacco by 15 percent (see table 2.2). The latter is the largest manufacturing subsector, contributing 11 percent to total 2010–13 GDP growth and 75 percent of growth in manufacturing output over the three-year period of the most recent data.

Although these figures are encouraging, it is too soon to declare a resurgence in manufacturing output. As such, it is vital that the recent growth in manufacturing output across most subsectors is given sufficient research and policy attention to support firms and workers, improve the business climate,

Table 2.2 Subsector Contributions to 2010–13 GDP Growth and Growth in Manufacturing

Manufacturing subsector	2010	2013	Real CAGR (%)	Contribution to 2010–13 GDP growth (%)	Contribution to 2010–13 manufacturing growth (%)
Plastic and rubber products	33.9	63.5	23.3	0.3	1.9
Basic metal, iron, and steel	44.5	76.5	19.8	0.3	2.0
Food, beverage, and tobacco	2,298.5	3,480.7	14.8	10.7	74.6
Cement	221.1	331.7	14.5	1.0	7.0
Pulp, paper, and paper products	24.4	36.5	14.4	0.1	0.8
Chemical and pharmaceutical products	25.2	37.6	14.3	0.1	0.8
Motor vehicles and assembly	21.9	31.8	13.3	0.1	0.6
Oil refining	255.2	358.3	12.0	0.9	6.5
Wood and wood products	123.4	169.9	11.3	0.4	2.9
Electrical and electronics	2.5	3.4	10.8	0.0	0.1
Nonmetallic products	59.5	74.3	7.7	0.1	0.9
Other manufacturing	116.1	139.2	6.2	0.2	1.5
Textiles, apparel, and footwear	352.5	360.1	0.7	0.1	0.5
Total manufacturing output	3,578.6	5,163.5	13.0	14.34	100

Source: National Bureau of Statistics data, various years; World Bank staff calculations.
Note: CAGR = compound annual growth rate; GDP = gross domestic product. Table sorted by real CAGR (2013 output figures were deflated to 2010 prices).

unleash positive localization and urbanization externalities by creating a functional urban system, and facilitate access to national and global markets and value chains.

The recent manufacturing growth has brought Nigeria's share of manufacturing to just 8 percent of GDP, in line with resource-dependent economies, but lower than economies at comparable levels of urbanization (figure 2.9).

The continuing weakness of the manufacturing sector is evident in the weakness of non-oil exports. Despite the growth and diversification of the economy, oil and gas continue to dominate Nigerian exports, averaging 95 percent of export revenues over the past decade and only slightly below this level in 2013 (table 2.3).

The paradox of strong economic growth but insufficient employment growth over the past two decades therefore can be attributed to a great extent to the

Figure 2.9 Manufacturing Share of Nigerian Economy as Compared to Other Countries by Urbanization

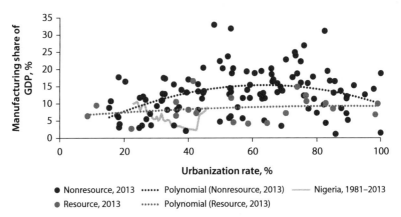

Source: World Bank, World Development Indicators; World Bank staff calculations.
Note: GDP = gross domestic product. Resource-dependent economies defined as those with 20 percent natural resource rents as share of GDP or higher.

Table 2.3 Share of Oil and Gas in Total Exports

Year	Share (%)
1995	91.6
2000	97.5
2005	96.4
2010	93.5
2013	93.4

Source: United Nations Conference on Trade and Development trade data.
Note: The following sectors were aggregated into the oil and gas sector by the UN's Standard International Trade Classification: [333] petroleum oils, oils from bitumen; materials, crude; [343] natural gas, whether or not liquefied; [334] petroleum oils or bituminous minerals >70 percent oil; [342] liquefied propane and butane; [344] petroleum gases, other gaseous hydrocarbons, n.e.s (Complete list available at http://unstats .un.org/unsd/cr/registry/regcst.asp?Cl=14).

weak performance of the manufacturing industry and the growth of the highly productive ICT, real estate, and oil and gas sectors. To generate the employment needed to reduce poverty and unemployment, especially youth unemployment, Nigeria urgently needs to develop and grow labor-intensive industries. The manufacturing sector and the urban industrial corridors in which they are located offer such an opportunity.

Growth and Employment in Regional and Urban Economies

An analysis of location quotients reveals important industrial specialization across regions. National-level data masks industrial concentrations across six Geopolitical Zones and metropolitan regions. State-level employment data by industry offers a plausible proxy for the industrial composition of metropolitan regions.[3]

The ICT and real estate sectors, together with oil and gas, drove over one-third of GDP growth over the last two decades, and are concentrated in the southwest of Nigeria. The ICT sector is highly concentrated, with nearly 60 percent of employment in the South West. Over 26 percent of total ICT employment is concentrated in Ogun State, and a further 18 percent in Lagos, together accounting for 44 percent of national ICT employment concentrated in the Lagos-Ibadan industrial corridor.

Ogun, as noted, is particularly specialized in ICT, with a location quotient of 7.2. The sector accounts for nearly 8 percent of total formal sector employment in the state (map 2.1). This is likely due to the cost of housing in Lagos, driving workers to neighboring Ogun State. The ICT sector also comprises a considerable 2 percent of total employment in Lagos. Although total ICT employment constitutes a minuscule share of total national employment, its concentration in the Lagos-Ibadan industrial corridor has considerable direct and indirect effects on Lagos and its surrounding economy.

The manufacturing sector is more spread out across the country, but nonetheless heavily concentrated within three major agglomerations: the Abuja-Kaduna-Kano industrial corridor in the North Central and North West Zones, the Lagos-Ibadan industrial corridor in the South West Zone, and a concentration reaching from Port Harcourt (Rivers State) in the South South Zone through Imo and Enugu states in the South East Zone. Lagos has the largest concentration of manufacturing small and medium enterprises (1,195), followed by the North West Zone around Kano, the largest city and commercial capital of Northern Nigeria, as illustrated in map 2.2.

Lagos has the highest number of manufacturing workers, with 545,000 manufacturing jobs, accounting for 15 percent of total state employment. The size of manufacturing employment in Lagos, however, is proportional to the size of its population, evident by a location quotient of 1.03. Other major manufacturing agglomerations are in Oyo and Ogun states, making the South West the largest manufacturing agglomeration with its three states accounting for 27 percent of national manufacturing employment,

Map 2.1 Manufacturing Employment Location Quotient by State, 2010

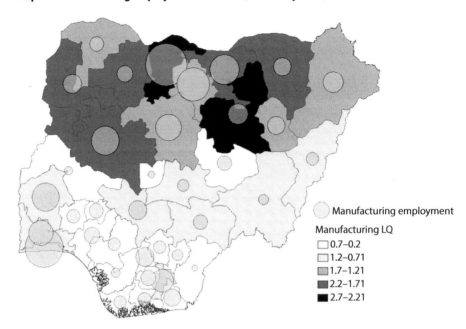

Source: Bloch, Makarem, and others 2015; data from National Bureau of Statistics 2010a.
Note: ICT = information and communication technology; LQ = location quotient.

predominantly concentrated in the Lagos-Ibadan industrial corridor through Ogun State.[4]

Kano State is the second largest manufacturing agglomeration, with 384,000 employees, and a location quotient of 1.23. Manufacturing here is principally located in Kano City, primarily in textiles and tanning and leather. However, these two subsectors are in decline and, moreover, are low productivity activities, as reflected in the state's low GDP per capita. Attempts to protect the manufacturing industry from imports have failed due to an inability to regulate and protect the border, which is flooded with "Made in Nigeria" imports from China. Jigawa and Kaduna are also major manufacturing employment centers, making the North West an important manufacturing zone, with the greatest concentration stretching along the Abuja-Kaduna-Kano industrial corridor.

The services industry is highly diversified and its subsectors are concentrated in the southwest, in and around Lagos. Three highly productive subsectors have driven the sector's growth over the past two decades: professional, scientific, and technical services; the public sector; and finance and insurance. Together, they accounted for almost 60 percent of growth in services from 1990 to 2010.

The professional, scientific, and technical services sector is highly concentrated in the South West. The subsector employs almost 780,000 workers, and is highly

Map 2.2 Location of Manufacturing SMEs at the State Level, 2010

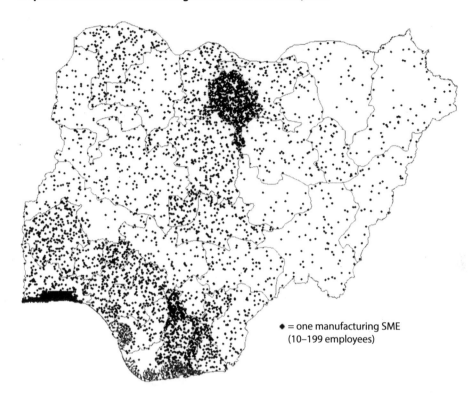

◆ = one manufacturing SME
(10–199 employees)

Source: Bloch, Makarem, and others 2015; data from Small and Medium Enterprises Development Agency of Nigeria 2010 Collaborative Survey; National Bureau of Statistics 2010b.
Note: SMEs = small and medium enterprises. Dots represent one firm in that state, not the exact location of a firm.

concentrated in Ogun State, with a location quotient of 4.1. It makes up a staggering 10 percent of state employment, or 20 percent of the subsector's national employment. The second largest concentration is in Lagos (126,000 workers), with a location quotient of 1.5 (16 percent of the subsector's national employment). The professional, scientific, and technical services industry clearly has positive employment and multiplier effects on the agglomerations in which it is concentrated, namely the Lagos-Ibadan industrial corridor (see map 2.3).

The sector offers high-end services to the oil and gas industry. The growth of the oil-related sector is likely consistent with evidence in the literature of the success of the government's increased local inputs into the oil and gas industry:

> From the Petroleum Act of 1965 to the directives in 1995 and 2005 mandating the use of local services of low-tech onshore supply of goods and services to Nigerian firms, government policies have paid off, evident by an estimated rise in local content within the Oil and Gas sector from 3 to 5 percent in 1970 to 20 percent in 2004 (UNCTAD/CALAG 2006) and to 39 percent in 2009.
>
> (Adewuyi and Oyejide 2012, 453)

Map 2.3 Professional, Scientific, and Technical Services Employment and Location Quotient by State, 2010

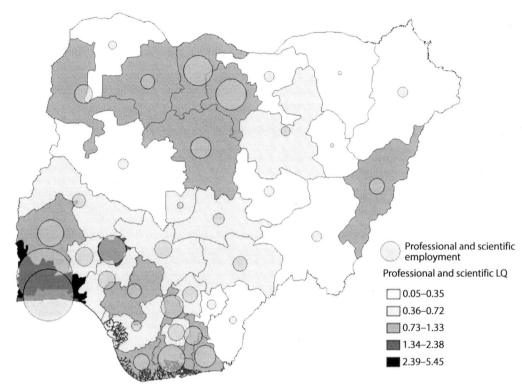

○ Professional and scientific employment

Professional and scientific LQ

☐ 0.05–0.35
☐ 0.36–0.72
▨ 0.73–1.33
▨ 1.34–2.38
■ 2.39–5.45

Source: Bloch, Fox, and others 2015; data from National Bureau of Statistics 2010a.
Note: LQ = location quotient.

The finance and insurance sector is also concentrated in Lagos. Although it employed just over 171,000 workers in 2010 (1 percent of services employment and 0.4 percent of national employment), some 27 percent, equivalent to 46,000 employees, is concentrated in Lagos (see map 2.4). Again, the disproportionately high concentration of productive workers has a positive impact on the wider regional economy of Lagos.

The Urban Informal Economy

High levels of unemployment and underemployment have contributed to the growth of the informal economy—and today the majority of Nigerians are employed informally. The informal economy, although a widespread phenomenon, is difficult to define. The National Bureau of Statistics uses an approach consistent with that of the International Labour Organization. It defines the informal economy as:

> …that which operates without binding official regulations (but it may or may not regulate itself internally) as well as one that operates under official regulations that do not compel rendition of official returns on its operations or production process
> (CBN/FOS/NISER 2001)

Map 2.4 Finance and Insurance Employment and Location Quotient by State, 2010

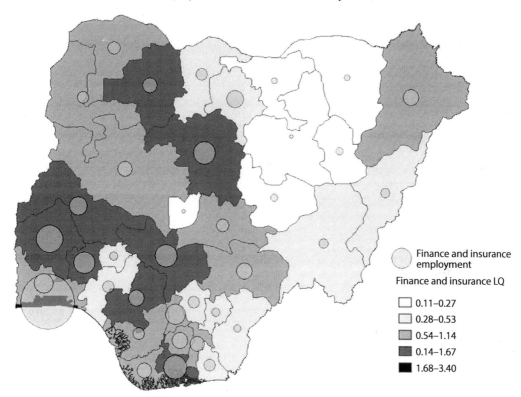

Finance and insurance
employment

Finance and insurance LQ

☐ 0.11–0.27
☐ 0.28–0.53
▨ 0.54–1.14
▨ 0.14–1.67
■ 1.68–3.40

Sources: Bloch, Makarem, and others 2015; data from National Bureau of Statistics 2010a.
Note: LQ = location quotient.

According to National Bureau of Statistics data, there is slightly more than one informal worker for every formal sector worker: 54.6 million informal workers versus 48.5 million formal sector workers. In other words, informal workers make up 53 percent of the active labor force.

A World Bank (2015) study, however, estimates the share of informal nonfarm employment as high as 84 percent. The study uses data from the 2010/11 General Household Survey and defines informal jobs as wage workers working without a contract and self-employed, and household enterprise workers in firms that are not registered with the authorities. While private sector jobs are almost exclusively (96 percent) informal, three quarters (74 percent) of public sector jobs are also informal, using this definition.

The largest concentrations of informality as a share of workers are found in the north, as illustrated in table 2.4 below ranking the six Geopolitical Zones by their average state location quotient of informal employment. However, there are exceptions to this trend, such as the Rivers State in the South South and Ogun in the South West (map 2.5).

Workers in the informal sector are classified into seven categories. The majority, 62 percent, are categorized as proprietors or partners. A large 17 percent are

Table 2.4 Average State Location Quotient in Informal Sector by Geopolitical Zone, 2010

Zone	Location quotient
North West	1.42
North East	1.19
North Central	1.02
South West	0.96
South South	0.81
South East	0.73

Source: World Bank staff calculations using National Bureau of Statistics data.

Map 2.5 Informal Employment by State, 2010

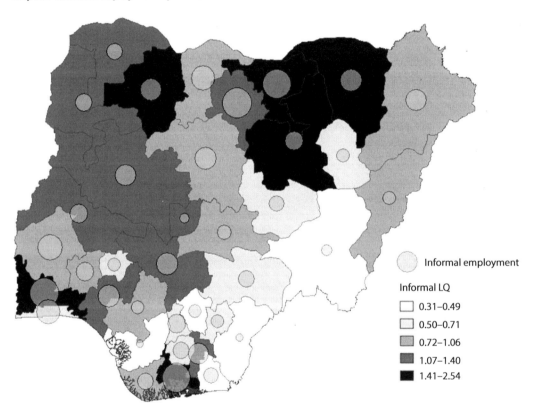

Informal employment

Informal LQ
- 0.31–0.49
- 0.50–0.71
- 0.72–1.06
- 1.07–1.40
- 1.41–2.54

Source: Block, Makarem, and others 2015; data from National Bureau of Statistics 2010a.
Note: LQ = location quotient.

unpaid workers, followed by apprentices (9 percent) and hired labor and casual workers/operatives (9 percent), as illustrated in figure 2.10.

Over 40 percent of informal workers are engaged in wholesale and retail, and repairing motor vehicles, by far the largest categories of informal businesses. Unlike the formal economy, manufacturing is the second largest informal sector, accounting for 17 percent of informal sector microenterprises, followed by other

Figure 2.10 Share of Informal Workers by Category of Worker
percent

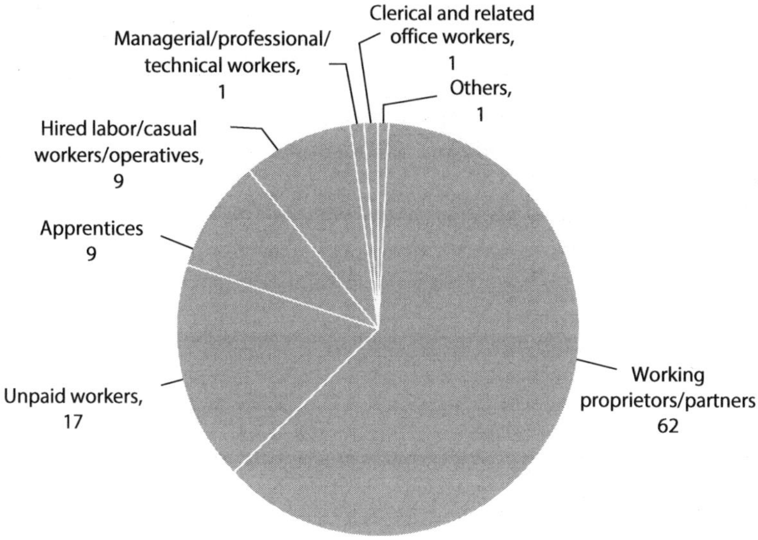

Source: National Bureau of Statistics data, various years.

social activities (11 percent), and accommodation and food services (10 percent). These four sectors comprise almost 80 percent of informal microenterprises. The agriculture, forestry, and fishing sector accounts for 7 percent, followed by transportation and storage (5 percent) and construction (2 percent).

Informality is the norm for a country at Nigeria's stage of development, and evidence from Latin America and Southeast Asia indicates that the share of informal employment may increase further with growth (World Bank 2015). As such, the share of jobs classified as informal is not necessarily a good indicator of the quality of employment opportunities. So rather than focusing on reducing informality, it is more important to raise productivity across all sectors, in formal as well as informal enterprises.

Informality of urban employment is associated with lower levels of productivity and lower tax revenue. Informal businesses are much less likely to grow given their lack of access to the formal legal system, thereby reducing the benefits of scale economies that urban environments can provide. Furthermore, informal enterprises avoid taxation, which limits the funds available for public use. This leads to a vicious circle of increased taxation and fees imposed on the formal sector, which reduces the competitiveness of formal firms, inducing further informality and reducing foreign direct investment (Mbaye 2014). Studies have found that, internationally, an increase of one standard deviation in the size of the informal sector corresponds to a 1–2 percentage point decline per capita GDP growth (Oviedo, Thomas, and Karakurum-Ozdemir 2009).

Average wages in the formal sector are about 70 percent higher than the informal sector, although there is overlap, with some informal workers earning more than some formal workers. Part of this formal sector premium is due to education: the returns to education are lower in the informal than the formal sector. This reflects the problem of underemployment in the Nigerian economy, whereby workers are unable to find employment that is well matched to their level of education or skills and end up working in low-productivity informal jobs where their education is not needed and hence not compensated (Behar 2013).

The distinction between formal and informal is, however, more complex than it first appears. Workers in the informal economy are not necessarily a residual comprised of disadvantaged workers rationed out of good jobs, but may have chosen voluntarily to pursue an entrepreneurial informal sector job. Conventional economic theory views informal workers as the less advantaged sector of a dualistic or segmented labor market, in which a lack of formal jobs and above market-clearing wages force workers into subsisting in informal jobs while they wait for an opportunity in the formal sector. However, although this may be the case for some, if not many informal workers, for others it is the optimal decision given their preferences, the constraints they face in their level of human capital, and the level of formal sector productivity in the country (Maloney 2004).

It is more appropriate to view formality as a continuum. Economic relations—of production, distribution, and employment—tend to fall at some point along a spectrum between pure "formal" relations (that is, regulated and protected) at one pole and pure "informal" (unregulated and unprotected) at the other, with many categories in between (Chen 2005). Many informal enterprises have a taxpayer ID number, and some maintain subcontractual relationships with multinational firms (Mbaye 2014). Importantly, it is possible to make the transition from formal to informal and, depending on their circumstances, firms and workers are known to move with varying ease and speed along the continuum or to operate simultaneously at different points on the continuum (Chen 2005).

That said, firms must overcome considerable barriers to enter the formal sector. Research exploring the determinants of informality drawing on a survey of micro, small, and medium enterprises in Côte d'Ivoire, Kenya, Nigeria, and Senegal confirms that corruption, which increases the cost of registration, is a determining factor in informality. The research also found that higher productivity firms, with better access to bank finance, are more likely to register and remain formal (Gajigo and Hallward-Driemeier 2012).

In other words, the drivers of informality are high formal costs to registration, corruption and a weak rule of law, low productivity, and low access to bank finance. Current economic conditions therefore provide few incentives for informal firms to grow, particularly given high corruption and little faith in the impartiality/effectiveness of the judiciary. Transparency International ranked Nigeria the most corrupt country in the world in 2000, and it is currently ranked 136th out of 175 countries.

The functioning of the urban economy in Nigeria reflects the continuum just described. Many links exist between formal and informal firms, further blurring the lines between the two sectors. For instance, many informal enterprises have production and distribution relationships with formal enterprises supplying inputs, finished goods, or services, either through direct transactions or subcontracting arrangements. In addition, many formal enterprises hire wage workers under informal employment relations. For example, many part-time workers, temporary workers, and homeworkers work for formal enterprises through informal or semiformal contracting or subcontracting arrangements.

The relationship between government and the informal sector in Nigeria is a complex one. On the one hand, policy makers and authorities have sought to "formalize" the informal economy, treating it as a social problem. In other cases, however, they have engaged with and recognized firms operating informally. Ways in which authorities have sought to formalize the informal sector include fines, closures of informal businesses, and repossessions of informal property. However, these methods are largely counterproductive as many informal firms do not have the means to formalize and the benefits of formally registering for a small firm are far outweighed by the costs. Ultimately treating the informal sector in this way creates barriers to growth for informal enterprises, reducing their productivity and ability to generate income for their owners and employees.

It is far more effective to engage with the informal sector. One way that government can do this is through engaging with local business associations that represent informal firms in a particular sector or location. An example of this is the interaction between informal ICT firms in the Otigba ICT cluster in Lagos and the Lagos state government, which relates with them through the Computer Allied Products Dealers Association of Nigeria and even collects taxes from firms (Oyelaran-Oyeyinka 2014).

Given the right conditions, informal firms can raise their productivity, increasing the wages and benefits for employees and, ultimately, make the transition to formality. The experience of informal enterprises in other parts of the developing world demonstrates the high productivity that informal sector enterprises can achieve through local economies of scale generated by multiple small enterprises. In China, for example, informal township and village enterprises, once their property rights were secured, increased investments in human and physical capital and established links with formal and informal enterprises. Local informal township and village enterprise clusters in small urban regions generated local scale economies with positive economic spillovers, playing a critical role in China's economic development.

Successful informal enterprise clusters exist in Nigeria. The Otigba ICT cluster, already cited, is a spontaneous cluster that has been described as the "Silicon Valley of West Africa." The cluster contains a variety of firms spanning the formal-informal continuum, from sole traders dealing in laptop accessories, to retailers and small repair shops and firms that make locally branded hardware products, including laptops and tablet computers, which are formally registered and even exported internationally. In 2005 the cluster contained about 3,500 firms, which between them employed about 10,000 people. And the numbers have grown since then. Moreover, in 2013, more than one-quarter of businesses were estimated to be worth between US$6,200 and US$31,000, and more than a tenth of businesses were worth over US$620,000 (Oyelaran-Oyeyinka 2014).

Other similar examples include the Nnewi Automotive Parts Industrial Cluster, the Aba shoe and garment clusters, the Ilorin weaving cluster, Kano leather tanneries, and the Onitsha Plastic Cluster (also known as the Osakwe Industrial Cluster).

Informal clusters in Nigeria share distinct characteristics that have contributed to their success. These include: (a) the existence or establishment of active business associations and social/popular networks; (b) the contributions of skills, learning spillovers, and entrepreneurship in creating opportunity and innovation; (c) significant interfirm links, specifically with large firms, (d) specialization and division of labor among individual firms, which enhances productivity; (e) engaging in workplace training in the form of apprenticeships; and (f) the sociocultural factors, which play an important role in the development of informal clusters in Nigeria, as a shared sociocultural identity provides a basis for trust and reciprocity in an informal setting (Bloch, Makarem, and others 2015).

The Urban Business Environment

The Nigerian urban business environment discourages investment and frustrates competitiveness. A large body of research on Nigeria has focused on the business climate and its constraining effects on firms in general and on manufacturing firms in particular.[5] Nigeria ranked 175th out of 189 countries in 2014 in the World Bank's Doing Business ratings. Its ranking was particularly bad for dealing with construction permits, getting electricity, registering property, paying taxes, and trading across borders.

A dysfunctional business climate undermines worker productivity. Although wages in Nigeria are lower than many of its competitors, this low productivity means that workers produce less, on average, than competitors, reducing competitiveness in the global economy.

The biggest constraint to productivity in Nigeria, as perceived by businesses, is power. Almost all Nigerian firms experience power outages, averaging 8 hours per calendar day, resulting in indirect costs equivalent to 4.3 percent of sales for manufacturing firms and 5.3 percent for retail firms (Iarossi and Clarke 2011). To address this situation, the majority of firms (88 percent) have their own generators, which adds significantly to their operating costs. Manufacturing firms reported that approximately 69 percent of their total electrical utilization comes not from the public grid, but from their own generators, with large manufacturers more dependent than smaller ones on generator power. The cost of acquiring and maintaining a generator amounts to 9 percent of the total value of a firm's equipment and machinery and 13 percent of its operating expenses (Iarossi and Clarke 2011).

The centrality of a poor infrastructure environment and particularly poor provision of electricity to business operations is confirmed in enterprise surveys. Nearly 80 percent of total firms identify electricity as a major constraint, well above the Sub-Saharan average of 50 percent (figure 2.11). However, compared to other countries in Sub-Saharan Africa, neither the cost nor the skill level of labor is seen as a major problem, although there is some evidence that wages in Nigeria are high relative to productivity, making them less competitive (World Bank 2014).

Transport problems are also a significant problem in Nigeria, accounting for annual sales losses of 2.4 percent (Iarossi and Clarke 2011). Road transport is the primary means of transport in the country and poor quality roads and congestion are the main cause of these losses. The cost and amount of time taken to process imports and exports is also higher than in other comparable countries. The cost of congestion is a significant fraction of GDP and varies across regions. Findings from a background paper for this report suggest that traffic congestion costs the Federal Capital Territory/Abuja, Kano, and Lagos US$389 million, US$673 million, and US$2.8 billion a year, respectively, in lost productivity—or 7.1 percent, 5.0 percent and 3.5 percent of these cities' regional GDP (figure 2.12).[6] Nationally, some US$5.51 billion is lost from congestion annually in the country's 14 largest cities.[7] This is some 1 percent of the country's GDP.

Access to finance and, to a lesser extent, the cost of finance are perceived by Nigerian firms as the third most important constraint to doing business (World Bank 2011). About 52 percent of firm managers said that access to finance was a serious constraint, and 46 percent of firm managers said the same about the cost of financing. Nigeria's businesses are starved of capital: only about 12 percent of Nigerian firms have an overdraft facility and only about 14 percent have an overdraft or loan. Collateral is also more likely to be required to obtain

Figure 2.11 Share of Firms Identifying Issue as "Major" or "Severe" Obstacle

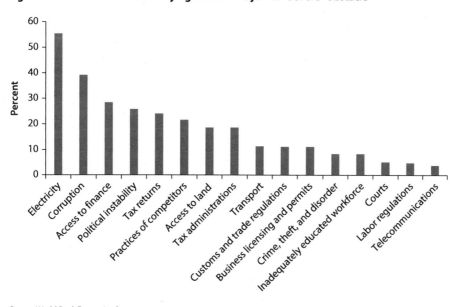

Source: World Bank Enterprise Surveys.

Figure 2.12 Annual Cost of Congestion as a Proportion of Regional GDP

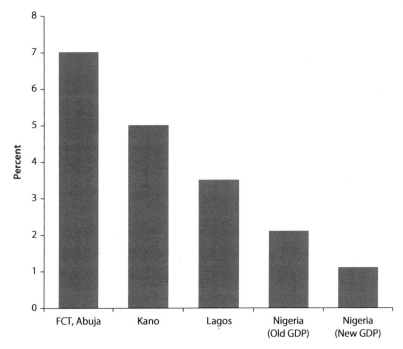

Sources: Travel demand surveys in the FCT/Abuja (2013), Kano (2012), and Lagos (2009, 2012), undertaken by
the Nigeria Infrastructure Advisory Facility (NIAF), funded by the U.K. Department for International
Development (DFID) Demand Survey.
Note: GDP = gross domestic product.

a loan and the amount of collateral required as a ratio of the loan was higher than
comparator countries (at 170 percent of the value of the loan). Even when firms
do manage to get a loan, the time they have to repay it is shorter than in comparator countries.

That the formal financial sector services a mere 1 percent of businesses' financial needs highlights the inadequacy of Nigeria's financial infrastructure. This
obstacle, however, does not affect all firms equally: the smaller the firm, the
greater the challenge of accessing capital (Iarossi and Clarke 2011).

Setting up a business is very difficult. In particular, land transactions are
very costly, lengthy, and complicated, discouraging both buyers and sellers
from the formal procedure. To transfer a real estate property in some jurisdictions, one has to pay stamp duty (2–3 percent of asset value), capital gains
tax (2 percent of land value), transfer tax (8–30 percent of land value as set
by states), and a registration fee (3 percent of asset value). Unlike most
countries, capital gains are taxed on the land value, not the gain. The transfer
tax percentage is significantly higher than in other countries, and registration
fees are a percentage of asset value, not a fixed amount (Iarossi and Clarke
2011). The cost of titling land alone in Lagos and Port Harcourt is 30 percent
of the construction cost.

Several of these obstacles to business development are particularly pertinent to urban labor-intensive manufacturing firms. Manufacturing industries are much more dependent on a constant and reliable flow of electricity than are real estate and service-sector firms. Congestion, expensive transport, and border barriers are most relevant for the tradable sectors. In other words, while Nigeria's poor business environment affects all firms, it has a disproportionate impact on the productivity of manufacturing firms.

On the other hand, some of these obstacles, namely bureaucratic trade barriers and infrastructure, play a lesser role as obstacles to the development of high-productivity sectors such as ICT; real estate and construction; professional, scientific, and technical services; entertainment; and finance and insurance, which have been important drivers of GDP growth over the past two decades. Growth of these sectors attests to the resilience and ingenuity of urban entrepreneurs who have successfully developed their businesses in these sectors in the face of severe challenges.

Trade, Connectivity, and Regional Development

A long and rich historical legacy of north-south trade in Nigeria is being undermined by poor and deteriorating transport infrastructure, dysfunctional institutions, and a lagging manufacturing sector. The "economic distance" between regions reduces firm competitiveness and diminished positive externalities from regional agglomeration economies. As a result, stark and growing disparities are evident in levels of economic development and living standards between the north and the south of the country.

A complex system of internal and cross-border trade networks exists in Nigeria, which is deeply rooted in cultural and historical ties. The structure of the present-day Nigerian spatial economy can trace its origins to the colonial period and the economic system that developed under colonial rule. Patterns of internal and cross-border trade can trace their origins back even further.

Nigeria enjoys a historical legacy of north-south trading relations dating to the precolonial era. In this period, a complex system of trade and urban economies existed, and was particularly evident in the north. The Hausa states and the Kanem Empire, centered on Borno, were part of a trade network stretching across South Sudan northwards to ports in North Africa and on to Europe.

The colonial era and subsequent policies pursued after independence saw the development of new patterns of internal trade and the reinforcing of north-south trade links.

Internal trade expanded with the construction of railways across the country. The western line between Lagos and Kano was finished in 1912 and an eastern line from Port Harcourt to Jos, which joined up with the western line in Kaduna, was finished in 1927. This substantially reduced transport times and costs from the north of the country to the coast. For example, the journey time from the tin mines in Jos to the coast decreased from 35 days to less than 35 hours, while costs fell by three-quarters (Mabogunje 1965).

The result was a huge increase in the production of agricultural and mineral commodities for export in the north of the country, with the direction of trade now channeled almost exclusively toward the ports of Lagos and Port Harcourt, which became the most important nodes in the transport network (Mabogunje 1965).

The spatial economy developed along the same patterns post-independence, though at that point the economy was based on manufacturing supported by the policy of import substitution. Kano and the surrounding area emerged as the most industrialized region of the country. Leather, textiles, and food production were the dominant industries. By the 1980s, before the onset of structural adjustment, 2,500 manufacturers were located in Kano (Miles 2013). At its height, the textiles industry employed over 350,000 workers in over 175 businesses that exported fabrics throughout West Africa (Miles 2013). Throughout this period manufacturing was concentrated primarily in four areas of the country:

- Southwest corridor between Lagos and Ibadan
- Southeast industrial zone: Onitsha, Port Harcourt, Enugu, Aba, Umuahia, and Calabar
- Northern industrial zone: Kano, Kaduna, Jos, and Zaria
- Midwest industrial zone: Benin City, Sapele, and Warri

However, the failure of import substitution, the deterioration of infrastructure, poor governance, and a dysfunctional business climate has taken a heavy toll on the manufacturing sector across the country.

Present-day trade in Nigeria is conducted predominantly along road corridors. These routes span the length and breadth of the country, as well as linking Nigeria with its neighbors. The Trans-African Highway network represents important trade corridors facilitating road freight movements to and from Benin, Cameroon, Chad, and Niger, stimulating regional trade and acting as particularly important connections for Nigeria's landlocked neighbors.

The key internal trade route is the Lagos-Kano corridor, which is the main channel for domestic, regional, and international trade. It spans approximately 1,000 kilometers, linking the country's two largest cities, and passing through Kaduna, Ilorin, and Ibadan. A newly renovated railway also links the same cities. The Lagos-Kano corridor is the main link between the north and south of the country.

Trade along this corridor flows mainly from south to north. It consists of imported consumer goods shipped through the port at Lagos, manufactured goods produced in the south, petroleum, and inputs for manufacturing firms in the north. North-south trade consists mainly of livestock and agricultural produce, as well as some manufactured goods produced in the north that are predominantly destined for export through Lagos.

The majority of Nigeria's trade with neighboring countries in West Africa is informal. Informal cross-border trade is estimated to be worth around 20 percent of Nigeria's GDP (Afrika and Ajumbo 2012). This trade is deeply rooted in the country's cultural history. To some extent, the historical trade networks persist in the present day. For example, the states of Kano and Katsina in the north and the province of Maradi in neighboring Niger form a vast, densely populated trading area based on the cultural area of the former Hausa states. An intensive trade in agricultural products thrives here, especially in livestock from Niger, cereals and manufactured products from Nigeria, and, above all, products reexported to Nigeria via Niger coming from Benin/Togo (OECD 2006).

Informal trade in food and consumer goods thrives along borders. From Benin, transborder trade is tilted in favor of the purchase of goods from across the border into Nigeria. Imported items are mainly consumer goods, while the main exports from Nigeria are plastics and petrol. Cotonou is the most popular place of purchase, mainly for used cars and spare parts. Purchases of frozen foodstuffs are made almost daily from Igolo. Major places of sale within Nigeria for foodstuffs and used cars are Idiroko, Lagos, and Sango-Otta; and the relatively less important markets are Ibadan, Sagamu, and Benin.

Connective infrastructure has played a pivotal role in the formation and development of modern day Nigeria, contributing to increased social, cultural, and economic integration and influencing the rate and pattern of urbanization across the country.

Today, however, poor connectivity is a constraint on interregional trade, limits integration, and inhibits the functioning of Nigeria's spatial economy. Poor transport infrastructure is reducing annual GDP by approximately 3 percent (World Bank 2007). Research indicates that there is strong correlation between the quantity, quality, and efficiency of a country's transport infrastructure and the level of economic development (World Bank 2004; WTO 2004).

Although Nigeria has an extensive transport network relative to other resource-rich African countries, much of it is in poor condition. In 2013, federal government expenditure on road and bridge, railway, aviation, inland waterway and maritime transport maintenance, and rehabilitation and reconstruction projects amounted to US$3 billion, of which roads and bridges accounted for 74 percent, railways 18 percent, aviation 7 percent, and inland waterways and maritime transport 2 percent.

The international benchmark comparison suggests that Nigeria should ideally look to spend a minimum of 1.8 percent of GDP (US$9.1 billion) annually on transport infrastructure, representing a 204 percent increase in the federal government expenditure on transport infrastructure in 2013. The analysis also indicates that 1.2 percent of GDP (US$6.3 billion) should ideally be allocated to roads, representing a 186 percent increase on 2013's expenditure.

Both paved and unpaved road densities are more than twice as high as comparable countries. However, the percentage of these roads in good or fair condition is lower. It is estimated that 40 percent of federal roads, 65 percent of state roads, and 85 percent of local government roads are in poor or bad condition requiring rehabilitation or reconstruction. The government is failing to maintain the roads built during the era of military rule. Due to the backlog of deferred roads maintenance because of sustained underfunding of routine and periodic road maintenance, it will cost an estimated US$18.8 billion, or 3.6 percent of GDP, to fully rehabilitate all federal roads in poor condition.

Highway accessibility, in the form of drive time to the nearest federal or state capital, highlights large regional variation in its quality, which arises from a combination of poor road conditions, urban congestion, and missing highway and bridge connections. In addition to the quality of road infrastructure, institutional constraints reduce interregional connectivity. On average, Nigeria has more than two roadblocks every 100 kilometers (see figure 2.13).

One-third of ongoing road and bridge projects account for some 80 percent of total travel time savings. But a backlog exists of over 250 ongoing federal road and bridge projects[8] arising from a combination of significant funding constraints, the persistent prioritization of rehabilitation and reconstruction expenditure activities over routine and periodic maintenance activities, and the absence of detailed project planning and prioritization activities. When ongoing federal road and bridge projects were reviewed in terms of accessibility-based prioritization it was revealed that not all ongoing projects are equal in their impact on improving accessibility to federal and state capitals.

Evidence from a study of the cattle and leather trade along the Lagos-Kano corridor reveals a variety of unjustified charges and barriers along the corridor increase transport and related costs by 18 percent and increase journey times by 23 percent (Coste 2014). The study found there were 23 roadblocks along the 990-kilometer route. Although the majority of these were operated by public authorities, such as police and other security forces and state revenue collection and other agencies, many roadblocks were not legitimate and were used to extort illegal charges from traders. In addition, roadblocks operated by criminal gangs took an average of US$42 per trader and caused delays of over 30 minutes

Figure 2.13 Number of Roadblocks per 100 Kilometers, Selected Countries, 2011

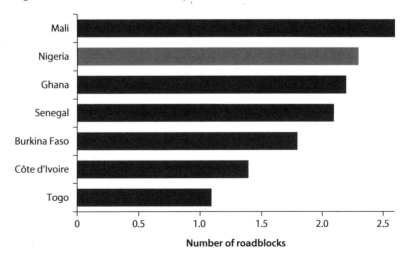

Number of roadblocks

Source: Coste 2014.

per journey. In addition to these facilitation payments at roadblocks, truck owners and drivers must pay to obtain a plethora of permits to operate in the successive states and local government areas (LGAs) that the corridor passes through. Many of these licenses were not mutually recognized between neighboring administrative authorities.

A study (USAID 2013) of the Lagos-Kano-Jibiya corridor (that is, the Lagos-Kano corridor plus the road to the border with Niger at Jibiya) found the corridor had 4.5 roadblocks on average and traders were required to pay an average of US$11.50 in bribes per 100 kilometers. This is substantially higher than other corridors in West Africa, even though many of these corridors cross national borders.

Evidence from a freight movement survey conducted by the Nigeria Infrastructure Advisory Facility on the A2 corridor between Abuja-Kaduna-Kano from December 2013 to May 2014 highlights additional inefficiencies that add to transport costs. A significant imbalance exists in compatible traffic flows between the north and south of the A2 corridor, which leads to freight vehicle overcapacity, vehicle underutilization, and excessive empty running. Empty running accounts for almost half of all truck movements on the corridor, with trucks often full on the journey north, but empty on the return journey south. Moreover, vehicles are mostly outdated and in poor condition, which reduces reliability and adds to fuel costs (NIAF-World Bank 2014). Box 2.2 summarizes the key findings of the survey.

Nigeria's rail network offers little alternative to poor road quality. The rail network, a legacy of the colonial era, stretches across the country, linking several major cities. However, due to deficient performance and erratic services, both passenger and freight traffic have been in long-term decline (see figure 2.14). As a result, traffic density is a tiny fraction of the already low levels found on other African railways (Foster and Puschak 2011), although, it has started to recover slightly in recent years.

One of the railways' most significant contributions to modern day Nigeria is the pattern of land use development that they have supported. In particular, the urbanization resulting from the emergence of "railway towns" in Lagos, Kano, Ibadan, Enugu, Jos, Kafanchan, Makurdi, Minna, Port Harcourt, Umuahia, and

---

Box 2.2 Key Findings of the Kaduna Freight Survey

The results of the NIAF-World Bank Freight Survey indicate priority action areas to improve inter-city freight movement nationwide.

Priority 1: Road Condition and En Route Facilities

Infrastructure bottlenecks and poor road condition raise the costs of goods and services. A lack of en route repair, service, and maintenance facilities lowers the resilience of both the network and Nigeria's road freight transport fleet. The lack of adequate off-road overnight parking

box continues next page

Box 2.2 Key Findings of the Kaduna Freight Survey *(continued)*

facilities poses accident risks to drivers, vehicles, loads, other road users, and local communities by encouraging drivers to park adjacent to or directly on the roads.

To reduce journey times, improve journey time reliability, road safety, and network efficiency, and reduce the cost of freight movement, appropriate facilities are needed to improve road conditions including as a minimum the development of a network of freight villages offering repair and maintenance and secure parking.

Priority 2: En Route Security

Security issues en route present a significant obstacle to nighttime freight transport in Nigeria and thereby affect overall network use and road freight operational efficiency. Safety and security for road freight vehicles traveling and parking along strategic routes needs to be improved.

Currently, due to security issues affecting drivers, vehicles, and loads, many operators do not run at night, which means narrower operating nighttime if nighttime operations were more secure.

Priority 3: Modernizing Fleet Operations and Management

Nigeria's road freight transport fleet has inherent operational inefficiencies, which raises the costs of goods and services. Vehicles are extremely aged or in poor condition, which is exacerbated further by inefficient operations such as a high percentage of empty return trips. Policy makers need to provide incentives for a more efficient trucking market, with the primary focus on improving fuel economy and their truck fleets, and reducing operating costs.

Guidance and training in management techniques should be provided as a countrywide initiative, aimed at improving industry expertise and raising the bar for performance. This should come in the form of hard copy and online support material.

Priority 4: Empty Running—Third-Party Logistics Coordination and Consolidation

Empty running is a huge drain on fleet efficiency and network usage, and is crippling the efficiency of Nigerian road freight operations. Weak coordination can also erode efficiency, increase delivery times, and drive up operating costs.

A system of third-party logistics needs to be developed whereby an expert contractor operates and controls elements of the supply chain to better coordinate trucking operations, remove overcapacity, and reduce chronic levels of empty running, ultimately driving down the cost of road freight transport. The use of third-party logistics providers is a well-tested and proven structure in mature European markets and North America.

More coordination by government and trade bodies could also improve utilization levels. Coordination and consolidation through a third- or fourth-party logistics provider—a major operator overseeing all freight movements for customers sometimes using managed subcontractors, but with visibility across a wide range of activities to identify opportunities for efficiencies—would reduce levels of empty running and increase industry performance levels.

Source: NIAF–World Bank 2014.

Figure 2.14 Performance of the Railways: Passenger and Freight, 1964–2013

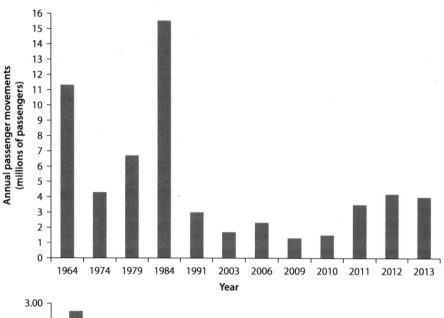

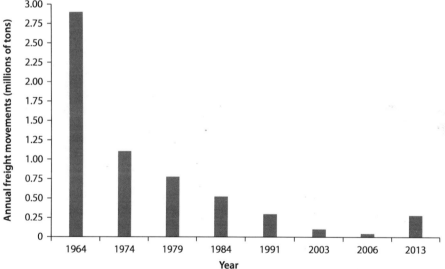

Sources: Federal Ministry of Transport; Nigerian Railway Corporation data.

Zaria, among others (Jaekel 1997). The railways also played an important role in the development of sea ports in Lagos and Port Harcourt, with the then railway administration being responsible for quayside cargo handling activities.

More recently, a renewed refocus on the need for the rehabilitation, renewal, and modernization of the nation's railways has seen increasing funds allocated to this sector, including an increased budget from the Subsidy Reinvestment and Empowerment Programme, culminating in the 2012 reopening of the Lagos-Kano segment of the western railway line, the ongoing rehabilitation of the eastern railway line and the remainder of the western railway line, the rehabilitation and completion of the central railway line, and the ongoing construction of a new standard gauge railway line from Abuja-Kaduna.

As a result of poor infrastructure and dysfunctional institutions, trade between regions is very costly. The consequence of these infrastructure and institutional constraints—delays from poor quality roads, the high number of roadblocks, the cost and delays caused by permits and fees (both legal and illegal)—is that transporting goods within Nigeria is more akin to cross-border trade than what should be cheap and efficient interregional trade. Illustrating this problem, the cost of transporting a ton of freight from one end of Nigeria to the other is greater than moving a ton of freight from China to Europe.

The burden of high transportation costs falls disproportionately on small and medium-size businesses. Evidence from the Lagos-Kano corridor found that the cost of importing a container of tanning chemicals through Lagos to Kano is US$4,300 per trip, equating to slightly over 10 percent of the total value of the goods. Of this, US$2,100 is incurred in port costs and US$2,200 in transportation costs from Lagos to Kano. These costs are more than three times the cost of transporting a container of leather products south from Kano to Lagos, due to the empty running of freight trucks from north to south, as already discussed. These costs are prohibitively high for smaller leather producers, who have reportedly resorted to shipping small orders of chemicals north on passenger buses (Coste 2014), and constitute a significant share of their overall cost structure (evident by the high share of the costs of inputs, as the Kano case study illustrates in box 2.2).

The "economic distance" between regions, especially those connecting the north and south of the country, disconnects firms and regional economies from national "home-market effects" and dramatically reduces internal and external economies of scale and scope. Given Nigeria's 170 million people and its growing urbanized middle class, firms, particularly manufacturing firms with tradable outputs, have a potentially massive home market they can tap into—not doing so constitutes a major opportunity cost, which manifests in rising unemployment rates and informal employment.

The inadequate access of producers to markets beyond their immediate localities, especially those in large urban agglomerations, significantly reduces the internal economies of scale they can exploit. Such limits on the extent of the markets producers can access reduce regional external economies of scale and scope. As a result, cities and metropolitan regions cannot specialize and develop clusters connected to extra-regional supply chains. This severely hampers firms' capacities to focus on their core competencies, to develop the capabilities and absorptive capacities required to compete in broader and more competitive markets (including export markets), to upgrade to more productive activities, and to develop new products and services.

Regional fragmentation is evident in significant price variations across the country, as illustrated in table 2.5. Market fragmentation is also seen in the fact that most businesses in Nigeria are locked into local markets (figure 2.15). About 50 percent of firms identify their main market as being within the same state.

Table 2.5 Coefficient of Variation in the Price of Basic Goods between and within Regions

	North Central	North East	North West	South East	South South	South West	Average CV within each region	National CV
Maize, white	0.22	0.24	0.18	0.18	0.30	0.19	0.22	0.43
Maize, yellow	0.22	0.19	0.19	0.20	0.29	0.18	0.21	0.41
Rice, imported	0.13	0.16	0.14	0.14	0.19	0.14	0.15	0.22
Rice, local	0.15	0.17	0.15	0.17	0.30	0.20	0.19	0.30
Sorghum	0.24	0.22	0.19	0.18	0.21	0.20	0.21	0.41
Cement	0.22	0.15	0.20	0.07	0.10	0.08	0.14	0.24
Water 1	0.11	0.24	0.21	0.18	0.21	0.20	0.19	0.25
Water 2	0.13	0.16	0.22	0.12	0.24	0.17	0.17	0.22

Source: Drawn from Etienne 2014.
Note: CV = coefficient of variation.

Figure 2.15 Distribution of Firm Size and Product Market Channels

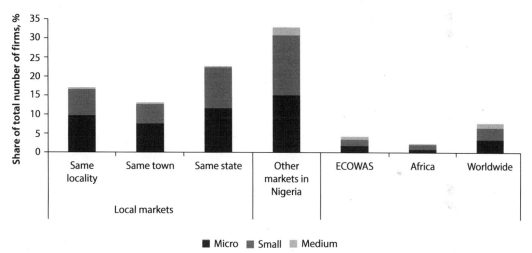

Source: World Bank team calculations using the Small and Medium Enterprises Development Agency of Nigeria (SMEDAN) 2010 survey.
Note: ECOWAS = Economic Community of West African States.

Most producers are therefore unable to scale up their production facilities and exploit greater economies of scale, and cities and metropolitan regions cannot specialize and grow their economies. Those that are able to overcome these constraints—and 50 percent of firms identify their main market as being within the same state—do so at a very high cost, according to the SMEDAN (Small and Medium Enterprises Development Agency of Nigeria) 2010 survey.

Poor connectivity and market fragmentation have contributed to growing regional inequalities in the country. Trucks running empty from the north of the country to the south is an illustration of how traditional north-south trade routes have been undermined by the recent industrial decline of northern states and the poor state of infrastructure connecting the north with the rest of the country. Box 2.3 details the rise and decline of manufacturing in Kano.

This growing inequality is reflected in the size of states' respective economies and incomes per capita (see map 2.6). With the exception of the Federal Capital Territory (Abuja), overall GDP is largely concentrated in the south, while GDP per capita is noticeably lower in the north, where it is just US$1,153 on average, compared to US$2,432 in the southern states and US$5,612 in the Federal Capital Territory. Data presented earlier also shows a significantly larger share of informal workers in the northern states.

Box 2.3 The Decline of Kano—The Industrial Capital of Northern Nigeria

With a rich history dating at least as far back as the end of the eleventh century, Kano is the commercial, industrial, and administrative center of Northern Nigerian. Since independence, Kano has witnessed tremendous rates of urbanization, population growth, and economic restructuring. Today its GDP is estimated at US$10 billion, equivalent to 4 percent of national output, but lower than its respective share of national population.

In the 1960s Kano was Nigeria's most industrialized state. Characterized by strong business-civic leadership and entrepreneurship, Kano was the economic powerhouse of the north, specializing in tanneries and leather work, textiles, agricultural processing, and, later, plastics. Formal sector manufacturing operations were located in five main industrial estates at Sharada, Challawa, Bompai, Tokarawa, and Zaria, which were originally serviced by the railway.

By the 1980s Lagos was the country's most industrialized city, but Kano still hosted over 2,500 manufacturing firms. Over the past two decades, however, the city has experienced major economic decline and deindustrialization. By 2011, two-thirds of its tanneries had closed, forcing over 16,000 workers out of the labor market. Only five tanneries were operational by 2013. The same story of decline characterizes Kano's leather and textiles industries.

Once known as the "Manchester of Africa" for its dynamic textile industry, the industry today has all but collapsed. At its peak Kano employed about 350,000 textile workers in 175 businesses; 30 textile firms were operating in 1990, employing about 50,000 workers. Today, a mere six factories survive, with only three operating at near full capacity.

Nigerian textile firms cannot compete with cheaper imports from China. The country's incapacity to regulate borders—despite a ban of textile imports—has resulted in more than US$2.2 billion worth of so-called Made in Nigeria apparel being smuggled into Nigeria through Benin every year. Nigeria's textile production has slumped to a mere US$40 million per year, disproportionately impacting the economy of the north and Kano in particular.

The entire state of Kano is currently host to just 350 large and medium manufacturing firms, the majority of which are in Kano City. Moreover, many of these are operating at low levels of capacity utilization, despite increasing manufacturing capacity utilization in Nigeria as a whole.

The competitiveness of manufacturing in Kano is adversely impacted by a weak business climate, in particular inadequate access to electricity. The state experiences the equivalent of 16 days of electricity outages per month, being the worst-hit state in the country, according to the Growth and Employment in States (GEM3) program financed by the World Bank and the

box continues next page

Box 2.3 The Decline of Kano—The Industrial Capital of Northern Nigeria *(continued)*

U.K. Department for International Development. The need for private power generators adds a substantial cost to businesses, and more so for larger firms: on average 15 percent of their operating costs.

The high costs of raw material and lack of government support for businesses are also major barriers (see table B2.3.1). It takes 40 percent more time to start a business and enforce contracts in Kano than in the rest of Nigeria.

Other problems highlighted through business surveys are the cost of capital, the difficulty of accessing financing for working capital, and, more recently, security concerns due to the conflict with Boko Haram. The business climate is also exacerbated by an inefficient and often dysfunctional political economy due to the rent-seeking, elite capture, and corruption endemic in many regional economies across Nigeria.

On a positive note, surveyed businesses in Kano consider the city to be a good place for running a business and are surprisingly optimistic about the future. A survey by the Manufacturing Association of Nigeria and the Nigerian Association of Small Scale Industries in

Table B2.3.1 Factors Affecting Business in Kano

Score	Factors affecting business
2.1	Road conditions
3.1	Traffic congestion
3.4	Water supply
4.2	Electricity/power
2.9	Drains and drainage
2.9	Solid waste collection
3.0	Security in Kano
3.6	Government assistance
2.2	Labor supply
2.3	Labor skills
2.3	Demand for products
3.5	Raw material costs
2.3	Transport to other cities
2.5	International connection
2.9	*Average for Kano*

■ Good in Kano
■ Neutral; neither especially good nor especially bad
▨ Bad in Kano

Source: Nigeria Infrastructure Advisory Facility Survey Kano (June 2013).
Note: N = 73. Respondents were asked to report on a scale where
1 = very good in Kano, and
5 = very bad in Kano.

box continues next page

From Oil to Cities • http://dx.doi.org/10.1596/978-1-4648-0792-3

Box 2.3 The Decline of Kano—The Industrial Capital of Northern Nigeria *(continued)*

2013 reveals that 80 percent of respondents considered Kano a good or very good place to run a business. Respondents drew attention to the region being a major center of commerce in the north, the growing size of its market, and that materials and labor, including skilled labor, were readily available. Their optimism is reflected in a small but substantial increase in the number of workers employed by surveyed firms from 2011 to 2013, which is consistent with the national growth of manufacturing subsectors for 2010–13.

Source: Miles 2013.

Map 2.6 GDP and GDP per Capita by State, 2010

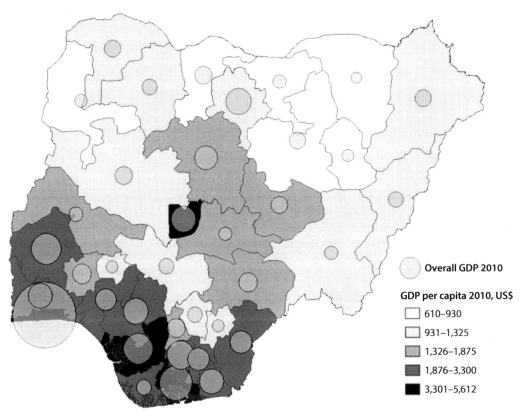

Overall GDP 2010

GDP per capita 2010, US$
- 610–930
- 931–1,325
- 1,326–1,875
- 1,876–3,300
- 3,301–5,612

Source: Bloch, Fox, and others 2015; Data from National Bureau of Statistics 2010a.
Note: GDP = gross domestic product.

Notes

1. Analysis in this chapter on the overall composition of the national, regional, and urban economies in the formal and informal sectors, and on the emerging spatial patterns of agglomeration, is drawn from the Urbanisation Research Nigeria 2014 report *Economic Development in Urban Nigeria* by Robin Bloch, Naji Makarem, Mohammed-Bello Yunusa, Nikolaos Papachristodoulou, and Matthew Crighton.

2. The widely-disseminated McKinsey figures claim real growth in manufacturing of 13 percent from 2010 to 2013 (McKinsey 2014, 11), but our calculations show that their figures are in fact nominal not inflation-adjusted.

3. Our analysis of industrial location was conducted excluding agriculture, and mining and quarrying (including oil and gas), as the location of these sectors is to a great extent driven by natural endowments.

4. National Bureau of Statistics manufacturing employment data was altered by reducing the number of stated manufacturing workers in the state of Katsina on the basis of interviews with key informants. The data initially showed Katsina to be the largest manufacturing agglomeration, which is widely recognized by industry experts and NBS professionals, but turned out to be incorrect.

5. See Ogun (2010), Foster and Puschak (2011), World Bank Doing Business in Nigeria 2012 and 2014 surveys, African Development Bank (2013).

6. Travel demand surveys in the FCT/Abuja (2013), Kano (2012), and Lagos (2009, 2012), undertaken by the Nigeria Infrastructure Advisory Facility, funded by the U.K. Department for International Development.

7. Defined here as the Federal Capital Territory/Abuja, Aba, Benin City, Enugu, Ibadan, Ilorin, Jos, Kaduna, Kano, Lagos, Maiduguri, Ogbomosho, Onitsha, and Port Harcourt.

8. The backlog of ongoing federal road and bridge projects encompasses the Federal Ministry of Works, Federal Roads Maintenance Agency, Ministry of Niger Delta Affairs, and the Subsidy Reinvestment Program road and bridge projects.

References

Adewuyi, A., and A. Oyejide. 2012. "Determinants of Backward Linkages of Oil and Gas Industry in the Nigerian Economy." *Resources Policy* 37 (4): 452–60.

African Development Bank. 2011. *The Middle of the Pyramid: Dynamics of the Middle Class in Africa*. Abidjan: African Development Bank.

———. 2013. *Nigeria Economic Report*. Abidjan: African Development Bank.

Afrika, J., and G. Ajumbo. 2012. "Informal Cross Border Trade in Africa: Implications and Policy Recommendations." Africa Economic Brief 3 (10), African Development Bank, Abidjan.

Behar, A. 2013. "Does the Nigerian Formal Sector Pay More than Its Informal Sector?" Working Paper WPS/2013-21, Centre for the Study of African Economies, Oxford University.

Bloch, R., S. Fox., J. Monroy, and A. Ojo. 2015. *Urbanisation and Urban Expansion in Nigeria*. Urbanisation Research Nigeria Research Report, ICF International, London.

Bloch, R., N. Makarem, M. Yunusa, N. Papachristodoulou, and M. Crighton. 2015. *Economic Development in Urban Nigeria*. Urbanisation Research Nigeria Research Report, ICF International, London.

CBN/FOS/NISER (Central Bank of Nigeria/Federal Office of Statistics/Nigerian Institute for Social and Economic Research). 2001. *A Study of Nigeria's Informal Sector, Volume 1: Statistics on Nigeria's Informal Sector*. Abuja: CBN.

Chen, M. A. 2005. "Rethinking the Informal Economy: Linkages with the Formal Economy and the Formal Regulatory Environment." Working Paper 10/2005, UNU-WIDER, Helsinki.

Coste, A. 2014. "Domestic Obstacles to Trade and Transport in Nigeria and Their Impact on Competitiveness." Africa Trade Policy Notes No. 42, World Bank, Washington, DC.

Federal Roads Maintenance Agency. 2011. "Nigerian Integrated Accessibility Model Visual Inspection Surveys."

Foster, V., and N. Puschak. 2011. "Nigeria's Infrastructure: A Continental Perspective." Policy Research Working Paper 5686, World Bank, Washington, DC.

Gajigo, O., and M. Hallward-Driemeier. 2012. "Why Do Some Firms Abandon Formality for Informality? Evidence from African Countries." Working Paper Series 437, African Development Bank, Tunis.

Jaekel, F. 1997. *The History of the Nigerian Railway*. Ibadan: Spectrum Books.

Leke, A., R. Fiorini, R. Dobbs, F. Thompson, A. Suleiman, and D. Wright. 2014. *Nigeria's Renewal: Delivering Inclusive Growth in Africa's Largest Economy*. New York: McKinsey Global Institute.

Mabogunje, A. 1965. "Urbanization in Nigeria: A Constraint on Economic Development." *Economic Development and Cultural Change* 13 (4): 413–38.

Maloney, W. 2004. "Informality Revisited." *World Development* 32 (7): 1159–1178.

Mbaye, M. 2014. "The Informal Sector, Growth, Employment, and Sustainable Development." Discussion Note, Organisation Internationale de la Francophonie, Paris.

Miles, N. 2013. "An Economic Analysis of Kano City and Its Immediate Region." Background study, Nigeria Infrastructure Advisory Facility.

National Bureau of Statistics. 2010a. *National Manpower Stock and Employment Generation Survey*. Report on Household and Micro Enterprise (Informal Sector). Lagos: National Bureau of Statistics.

———. 2010b. *National MSME Collaborative Survey*. Lagos: National Bureau of Statistics.

NIAF (Nigeria Infrastructure Advisory Facility)-World Bank. 2014. "World Bank Freight Survey Kaduna." Background survey.

OECD (Organisation for Economic Co-operation and Development). 2006. "Food Security and Cross-border Trade in the Kano-Katsina-Maradi K²M Corridor." Joint Mission Report, Sahel and West Africa Club Secretariat/OECD.

Ogun, T. P. 2010. "Infrastructure and Poverty Reduction." Working Paper 43/2010, UNU-WIDER, Helsinki.

Oviedo, Ana Maria, Mark R. Thomas, and Kamer Karakurum-Ozdemir. 2009. "Economic Informality: Causes, Costs, and Policies—A Literature Survey." Working Paper 167, World Bank, Washington, DC.

Oyelaran-Oyeyinka, O. 2014. "Informal Sector Employment, Industrial Clusters, and Urban Poverty in Africa: A Lagos Case Study." Urban Opportunities: Perspectives on Climate Change, Resilience, Inclusion, and the Informal Economy, Wilson Center, Washington, DC.

SMEDAN (Small and Medium Enterprises Development Agency of Nigeria). 2010. "Survey." United Nations Conference on Trade and Development.

USAID (United States Agency for International Development). 2013. *Lagos-Kano-Jibiya (LAKAJI) Corridor Performance: Baseline Assessment Report on the Time and Cost to Transport Goods*. http://www.carana.com/images/summary_of_findings.pdf.

Walther, O. 2011. "Integration of Informal Economic Cross-Border Networks in West Africa." Presentation at West African Futures conference, Paris, October 27–28.

World Bank. 2004. *The Effects of Infrastructure Development on Growth and Income Distribution*. Washington, DC: World Bank.

———. 2007. "Nigeria—Competitiveness and Growth: Country Economic Memorandum, Vol. 2, Main Report." Washington, DC, World Bank.

———. 2011. "Nigeria 2011: An Assessment of the Investment Climate in 26 States." World Bank, Washington, DC. http://www-wds.worldbank.org/external/default /WDSContentServer/WDSP/IB/2012/08/17/000386194_20120817041046 /Rendered/PDF/718910WP0Box370Climate0in0260States.pdf.

———. 2014. *Nigeria Economic Report. No. 2*. Washington, DC: World Bank.

———. 2015. *Nigeria Jobs Report*. Washington, DC: World Bank.

WTO (World Trade Organization). 2004. *Infrastructure in Trade and Economic Development*. Geneva: WTO.

CHAPTER 3

Land, Urban Planning, and Housing

Nigeria's states and local governments often work hard to deliver land regulations, urban plans, planning codes and municipal services, and infrastructure. They have, however, inadequate knowledge of the economic potential of their cities, a weak ability to understand rising land values, and insufficient capacity to facilitate public and private investments at the scale needed. The costs of settling businesses or households on serviced, accessible, and secure land are often much higher than necessary and hinder public sector efforts to service and formalize land, holding back the potential of the cities.

This chapter summarizes existing arrangements for land management, urban planning, and housing in Nigeria, identifies key sector challenges, and suggests interventions that could contribute to more efficient and equitable urban development.

Land Ownership and Land Values

The national legislative instruments that have the greatest influence on the development of urban land and planning are the Land Use Act (LUA) of 1978, which governs land ownership rights and transactions, and the Urban and Regional Planning Act, Decree No. 88 of 1992, which governs development planning and permitting issues.

The LUA aims to ensure social justice in the distribution of land, reduce opportunities for land speculation, ensure equitable social development through the ability of state governments to acquire land for developmental purposes, and improve security of tenure. The act sought to remove traditional powers of land management, administration, and title from families, community heads, and chiefs, vesting these with state governors. It also invokes the right of eminent domain, through which the state can acquire land through compulsory acquisition for serving overriding public interests.

The LUA is incorporated into the 1999 constitution, making it difficult to revise or replace. It harmonizes the land management and tenure system across the country under a uniform set of rules, with rights to land in each state vested in the respective state governor to hold in trust and administer for the benefit of all Nigerians.

Prior to the enactment of the LUA, land tenure was largely guided by traditional administration and ownership systems, which valued land in terms of custom, use, and employment, and differed among regions and ethnic groups. However, elements of these traditional customary practices of land management and administration continue to work alongside, and can be said now to effectively coexist, with the modern legal system of land administration.

In Nigeria's cities, friction in the systems delivering land information, titling, and transactions places severe constraints on the healthy development of the property. The current system for land management is costly and does not encompass traditional tenure types. As a result, collecting information on property, uses, and ownership is difficult. Furthermore, without mechanisms to formally recognize property systems, little to no tenure security exists, and the threat of displacement is high.

The dearth of information on land values and ownership stems from systemic weaknesses in the laws and governance of land, including the bifurcation between urban and rural land management and the concentration of power at the governor level. Only 3 percent of properties are estimated to be formally registered (Birner and Okumo 2011). The tenure status of many of these unregistered properties falls along a wide spectrum of customary ownership and usage rights.

The adjudication of land tenure in each state is categorized as either urban or non-urban. The governor in each state controls and manages land in the urban areas, while non-urban lands are to be managed by the local governments. However, rights to land are held under a long lease of 99 years titled with a Certificate of Occupancy. This right is to be granted by the state governor for both urban and non-urban lands.

Legal limbo on the peripheries and edges of cities and towns is one result of the sharp administrative division between urban and rural land. Urbanization pressures, creating the need for transferable titles and development, are the source of much land conflict. Rights of occupancy are typically respected in smaller communities, but when pressure from urban expansion or industrial projects occurs, these rights are typically not respected and are taken or acquired at a low price by a land consolidator.

The disconnect between social recognition and legal status expanded significantly with the nationalization of the land code in 1978. The current land code only recognizes two types of tenure: statuary and customary occupancy. Widespread community allocation systems have been officially replaced by the government, specifically the state governor, which can grant or waive both statutory and customary occupancy.

As a result, customary tenure remains the most widespread, in spite of several generations of land reforms. Nearly all customary systems are characterized by their recognition of a wide spectrum of tenure rights, which build on the customary valuing of land as a base for housing, food, and employment. In determining allocation, most customary systems also place higher value on the rights of the community or the larger family over those of the individual. Permanent freehold was first introduced nationally under colonial rule. Freehold overlays now and then come into conflict with the more diverse classifications in customary law.

The current LUA more clearly identifies responsibilities, although it has been criticized for failing to promote security of tenure and fair takings, especially in areas where development pressures exist. The LUA regulates the management and planning of urban and rural lands and in theory divides responsibilities between state and local government.

Under the LUA, the Certificate of Occupancy is the sole legal proof of occupancy. Governors determine rights and allocations of urban land and grant all statutory rights of occupancy. In addition, the LUA explicitly vests all land in the hands of the governor such that the state can revoke prior claims and rights of occupancy, even if granted by local government, as long as a clear case can be made for public purpose.

Nascent land valuation systems have little information to work with. As a result, public valuation remains skewed, and the fixed formulas driving public valuation for taxes miss the dynamism of urban land markets. Because of this, valuation formulas and information skew taxation strategy and implementation. Valuation formulas also have little flexibility to capture the differences between urban property markets. Local government administrations (LGAs) are in charge of property assessment, but formulas are typically set by states. LGAs are also responsible for collecting taxes, but these go to the state government. Some private valuation occurs for high-end properties for mortgages.

The "building blocks" of information needed as inputs for valuation formulas are weak, undermining the ability to gauge true value. The sales comparison approach is the most widely used and preferred method of valuation of real estate, land inclusive, in Nigeria today. All land valuation methods require a certain degree of comparison with other parcels of land that have been recently transacted, to determine either the comparability of the features or the yield. Effective comparison relies on access to data and recent market transactions.

In most cities in Nigeria, however, evidence of sales of comparable land is rare. As a result, values are often estimated—with unpredictable monetary values placed on those property characteristics thought to drive a potential difference in price. Recent sales transactions are similarly difficult to acquire, in part due to the reluctance toward disclosure.

More transparent valuation is needed, ideally, through adherence to a standardized valuation scheme and readily available information. The elements of the existing valuation system are unreliable, and even if it falls back on a "sales comparison" approach the inputs are not reliable. Furthermore, in instances of expropriation, no formal structures exist for compensation. To improve on the valuation system, tenure types need reevaluation so that they adhere more closely to the existing diversity, and to protect community allocation while also enabling individuals to undertake land acquisitions and other transactions.

Improved and clear information on land ownership and transparent valuation systems can reduce transaction costs and insecurity for the property market in urban Nigeria. Furthermore, transparent valuation is a crucial ingredient for cities to unlock effective coordination between land use and basic services, as well as leveraging the private resources that can help fund and implement sustainable urban expansion. Stronger regulatory and institutional frameworks that clarify land ownership and values in turn require strengthening building blocks in land rights, transactions, subdivision, and planning and information systems.

In fact, some states are making gradual improvements. In Lagos, in the context of two World Bank–financed development policy operations, the state government introduced a series of reforms including the following:

- Simplification of procedures for assignment and mortgage transactions
- Regularization of lands without formal titles, which applies to properties that comply with the existing schemes and layout plans for some of the regularization areas
- Introduction of electronic certificates of occupancy.

These land registration reforms aimed to facilitate an increase in the investment attractiveness of Lagos to promote sustainable economic growth. According to the recently conducted Poverty and Social Impact Analysis for these development policy operations, the Lagos state government adopted policy measures to streamline approval of land-related transactions. This included the delegation of the governor's prerogative to grant consent to four commissioners (since expanded to seven) within a 48-hour time frame, along with other streamlined administrative procedures. The electronic Certificate of Occupancy system was formally launched in February 2014, but is not yet fully operational.[1]

In general, however, the existing governing structure for urban and rural land management may well need to be reconsidered and enhanced for improving land development. Empowering LGAs and decentralizing the control of governors over land tenure could begin to address some of the challenges in land tenure and formalization. At the same time, it can address the divide in urban and rural management and the balance between urban and rural development, as well as protect against development pressures on rural land bordering cities and towns.

The Challenges of Land Tenure

The LUA recognizes three official tenure types. The first, the statutory right of occupancy as defined in section 5 (1) (a), is formally a leasehold of 99 years. Only state governors can grant this statutory right and, in nearly all cases, it overrules all other claims, including those formalized by local or national authorities. The second is the deemed customary right of occupancy, with no time limit on claims as written in section 5 (1) (b). These are only available to households which happened to have a formal title before the law came into effect, and are eligible to apply for the Certificate of Occupancy without state permission. And third, the law recognizes deemed statutory right of occupancy.

Most lands in Nigeria fall into these three categories, but many types of claims are neither statutory nor customary occupancy. In practice, most lands in non-urban areas continue to be held under customary law, but lack the official Certificate of Occupancy. Especially in areas without development pressure, access and use of land has continued under an array of traditional systems, many of which are not encompassed by the customary definition.

The statutory right of occupancy granted by states supersedes all other formal claims on land recognized by other levels of government. State governments, under section 28 of the LUA, have the ability to "issue a statutory right of occupancy to any person for all purposes whether or not in urban areas." Section 28 consequently allows the state to revoke any right of occupancy, even those granted by the local government, thus establishing the state governor as the most influential in land alienation processes.

Specific sections of the LUA delegate more powers to local government, but in practice this has not been implemented. If a local government requires land for development, it has to consult with local customary chiefs or land-owning families and then seek a statutory right of occupancy from the state government.

Similarly, section 6 (3) of the LUA gives the local government power to enter any land within its area of jurisdiction for public purposes. However, the law does not give any guidance to the local government on its exercise of this power. As a result, the rights of revocation in practice have remained solely with and have been extensively utilized by state governors. In any land acquisition, a buyer-beware principle holds to forewarn buyers that they need to ensure that the title to the land they are planning to buy is free from government acquisition.

The LUA requires state governor consent for all formal transactions, but this triggers the right of the states to collect a ground rent, which acts as a disincentive. Ground rents are one of the primary mechanisms by which the LUA drives up the cost of formality. Under section 5 (1) (a–c), state governors can charge ground rents on any land that has been granted a right of occupancy by the governor. Because nearly all plots that are newly registered or were subdivided must be granted a right of occupancy, they fall subject to ground rents, creating a major disincentive to formalization.

Further criticism of the LUA highlights how, in certain instances, state takings create uncertainty and distort urban land markets. A recent study suggests the overall effect of the act's consent provision on land acquisition is to weaken land markets in Nigerian urban areas, making access to land more difficult and encouraging the proliferation of informal land transactions in the non-urban areas (Federal Republic of Nigeria 2012).

Pathways to formalization—registering occupancy rights, transactions, inheritance, and dispute resolution—are tedious, costly, and complex. The process for regularizing tenure through a Certificate of Occupancy is estimated to cost 27 percent of the property value on average and 10 percent at a minimum.

These costs come from official fees, which are often difficult to know about in advance, a factor adding further risk to landholders hoping to formalize. State governments often link formalization processes to revenue generation drives. In a standard process, applicants will encounter a mix of regular fees and unexpected charges, including consent fees, sampling fees, registration fees, taxes, and levies. Furthermore, as the permission and approval processes are not clearly defined in many states, these fees are spread over multiple regulatory agencies with conflicting requirements, often with their own revenue generating initiatives.

The significant time and expertise needed to register or change property deeds further drives up costs. In most areas, considerable expertise is needed to navigate the multiple regulations and institutions that govern the process. Delays of up to 130 days to acquire a Certificate of Occupancy are common across Nigeria. Backlogs compound delays, as the volume of land market transaction is such that the demand for the consent outstrips the capacity of most governors. This also leads to a market for backdoor transactions.

Ogun State has tried to address this issue by delegating the power of consent to commissioners of justice. For most households, the combination of the time, money, and expertise appear insurmountable, and as a result most land continues to be held informally, transmitting the costs of insecurity down the value chain to transactions and development.

Difficulties in land transactions are aggravated by the institutional oversight required. Transactions of properties without a Certificate of Occupancy require permission of the governor, and in many areas customary rights have limited frameworks for transactions because they were traditionally centralized allocations and not considered a right of the individual landholder.

Transaction costs for land are high; formal fees alone range from 12 to 36 percent of the value of the property. Fees typically include registration fees and stamp duties each equaling 2–3 percent of the asset value, capital gains of 2–3 percent of the net land sale proceeds, and a transfer fee that can range from 8 to 30 percent of the value of the property, depending on the state. High transaction costs hinder the efficiency of the property market and likely fuel Nigeria's widespread unregistered land ownership and tenure insecurity.

Even if a property has an official Certificate of Occupancy, the formal expansion of cities requires an official process to approve parcel subdivision, especially in land that is being converted from rural to urban. Acquiring planning permission to subdivide and develop is lengthy and costly. For example, to acquire a building permit in Jos took an average of 36 days and an additional 48 days to install services and pass inspections, according to the World Bank's *Doing Business* report and as table 3.1 demonstrates.

Because of these costs, a spectrum of intermediaries emerged which purchase, bundle, formalize, and resell land (but often without title). Such intermediaries include property societies, government direct developments, subdevelopers, housing societies, and employer-based associations.

These entities use revenue from a large number of parcels to navigate the fees and regulations. The process is nearly impossible for individual households to

Table 3.1 Official Fees in Jos to Acquire a Permit to Build a Warehouse

Prior to and during construction	Associated fees	Time
Environmental impact assessment from MDB or private registered professional	70,000	36 days to acquire building permit
Development permit	175,000	
Inspection fees (3)	30,000	

Prior to occupancy	Associated fees	Total time
Telephone	6,000	48 days (including inspections)
Electricity meter	52,500	
Electricity connection	20,000	
Equipment rental	300,000	
Materials and labor	170,000	
Geophysics tests	30,000	

Source: World Bank 2013a.

Table 3.2 One-Time Payments for Basic Service Connection in Oyun City (Osun State), 2014

Formal service connection[a]	Fixed cost
Electricity installation	₦52,500 (US$323)
Water connection	₦200,000 (US$1,232)

Source: World Bank 2014.
a. Costs calculated for a warehouse in Oyun City to install permanent electricity connection from the Power Holding Company of Nigeria. Water connection costs are estimated from the costs of digging a borehole, as public water supply is limited and unreliable.

undertake or to pay for, given how disproportionate associated fees are in comparison to average incomes, as demonstrated in table 3.2. Formalization takes place only when there are significant enough gains to hire an intermediary, which incurs further costs (see box 3.1). As a result, formal areas and formal new developments are primarily accessible only to those with high incomes.

Even when properties are formally registered, planned, and subdivided, tenure insecurity remains high. The extensive rights of the state over land, and land-conflict arbitration, further slow the functioning of the property market, increase insecurity, and appear to be a key source of conflict. Decades of ongoing state claims on property create further conflict and contested claims. And urbanization accelerates this. Moreover, according to Transparency International (2009, 2010), in 2009 one-third of households surveyed said they paid a bribe to the land services to acquire land rights, and nearly half perceived land matters as distorted by political corruption.

Although LGAs have rights to expropriate, public acquisition of lands is primarily done by state governors. Sections 6, 28, and 38 of the LUA give governors the power to revoke any right of occupancy over land within their state if it is in their overriding public interest. Such land then legally becomes government land "acquisition" (in local parlance), charted by the government's surveyor, and recorded for public notice in the government gazette.

Box 3.1   Intermediaries and the Cost of Low Information on Land Prices in Ota

A recent study on land prices in Ota, an industrial town on the northern boundary of Lagos State, revealed that across all transactions and locations, accessibility to a major road almost always led to an increase in land prices (Butler 2012). The study further showed that an average 13 percent increase in land prices could be attributed to sales to an out-of-state buyer.

Buyer information on the local market could reduce land prices, because local real estate developers tend to pay less (an average of 0.6 percent less than the base price) for land because their experience in local land purchases gives them a bargaining advantage.

Across Ota, in Ogun State, it was found that being introduced by a land agent could lead to substantial price increases. Although anecdotal evidence suggests that the conventional fees due to a land agent on land sales was a 10 percent commission "loaded" on the land price, the study showed that land agents' activities could lead to as high as an average 41 percent increase in land prices. Collusion between land agents and sellers is a factor. In this, land agents profile buyers to gauge their experience in land acquisition and their level of knowledge of prevailing local market conditions, then propose the price of land to be charged to the land owner in advance of negotiations with the buyer. Market information for buyers could reduce this practice.

Source: Butler 2012.

Subsequent market transactions without the participation of government are not considered legal. Compensation systems remain undeveloped, and correct valuation is a key constraint to acquisition for key infrastructure projects. Determining compensation amounts and time lags between the period of compensation and actual utilization of land is viewed as a primary bottleneck to the consolidation of land parcels for projects.

City zoning and strict regulations place further barriers to formal development of urban regulations on use and density appear to repress the development of higher density, value, and mixed use. Zoning often has little correspondence to actual usage. In a 2000 study of Ibadan, 83 percent of homes were noncompliant with city zoning regulations (Arimah and Adeagbo 2000).

A survey of developers in Lagos suggests that the most commonly breached planning regulations are setbacks, site coverage, and zoning. Registering formal developments with zoning is costly. Planners are also said to find zoning a bothersome, time-consuming, and highly technical distraction from what they regard as their more important planning function (that is, charting an area's future) (Otubu 2009).

The number of submissions for processing to obtain certificates of occupancy far outnumber approvals granted. This indicates that the rate of construction lags behind demand. Failure to obtain a governor's consent is generally associated with incomplete documentation, irregular signatures, or other administrative bottlenecks. Obtaining approval from government offices also involves a number of direct and indirect costs, including uncertainty, corruption, travel costs to government offices, and opportunity costs such as loss of wages (Aluko 2011). Bottlenecks create lengthy delays and require undue investment from beneficiaries to be processed (Aluko 2011).

Because of the few approvals of Certificate of Occupancy applications, the rate of construction can be low compared to demand. Planned redevelopment is scarce, although some examples exist. In Ibadan, the Oluyole industrial layout was resubdivided into mixed development and an older, single-use residential estate in Bodija now includes several commercial, light industrial, religious, recreational, office, hotel, and hospitality facilities, among others.

All of these high costs and uncertainties create significant distortions in the land and housing markets. The result is that informal land transactions remain the norm. With the statutory allocating rights of government hanging over customary possession, distress sales by customary title holders are common, which may lead to unjustified asset-price bubbles. The land sales market in urban areas, in particular, is known to have sprouted speculative purchases of large tracts of land from customary land owners eager to sell off their only assets and unaware of the consequences of their actions.

Even though under customary systems land was not traditionally alienable, today most customary communities permit land sales if all principal family members agree. Research has shown that leasing transactions are more common in customary land and that land transactions in the informal sector continue to be attractive to buyers given the difficulty inherent in registering titles after land transactions, as stipulated in the LUA. Current systems of customary land transaction need to be integrated into the formal framework—and to recognize that the customary system has legitimacy for a significant portion of the people.

The informal market thus provides land for housing for most Nigerians, but this has negative impacts on households. The informal land market tends to bypass the bureaucracies associated with the formal mechanisms already discussed, such as land registration, titling, and arrangement of funds. For this reason, it is more popular than the formal land market among "poor" rural dwellers within the customary tenure system. Some of the difficulties associated with the informal market include issues of fraudulent or double sales, the legality of sales, nondocumentation or nonregistration of land titles, fragmentation of landholdings such that land assemblage for development purposes might also be more expensive, and over acquisition by government for development purposes.

State land prices are believed to be significantly lower than market prices, which may encourage speculation and underutilization. Prices typically reflect a combination of an infrastructure charge and a price for the land itself. The infrastructure charge, based on cost recapture, is the primary component of the state land price in Nigeria and may be the only price in the case of residential schemes for lower-income people (Butler 2012). Some land administration officials estimate that prices for state land grants are 40 percent below prices for equivalent parcels in the private secondary market.

Land Use and Urban Planning

The Nigeria Urban and Regional Planning Decree No. 88 of 1992 was designed to reinvigorate a rigid planning system perpetuated since the 1978 LUA and to ease land allocation, transfer, and development. However, all land-related issues in the decree refer to the LUA and its provisions. For instance, granting a development permit by a Development Control Department must conform to the issue of Certificate of Occupancy. In addition, any revocation of acquired occupancy must be in accordance with the provisions of the LUA (Aluko 2011). Because all development takes place on land, the decree does not help to ease planning concerns since all land-related issues must be in accordance with the provisions of the LUA (Aluko 2011).

In many states, planning laws and regulations are enforced through the development control activities of planning agencies (see, for example, section 38 and all sections in part V of the 2010 Lagos State Law). The extent of enforcement depends on the nature and contents of the laws and regulations, public understanding of the perception of the laws, the competence of the enforcement officers, and the availability of manpower to ensure that any form of development conforms to the approved guidelines (Aluko 2011).

Consequently, service provision decisions are not coordinated by municipal plans, but made by a wide spectrum of entities. Basic services are funded and coordinated by a large number of agencies spread across levels of government. LGAs, slowed by low capacity and complex approval requirements from the state, struggle to fulfill their significant responsibilities in water, sanitation, solid waste, health, and education. State governments receive and distribute most funds for major infrastructure projects, and continue to subsidize the provision of water, sanitation, and waste, but efforts are often bogged down because of the multiple agencies involved. In addition to setting the strategic priorities, the federal government aims to ensure sufficient supply of water, power, and housing. In all these sectors, though, large supply-side subsidies have resulted in less effective market function and do not appear to improve equity outcomes.

Nigeria's urban and physical planning is in legal and administrative flux, and the plans that do exist are not coordinated with service provision. The 1999 constitution gave power to states to legislate on planning issues. The Supreme Court ruled in 2004 that the 1992 Urban and Regional Planning Decree should no longer be implemented as national legislation. These two conflicting mandates and lack of planning legislation have created a legal vacuum for land use planning and development control at the state and LGA levels. Clouding matters further, state authorities often alternate control over planning between state ministries, and occasionally delegate down to temporary metropolitan boards (Wapwera and Egbu 2013). As a result, current physical planning occurs through ad hoc efforts and in an uncertain climate.

New land use plans are often for aspirational suburban and peri-urban full-service developments. Detailed land use planning appears now to be concentrated on new medium- to high-end multiuse developments. Rivers State has developed one of the most ambitious long-term land use plans for Greater Port Harcourt, launched in 2009 with a 50-year scheme for growth that covers 40,000 hectares and projects housing 2 million residents.[2] The first phase aims to construct a modern city with 24/7 service provision at the outskirts of the existing urban area, with 30,000 units in the initial implementation. Eventually, the modern city is designed to gradually "de-densify" the existing city, with the eventual goal of replacing current infrastructure. As of 2014, 1,110 housing units had been completed under the new plan, with owners receiving Certificates of Occupancy (Watson and Agbola 2013). Although the language of the plan included lower-income earners, it has come under some criticism for not envisaging affordable housing.

Significant implicit and explicit subsidies have been created in alignment with Nigeria's new master plans and developments. Among other incentives, the Rivers State and the Greater Port Harcourt Development Agency offer tiered packages of free land, five years of state tax relief, and, for companies building more than 300 housing units, off-take guarantees for projects. Rewards for "green" carbon neutral building and technological enterprises are also eligible for additional support from the state.

Exacerbating impacts from land issues, the poor provision of services in cities drives up prices of formal housing, limiting access of affordable units to upper-income residents. The costs of acquiring a land parcel with a clear title and building formally are high. Securing services for these new developments is an additional challenge. Because public provision is so erratic, many formal developments opt to create private independent networks for water and sanitation, for example. Urban growth has made the provision of public services even more challenging. In Owerri City, the state water corporation covered all wards in the early 1990s, but by 2011 reached just 20 percent of residents; to make up the shortfall, commercial bore-wells, and a few community-based wells, sell water to the bulk of residents (Onyenechere 2011).

Missed opportunities to coordinate new development at a city level have resulted in expensive housing and additional costs to commerce and industry. Metropolitan plans can provide a framework for service provision coordinated with land development and housing. The metropolitan scale encompasses the actual urban footprint as well as where cities are likely to grow. Planning at the metropolitan or urban level is regulated by the 1946 Town and Country Planning Laws, along with the Regional Planning Law of 1992 and the Federal Capital Development Act of 2007 (Otubu 2009). However, only a few cities currently have active metropolitan-scale plans for land and service network development. While such strategic plans were established for some cities in the decades following the Town and Country Planning Laws of 1946, they were infrequently followed and had few regulatory instruments to enforce compliance.

Metropolitan-level planning organizations only exist for a handful of cities, primarily in the north, where they are termed Metropolitan Development Boards.

These regulate new formal construction, and their activities are often profit-generating and self-financing. In Jos, the Metropolitan Development Board garnered ₦12.7 million in revenue in 2012 from rents, processing fees for building plans, and fines (Business Day 2013). Furthermore, although developers can choose to hire private planners, many companies also opt to hire employees of the metropolitan boards to supervise development (World Bank 2013b).

Improving Urban Land Management—Recognizing the Value of Formal and Informal Systems

Although it is true that the LUA lies at the heart of constraints to improving urban land management and the effectiveness of urban planning, changing the LUA (which is incorporated in the constitution) is likely to present significant political and administrative hurdles.

Furthermore, despite general agreement on the imperfections of the LUA, consensus is lacking on how to reform it. A recent national conference on the LUA recommended its retention within the constitution, with only minor amendments. Still, value is to be had in establishing a policy dialogue with the new federal government on the LUA to help develop proposals for improving its effectiveness.

Current national urban development policy also proposes reforms to land management, as box 3.2 illustrates.

In addition, much can be achieved by supporting the development of institutional structures and instruments that can improve the effectiveness and efficiency of land management and planning within the existing legislative

---

Box 3.2 The New Urban Development Policy

The Federal Executive Council approved the National Urban Development Policy in June 2012. Chapter 4 captures the new policy on access to land, with the stated goal being to "ensure that land is made available for the purposes of promoting controlled and orderly development in the urban centers." It laments the "tortuous process of land acquisition by both individuals and corporate bodies for building purposes under the Land Use Act," linking the inefficiencies of the law to the lack of speedy and well-controlled urban development. The policy also identifies the major impediments to land acquisition as "high rates of land speculation, poor administration of land records, lack of cadastral, high cost of obtaining certificate of occupancy, and high land values, which the poor and their vulnerable groups cannot afford."

The policy lists six strategies for the federal government to accelerate the growth of urban centers through easy access to large tracts of land with secure title, and also to ensure access

box continues next page

Box 3.2 The New Urban Development Policy *(continued)*

to land in suitable and planned locations to reduce the social and economic costs of unplanned development and the continued proliferation of slums and shanties:

- Facilitate cooperation and ensure the collaboration between state governors and appropriate federal agencies to facilitate easy access to land for development by individuals and corporate bodies.
- Build and strengthen the capacities of the ministries, departments, and agencies in charge of land administration to facilitate and ensure that private sector developers have easy access to land for real estate development.
- Provide necessary support and incentives to the private sector to effectively participate in urban development programs.
- Promote public-private partnership to ensure rapid and effective urban development.
- Review existing town planning regulations and practices, and remove bottlenecks, to facilitate private sector participation in urban development.
- Build and strengthen the capacities of state planning boards and local planning authorities to implement the provisions of the urban and regional planning laws to achieve orderly and sustainable development of cities and towns.

Source: Federal Republic of Nigeria 2012.

---

framework. In particular, efforts need to recognize the importance of the existing informal urban land market and management systems. The integration of modern and customary systems can only be successful if the fundamentally different conceptions between the systems with regard to the role of land and land tenure in society are both recognized and rationalized. Consequently, support should be provided to strengthen the nexus between the formal land development process, the informal process, and the planning system. Actions could include the following:

- Support for a better understanding of how the array of traditional systems and existing informal adaptations work, so that they can be better accounted for in customary definitions and in adapting informal land management systems.
- Assistance in integrating current systems of customary land transaction into the formal framework (recognizing that the customary system holds some legitimacy).
- Supporting the development of bridging (or hybridization) strategies between formal and informal urban land development sectors that can benefit from the advantages of each.
- Supporting local planning authorities in providing local land-selling chiefs and individuals with basic standards for setting out plots and demarcating rights of way for local roads and basic infrastructure in accordance with urban area-wide structure plans.

- Improving the transparency, reliability, and predictability of land information and valuation systems to help reduce the current high costs and risks attached to land transactions.
- Assistance for developing transparent systems and processes for ownership, oversight, spatial regulation, and valuation of land parcels in and around cities.
- Assistance in developing systems to promote greater coordination between and among public entities inside cities, and between the local, state, and national authorities to promote better alignment between formal and informal land development, and infrastructure and service provision.
- Supporting the rollout of initiatives to guide informal land and housing developments through a process of "formalization" or "regularization," by which informal developments can, in principle, apply for a Certificate of Occupancy retrospectively.
- Supporting decentralized approaches to urban land development. Land development approaches vary between regions, and states and cities must find what works best under their unique social, economic, and political circumstances.
- Assisting in adapting the legal framework to encompass a broader spectrum of ownership types, such as use rights, grazing, or communal ownership, to enable marginalized groups to invest in assets and eventually access finance by using their land as collateral.
- Supporting capacity development, including professionalizing the Land Use and Allocation Committee and other land administration bodies.

Helping to Establish an Urban Planning System that Works

Nigeria's current urban planning system does not work. New planning mechanisms need to be developed—initially within the existing urban planning framework—that provide a more flexible and responsive tool to guide development and support the "hybrid" approach to land development, which combines the best aspects of the existing formal and informal urban land development processes.

Support in urban planning should focus on:

- Assistance to government and cities in moving away from rigid urban masterplans to more flexible urban planning frameworks that include a structure plan and, within this, development of local area plans for those districts that are the focus of development.
- Supporting cities in the development of land use transportation plans to better integrate the urban transportation implications of development decisions into planning decision making.
- Encouraging greater exchange of experience among cities in adopting newly piloted planning approaches, thus contributing to more quickly and effectively advancing the development of cities nationwide.

- Supporting the establishment of a unit of governance and coordination at the metropolitan level to better coordinate land use planning with infrastructure and service provision and to help build the capacity to operate such a unit.
- Assisting state governments in developing mechanisms for the delegation and decentralization of land management and administration responsibilities away from the governor.
- Assisting in the review, updating, and optimization of city zoning codes to support more efficient land use and socioeconomic development.
- Assisting in improving the integration of providing local land development and infrastructure, and in developing mechanisms to make better use of infrastructure to guide urban development.
- Assisting in the development of mechanisms to progressively introduce urban services to established informal developments that are without access to basic urban services.

Housing and Affordability

As urbanization increases, demographic changes will influence housing needs. Average household sizes in Nigeria have declined over the last decade, from 5.0 people in 2003 to 4.8 in 2013, though in urban areas the average is significantly lower at 4.2.[3] From 2003 to 2008, average urban household sizes declined by 13 percent. This trend toward smaller household sizes, especially among urban households, is expected and is associated with the higher cost of city living.

A survey of middle class (Renaissance Capital 2011)[4] households found that household sizes were even smaller, averaging 3.7 members with an average of 1.6 children versus 3.0 children nationally. At the same time, Nigeria's demographic profile is overwhelmingly young: the majority of the population (68.1 percent) is aged 24 years or less.[5] Similarly, the dependency ratio, a measure of workforce participation, has reached 89 percent and is expected to increase.[6]

These trends suggest that demographic shifts will correspond with the potential for economic growth and sustained rates of urbanization. The current and future demographic profile of the country suggests that new household formation and the accompanying demand for housing will be important characteristics of urban growth in the near future.

The quality and location of housing has long-term consequences for inclusive growth. For most household members, a house is the most valuable asset they will ever have. A home is also an investment vehicle that can appreciate in value over time, be used for collateral for borrowing, and, through inheritance, be an important component of intergenerational wealth transfer. The location of a house relative to schools, jobs, and transit access directly affects the quality of urban life and prospects for social mobility (World Bank 2013b).

Urban housing tends to be least expensive when it is located in undesirable areas and is of poor construction quality. Typically, this is on the fringes where land is not expensive or occupation will go unnoticed by landowners. While housing options in these areas may be affordable to the urban poor, the additional burdens imposed by long commute times, public health problems from inadequate water and sanitation, and the lack of education and health services are substantial indirect costs.

The housing sector is an important component of national economic growth. Housing stocks, along with investment and employment in related construction and finance industries, constitutes a major component of national wealth. For most countries, housing comprises 2–8 percent of gross domestic product (GDP); housing services may account for an additional 7–18 percent of GDP (Kessides 2006).

In Nigeria, however, housing investment constitutes only 0.05 percent of GDP (US$1.42 billion in 2011). Dasgupta, Lall, and Gracia-Lozano (2014) find that the rate of overall investment in housing as a share of GDP is highest when a country's income per capita income rises to between US$3,000 and US$36,000. Where, as in Nigeria, income levels are outside this range, investment levels even out as spending on housing competes with other needs. However, in 2014, Nigeria's GDP per capita was US$3,005, which suggests that total investment in housing will likely increase along with income gains.

Estimates suggest a large formal housing deficit in Nigeria. Estimates of formal housing supply suggest a current deficit from 17 million to 30 million housing units (Federal Republic of Nigeria 2012).[7] The variation of the estimates is due to several weaknesses in data availability and assumptions about housing needs. For example, estimates suggesting that 80 percent of the population lives in informal or self-built unserved dwellings puts the deficit estimate at 30 million.

Nigeria's chronic housing challenge is more complex than an undersupply of new formal units. Housing deficit estimates are not an accurate assessment of housing need, both because unit size and quality standards are not defined or distinguished within the current stock. Informal housing covers a range of physical durability and legal statuses, and typically lacks the infrastructure connections that formal units enjoy. Attention is needed for improving housing stock quality, its connections to infrastructure, and overcrowding rather than simply building new units that most people cannot afford.

Available data capture only a portion of the housing sector. This is because most housing is produced and consumed through informal channels. Data are scarce on market trends and prices, in part because of the limited penetration of formal finance tools such as mortgages, but also because of the tendency for houses to be retained and transferred among family members.

Most housing is also built incrementally, with savings and informal loans, which makes this type of housing investment difficult to track. Moreover, sales or rental transactions are often in cash and not reported, which makes it difficult to understand market volumes and price trends. The lack of data makes it difficult to establish a basis for affordability criteria or estimate effective demand based on prices and observed market activity.

This lack of data is a weakness for both government and private sector stakeholders in the housing sector. Limited data on housing prices and consumer investment decisions undermines the ability of subsidy programs to identify and target those who need them the most. And finance institutions and developers are reluctant to develop alternative finance instruments or housing products for lower-income groups.

Ownership is the most commonly reported type of housing tenure. The 2006 census records 28,197,085 regular housing units, and, based on population figures, 4.98 people per housing unit.

Figure 3.1 shows the distribution of housing types identified by the census, demonstrating that the majority of households reside in detached structures on separate land plots. Rental rooms in multiunit structures and traditional dwellings are the other most common structure types.

Figure 3.2 summarizes the distribution of tenure for households based on the 2006 census. The vast majority of households—83 percent—live in family-owned houses, which suggests a large segment of households rent or live rent-free with family members, as 68.5 percent of households report being the owner-occupiers of their house. However, although many may own their house, not all households hold secure tenure claims to the land on which it is built, due to the prevalence of customary tenure systems and weaknesses in the cadaster. Private rentals constitute about half of all renter households, suggesting about 10 percent of households live rent free. A very small portion, just 2.3 percent, had a mortgage or unpaid housing loan.

Figure 3.1 Distribution of Housing Types, 2006
percent

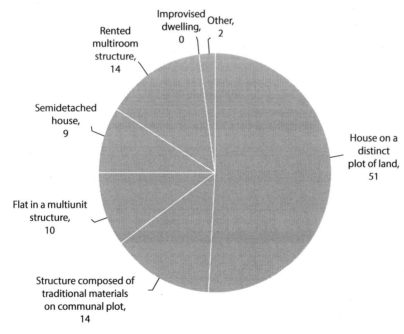

Source: Federal Republic of Nigeria 2006.

**Figure 3.2 Distribution of Regular Households by Tenure Status
of Dwelling, 2006**
percent

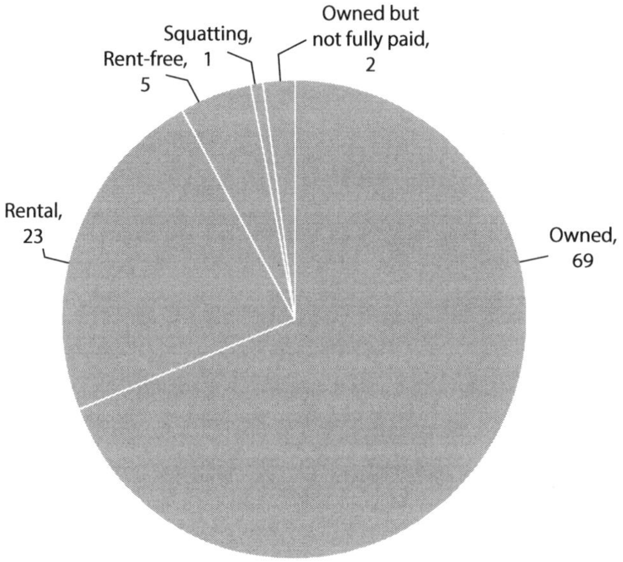

Renters are concentrated in urban areas, as most urban households rent, in contrast to rural households. In Lagos and Abuja, for example, renters are the majority (75.7 and 53.3 percent, respectively).[8] Overall, 85 percent of the urban population are renters, due in part to the high costs of land and the lack of secure land tenure title (Centre for Affordable Housing Finance Africa 2013). Households most commonly rent rooms or an apartment; renting a house often requires an advance payment of one year's rent. Land is prohibitively expensive to rent unless it is in peripheral areas and lacks services.

Public and social housing production has had limited success in meeting the need for affordable housing. The Federal Housing Authority (FHA), established in 1973, is the primary public agency charged with housing production. Its activities have been structured by a series of National Development Plans to supply 261,000 housing units across the nation.

By 2012 and over the course of three Development Plans, the FHA had delivered 41,000 units, or only about 15 percent of its total targets. This experience in the direct provision of public housing parallels the outcomes of many other countries with similar plans. In such cases, governments have been no better equipped to overcome many of the same obstacles private developers also face, such as expensive materials, construction firms with limited capacity, and scarce financial resources for bringing projects to scale.

The government also subsidizes mortgages through a housing provident fund, though the benefits are concentrated in the formal sector. The National Housing

Fund was established in 1992 to enhance access to housing among low-income groups by increasing and stabilizing the supply of home loans. The fund operates under mandatory contributions from nearly all salaried workers making at least ₦3,000 per year, and is operated by the Federal Mortgage Bank of Nigeria. Banks and insurance funds are also required to contribute to the fund.

In exchange, the program offers below-market interest rates (6 percent, 10 percent down payment, and up to a 30-year tenor) of up to ₦5 million. But because it requires contribution from salaried workers, by definition it excludes informal laborers, who cannot access the subsidized loans (Chiquier 2009). Instead, most of the loans go to higher-income groups, and, at the time of writing, only 12,000 mortgages out of 3.8 million contributors have been disbursed.

Efforts to privatize the FHA have also not improved the affordability of public housing. The authority currently directs much of its activity to coordinating with the private sector in the construction of housing. Engaging in this way is an important component of broadening the range of options for affordable housing. To date, however, housing units are still expensive; for example, the cheapest cost ₦5.5 million (US$33,000). Under the assumption such a unit was purchased with a Federal Mortgage Bank of Nigeria subsidized mortgage, the monthly mortgage cost of US$182 would be nearly twice the national minimum wage—out of reach of the targeted beneficiary group.

The gap between estimated housing needs and the current formal supply clearly indicates that affordability is a key challenge. Housing, like any other good, is not inherently affordable. Rather, "affordability" refers to reasonable household expenditure on a quality dwelling unit. International experience, based on the assumption of mortgage finance and widely available prices, suggests an affordability threshold of 25–30 percent of total household expenditures, or a housing purchase of 3–5 times total household income. Since GDP per capita in Nigeria in 2014 was US$3,005, this would mean that the average person would spend no more than US$83 per month on shelter expenses or to purchase a house of up to US$15,000.

By typical affordability standards, the cost of formal housing is very high and unaffordable for most, especially in urban areas. The majority of Nigerians (78 percent) subsist on less than US$60 per month. A low-cost house at US$16,700 would be more than four times too expensive for households, earning the minimum wage of US$109 per month, to afford (Centre for Affordable Housing Finance Africa 2013, 2014). Expenditure data suggests that monthly expenditures for households are already very constrained. Per capita spending on housing in urban areas is about 5 percent for all expenditure quintiles, while expenditure on food for the two lowest quintiles makes up 55–70 percent of total expenditure (Lozano-Gracia and Young 2014). These conventional measures may even understate the affordability gap, because poor households may not even have 30 percent of their income to spend on housing after accounting for other necessary expenses.

Formal housing options in major cities are far outside affordability thresholds. Available data suggests that residential markets tightly skewed to upper-income groups and foreign investors are clustered around Lagos and Abuja. A sample of 6,812 listings in August 2014 showed that only 75 were priced below ₦5 million (US$30,000). More than 4,000 listings were priced above ₦10 million, half of which were above US$300,000. This shows that even the least expensive formal properties are beyond the reach of most residents.

While most urban dwellers rent, formal rental options are also often unaffordable for most Nigerians. Furthermore, the typical practice in formal markets is to pay annual rent in advance, a significant expenditure for most households. Abuja commands the highest rents, partly due to restrictions on supply because of planning and land restrictions. A survey of estate agents in the city found that from 1998 to 2007 rents for three-bedroom apartments tripled, those for four-bedroom apartments tripled, and those for five-bedroom duplexes quintupled (Makama and Ishaya 2007).

Table 3.3 shows annual rental costs for apartments in select urban districts. It shows that listed rental properties in Abuja are about twice the average annual income and equivalent to the annual salary of middle-income earners.[9] However, in the northern city of Kaduna, a 2010 household survey showed that while half of respondents rented, median rent was only about US$11 per month. In this city, only about 5 percent of renters paid more than US$85 per month or ₦160,000 per year (Max Lock Consultancy 2010). This demonstrates that urban housing costs consume a much larger portion of household expenditure than do the rural, where rents are lower and homeownership is more common.

Due to affordability constraints, Nigeria's urban majority consumes housing informally, and 80–90 percent of housing can be classified as informal

Table 3.3 Lowest Annual Apartment Rental Cost in Select Urban Districts, 2011

City and districts	Annual rental cost (Naira per year)
Ibadan	
Sango, Moniya, and Eleyele	150,000–200,000
Lagos	
Ikorodu, Agege, and Ebute Metta	150,000–200,000
Uyo	
Idoro and Ikot-Ekpene Road	200,000–250,000
Enugu	
Abakpa and Asata	250,000–300,000
Port Harcourt	
Ada George, Iwofe, and Woji	350,000–400,000
Kaduna	
Barnawa, Narayi, Nassarawa, and Kabala	500,000–600,000
Abuja	
Nyanya, Karu, and Kubwa	400,000–700,000

Source: Private Property 2014.

(Boleat and Walley 2008; Lloyd-Jones and others 2014). Informal housing is distinguished from formal housing by having some element in its production or consumption that falls outside legal, financial, and regulatory institutions (UN-Habitat 2003). Informal housing typically has one or more of the following characteristics: irregular or absent land title claims or building permit approvals, incremental construction by owners or informal laborers, and substandard connections to utility and infrastructure facilities.

The term informal here only refers to aspects of housing that are extralegal or outside of official record, such as a squatter's temporary shelter or large, self-built brick home constructed without permits. In Nigeria, housing informality and poverty are not necessarily correlated: middle-class families may also live in informal settlements or build their homes incrementally without all the necessary permits or in ways that are outside of official design and development standards (box 3.3). Because informal housing conditions encompass a diversity of shelter types, infrastructure access levels, household income ranges, and tenure arrangements, policy attention must be directed toward overlapping interventions in finance, infrastructure, land, and construction materials.

Box 3.3 Informality and Incremental Construction: The Case of Kaduna

The northwestern city of Kaduna has grown rapidly, increasing demand for land and housing on the urban periphery. A 2009 survey found that 2,286 hectares of peripheral land, mostly under agricultural use, was subdivided into plots for future development (Mutter, Lloyd-Jones, and Gusah). Improvements have also occurred unevenly and sporadically, making residential density low. Formal planning regulations, land administration practices, and infrastructure investments have not kept pace with demand, but have nonetheless influenced market dynamics. In 2009, individual investments in land plots in Kaduna were between ₦15 billion to ₦25 billion (US$100 million–US$167 million), covering both legal and illegal plot subdivisions.

The location, tenure, and type of land directly influences market value. Formal and informal plot layouts have a direct impact on prices. A plot within a formal layout has road infrastructure, while informal layouts (which may not be designated for subdivision) do not. Prices for a 15 by 30-meter plot range from ₦120,000 to ₦360,000 (US$600–US$1,800) in informal layouts; plots that are part of formal layouts have much higher prices, ranging from ₦240,000 to ₦1,200,000 (US$1,200–US$6,000).

Housing costs also vary depending on the size and materials of the unit. For example, a two-bedroom mud-brick unit with a corrugated zinc roof costs about ₦1 million (US$6,000). A higher quality unit of cement blocks and corrugated aluminum would increase the cost by 50 to 100 percent. This would place the total cost of a house on an informal layout plot between US$10,000 and US$15,000 (₦2,000,000 and ₦3,000,000, respectively). By contrast, housing available on formal layouts is much more expensive: a government-built apartment of similar size on the outskirts of Kano is priced at ₦7 million (US$40,000).

box continues next page

From Oil to Cities • http://dx.doi.org/10.1596/978-1-4648-0792-3

Box 3.3 Informality and Incremental Construction: The Case of Kaduna *(continued)*

The difference illustrates how planning designations and infrastructure access confer large price premiums on land and housing values even in areas that lack density and are far from central city districts.

Land use planning and infrastructure investments require careful coordination. The expansion of both Kaduna and Kano on the urban fringes takes advantage of low-cost land, but the lack of amenities, services, and formal tenure security will likely present long-term costs and challenges to poor residents in terms of mobility, access to employment, and quality of life. Land use planning and infrastructure investment should be concentrated and support the efficient use of land to reduce the cost of connecting new residents.

The prominence of the self-build sector also demonstrates that interventions to improve the scale and quality of housing provision must take incremental development as a starting point, and be supported and improved rather than stigmatized. Improving technical capacities (such as certifications), reducing the cost of materials, and providing more sources of finance can all stimulate the informal construction sector, providing both employment and investment opportunities.

A substantial portion of the population lives in informal or substandard housing. This constitutes a wide spectrum of housing conditions, ranging from temporary or nonaffixed structures to titled, well-maintained properties that may not conform to current standards and regulations. "Slum" and "informal settlement" definitions concern the quality and regulatory status of built environments, and are not necessarily linked to poverty rates or security issues.

Informal settlements can thus include households from a wide segment of income classes and ethnic groups that live in a range of building types and ages. Informal settlements tend to have one or more of the following conditions: illegal or insecure land tenure claims; buildings that are impermanent or of substandard construction quality; and lack of access to infrastructure such as proper drainage, water and sewer systems, streets, and public services (UN-Habitat 2007).

According to United Nations (UN) estimates, the majority of Nigeria's population lives in slums (64.2 percent in 2007). From 1990 to 2007, the estimated urban population doubled from 33 million to more than 70 million, bringing the absolute number of slum dwellers to about 45.3 million or more than one-third of the population (DHS 2013). Others have estimated that the population living without secure housing tenure or in rented substandard dwellings is 72 million (Omrin 2007; Ubom and Ubom 2014).

Informal settlements include a range of income groups and quality of housing. Slums cover a diverse range of the country's shelter, income categories, and tenure conditions. For example, middle-class households may live in informal settlements alongside lower-income groups. In major cities approximately 20–30 percent of slum conditions are found in dense neighborhoods, and 15–30 percent of slums are interspersed within middle- and upper-income areas.

Residents in these areas typically do not have piped sewerage connections, but due to the proximity to wealthier neighborhoods are likely to have piped water and large plot sizes.

Demographic and Health Survey data shows that from 2008 to 2013 the proportion of households in one-room units for sleeping has fallen from 43 percent to 39 percent, suggesting a decline in the level of overcrowding (DHS 2013). The layout and density of informal settlements are also distinct: plot sizes tend to be large, population densities low, and, despite many households lacking the necessary Certificates of Occupancy, are allayed in an orderly pattern that permits pedestrian and vehicle circulation.[10] These settlements are much denser in central and waterfront zones of cities such as Lagos, Warri, and Port Harcourt, where land values are much higher and available space is absent.

The lack of access to improved water and sanitation systems are the most common housing deficiencies.[11] Only 15 percent of dwelling units have flush toilets and about half of all units use pit latrines. Among urban dwellers, only 6 percent of households—typically the wealthiest—have a toilet connected to a sewer system. About 11 percent of urban residents use septic tanks, which corresponds to a middle-income level. More than one-third of households obtain water from unimproved sources, putting them at risk for consuming contaminated water. About 65 percent of urban households (approximately 57 million people or 13 million households) have or share a pit latrine, higher than the national share of 49 percent. Sharing these facilities is common due to rental agreements. In urban areas, only 36 percent of households have improved private toilet facilities (DHS 2013).

Upgrading informal settlements to improve water and sanitation presents a number of interrelated challenges. The reliability of the power grid and its coverage must be extended to support pumps for piped water, and piped water increases the need for concurrent improvements in drainage systems. Drainage improvements may require paved roads to channel storm and waste water away from settlements. But outside of middle-class urban neighborhoods, most roads and streets are not paved. Furthermore, both piped water and poorly channeled storm water can flood septic and latrine facilities that most people use. These infrastructure deficiencies present both immediate and long-term costs to low-income groups. Firstly, there is the added time and cost of obtaining trucked or bottled water or acquiring water from a shared standpipe or pump. Secondly, the lack of controlled drainage and sewerage systems presents broad public health risks from water-borne diseases and soil contamination.

Durable construction materials are increasingly common, though remain costly. The most common residential building is constructed from bricks and has a corrugated metal roof. Census data show that cement and bricks (48 percent) are the most common materials for wall construction,[12] followed by corrugated metal/zinc (42 percent) for roof material.[13] More durable materials such as cement bricks, precast forms, and sheet metals are increasingly common, though expensive,[14] because they are manufactured abroad and imported.

From Oil to Cities • http://dx.doi.org/10.1596/978-1-4648-0792-3

Cement is an exception. From 2005 to 2013 the domestic cement industry grew 95 percent and supply increased to meet about 90 percent of demand. But despite the increase in domestic capacity, prices remain high, perhaps in part due to a lack of competition among the two main producers. For example, in 2013, a 50-kilogram bag of cement cost up to ₦1,800 which was 36 percent more expensive than in neighboring Ghana. A lack of quality control has also resulted in the mixing and use of inferior quality cement, which has likely emerged as a way to compensate for the high cost of regular cement. This illustrates a general lack of national building regulations enforced at the state and local level.

The formal housing delivery system covers a small portion of the Nigerian housing market. In developed economies, credit institutions finance housing units, which are built at scale by construction firms that follow building and land use standards. Consumers purchase homes with commercial mortgages or rent units under binding legal agreements. This form of housing production and consumption is not common in Nigeria and constitutes about 15 percent of the housing market (Finmark Trust 2011). The annual supply of housing built by private developers or government producers is 100,000 units, compared to the estimated 900,000 units the informal sector has built.

The construction sector itself is small and constitutes only 3.1 percent of GDP.[15] Private developers are concentrated in major cities and, apart from building activity in residential, commercial, hotel, and office properties, much of this sector's activity is in publicly funded infrastructure projects. More common private development activities are centered on the acquisition and subdivision of government land for sale in plots of around 450 square meters, often in rural areas or the urban periphery. As most housing is self-built, owners may remove or replace any existing structures on the plot and construct a new house to their preference.

Most sources of finance for housing are outside commercial banks and primary mortgage institutions. Among the poorest 40 percent of the adult population, only one-third have an account at a formal financial institution (World Bank 2014). By contrast, the most common borrowing sources in 2011 for households were savings groups and family members (both 44 percent). This suggests that most sources of finance for housing are informal and support incremental investment. Indeed, 41 million people are estimated to participate in savings groups and cooperatives, which provide a source of finance for small businesses, housing, education, and other large or unexpected household expenses (Napier 2009).

Similarly, remittances from migrants abroad form a significant source of income for many households. In 2012, these remittances totaled US$20.6 billion, about 4.5 percent of GDP. This is more than twice the amount of official overseas development assistance, which peaked at 8 percent in 2006. Remittances are an important source of income that households can use for day-to-day expenses or to save for larger investments (Oluwafemi and Ayandibu 2014).

The lack of mortgage finance restricts formal housing development to new supply. In 2012, mortgages accounted for less than 0.5 percent of GDP (less than US$1.5 billion).[16] Mortgage interest rates tend to be high: since 2008 interest rates have averaged 9.5 percent. Figure 3.3 indicates the most common sources of finance based on household survey data. The data show that at least half of the population has no access to formal mortgages and relies either on household savings, loans from family, or microfinance and savings groups (including traditional credit arrangements, such as *ajo* and *esusu*). The lowest 30 percent of the population lacks the capacity to borrow for incremental improvements and likely relies on informal rentals or subsidized public housing (Omrin 2007). The lack of mortgage finance also prohibits the growth of a secondary or resale market for housing. Most people prefer to retain their homes for a long time or transfer them among family members rather than sell them. The data on informal market transfers are limited, but it is likely most of these are cash transactions.

Formal housing development carries significant risks for both developers and consumers, due in part to weaknesses across housing delivery supply chains. Developers that do build homes can obtain finance from banks at interest rates of 16–20 percent. Homes are sold "off-plan," with a 20 percent buyers' down payment that the developer uses for land acquisition, construction costs, or debt service. In larger, more prosperous cities such as Lagos, Abuja, and Port Harcourt, banks and building societies have partnered with some developers to provide development finance, assemble potential buyers, and take on the role of intermediaries by acting as an escrow agent.[17] In each case, however, little oversight in how down payments are spent puts consumers at risk and if the housing development is not completed, the deposit is lost. Furthermore, since tenure security is

Figure 3.3 Distribution of Access to Housing Finance, 2007

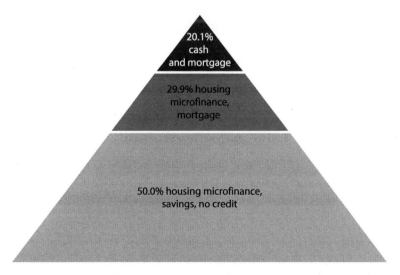

20.1% cash and mortgage

29.9% housing microfinance, mortgage

50.0% housing microfinance, savings, no credit

Source: EFInA and FinMark Trust 2011.
Note: Estimates are approximate and derived from Finmark's analysis of data from the National Bureau of Statistics for 2007 and the Nigeria Living Standard Survey in 2004.

weak, construction materials and development finance are expensive. As a result, it is common for new building projects to fail or to be partially completed.

A liquidity facility could improve the formal housing finance sector. In 2013, in partnership with the government, the World Bank contributed to the launch of the Nigerian Housing Finance Development Program, a suite of three overlapping programs to support investment in land and development. The project allocates US$250 million to support the Nigerian Mortgage Refinance Company, a liquidity facility aimed at improving the access of banks to long-term sources of finance for primary mortgages.[18]

The success of the facility depends in turn on a well-regulated and active primary mortgage market. In this respect, technical assistance has addressed important regulatory and institutional shortcomings. For example, the project's initial achievements include the completion of mortgage underwriting standards that will be applied across the sector and improve mortgage lending by clarifying requirements and obligations between banks and borrowers.

Housing is an important component of inclusive growth. The location and quality of housing has a direct relationship to the quality of urban life and access to services and jobs. A robust housing sector also provides jobs in construction, building materials supply, finance, and property management, and can be a key national economic driver.

Housing policy should place the government in the role of an enabler rather than direct provider, though this is not to discount or dismiss the role of government in housing provision (Kaivani and Werna 2001). But given the existing weaknesses in the private markets that supply materials, skilled labor, and consumer and developer finance, improving housing affordability for Nigeria's urban poor will require strategic investments and regulatory reforms to expand both the supply and demand sides of housing provision. As most housing is developed through informal channels and built incrementally, governments need to recognize and support this provision system alongside interventions to strengthen the formal sector.

An enabling approach can support housing affordability in three complementary areas. First, governments in Nigeria, especially at the local level, have an important role to play in setting and enforcing land use rights and development standards, simplifying title registration and strengthening cadaster records, and guiding growth with strategic infrastructure investments. Each of these measures would improve housing affordability, regardless of income level, by reducing the cost of important supply-side inputs, namely land and infrastructure.

Second, policies should engage the informal housing sector, recognizing that it is largely a response to the high cost of materials, the price of land, and the scarcity of credit. Graduated support for building standards, support for renting, and affordable home loan alternatives such as microfinance could improve the quality and lower the cost of self-built housing units.

Finally, strengthening the formal finance sector by enabling banks to obtain longer-term credit and greater levels of liquidity and establishing a housing market data observatory can enable a wider and more competitive lending market.

Urban planning and infrastructure investments should be coordinated to support density and diversity, and target neighborhoods with the greatest deficiencies. Coordinating land use regulations that support a density and diversity of use can both reduce the cost of network infrastructure connections and improve mobility. An integrated approach is necessary to improve water and sanitation conditions in informal settlements because the function of each is interdependent. Sewerage systems can be extended to densely populated areas where economies of scale can reduce the hook-up costs to trunk lines. In lower density informal settlements, where incomes tend to be lower and housing units more dispersed, interim solutions that allow for the improvement and management of existing septic tanks and latrines are more appropriate. Targeted subsidies and support to community and private sector organizations for upgrading deficient areas are options worth exploring.

Governments must also engage with the informal sector and expand access to new finance sources that enable incremental development. Most housing is built by owners or through small contractors. Without support for this component of the housing delivery system, the disparity in access to quality housing will not change for the majority of urban residents. Mortgage alternatives, such as housing microfinance, can play a more significant role in improving housing quality and infrastructure upgrading.

The Central Bank of Nigeria (2012) reforms to microfinance banking could improve the variety of options for finance available to lower-income groups, especially if paired with in-kind discounts on building materials and technical assistance. Housing microfinance loans would be larger and have longer tenors (around five years) than typical small business loans, but would be for smaller amounts and shorter tenors than current mortgage products (Daphis and Ferguson 2004). Housing microfinance is currently very limited in Nigeria and Sub-Saharan Africa, in part due to the lack of lending familiarity with these products by institutions, as well as a scarcity of secondary finance sources needed to develop them.

In spite of its weaknesses as a housing producer, the FHA could improve the affordability and location of housing in partnership with private developers. In partnering with private developers, the FHA could use its advantages to more easily assemble and convey land to the private sector in exchange for set asides like affordable units. The FHA's role should be distinct from a private developer, but supportive of affordable housing development. The power the FHA has in assembling land and securing property entitlements makes it an ideal organization for cultivating partnerships with private and nonprofit housing developers that can build houses. The FHA negotiates with each state government and can obtain up to 300 hectares of land at little or no cost. Also, the property rights the FHA assigns to beneficiaries, and a Certificate of Occupancy for land and an Allocation Letter or Deed of Assignment for individual houses, carry significant credibility and security. In contrast, obtaining these entitlements is difficult and burdensome for private sector developers and reduces investor confidence in their projects.

Rental housing is a prevalent tenure type and worthy of additional policy support to improve affordability and protections for tenants and landlords alike. This can be done by providing subsidies or grants to petty landlords for improving small-scale rentals, such as spare rooms or backyard ancillary units, provided they meet certain building standards or live on site (Martin and Nell 2002). Strengthening eviction protections and clarifying adjudication procedures can also encourage more owners to rent space. In addition, the government, through the FHA, can encourage the production of new rental units through targeted subsidies for development finance or through requirements in exchange for land assembly for private developers.

The formal housing sector would benefit from policy support that allows for lending protection and access to long-term finance. Apart from support for microfinance institutions to develop housing products, the central bank should also take the lead in helping primary mortgage institutions better secure access to secondary finance to help catalyze a more competitive commercial mortgage market. This would also require complementary reforms to improve creditworthiness assessments and foreclosure proceedings. The existing provident fund can be reformed to set aside a certain share of funding for low-income groups provided they meet certain requirements, such as proof of title or meeting a savings threshold. High down-payment requirements can be reduced by government investment in a mortgage insurance scheme. This would reduce the risk commercial banks face in lending to consumers (Finmark Trust 2011).

Collecting data on a broad set of indicators can help both the targeting of subsidies and improve private investment in housing. Data and information on land and property transactions, including prices, volumes, and submarket locations, should be established to track housing market activity. Such a database would provide a valuable resource for public subsidies targeted to low-income groups and, along with census or survey data, could help identify cities or neighborhoods where affordability or infrastructure gaps are particularly acute.

Such data would also be useful for guiding the investment decisions of lenders and developers. Public and professional organizations such as the Central Bank of Nigeria, the Mortgage Bankers Association of Nigeria, and the Housing Finance Professionals Association of Nigeria can also collaborate to develop training and certification programs with the help of local universities to improve capacity in housing finance and overlapping sectors (Finmark Trust 2011).

Notes

1. Poverty and Social Impact Analysis notes that the impacts of these reforms can be limiting, partly because these reform measures are not widely known to Lagosians and thus underused.

2. For more information on the Greater Port Harcourt City Development Authority, see its website at http://www.gphcity.com/about/authority.php.

3. According to the National Bureau of Statistics, household sizes across states vary widely; from an average 3.1 individuals in Ondo and Kogi to 6.6 in Jigawa and 6.0 in Bauchi. Abuja, at 4.5, is near the mean. Estimates suggest there are approximately 36.5 million households in the country.

4. The survey of 1,004 households was conducted by Renaissance Capital. The report defines middle class as those who make between ₦75,000 and ₦100,000 (US$480–US$645) per month.

5. Index Mundi, Nigeria's Demographics Profile 2014. http://www.indexmundi.com /nigeria/demographics_profile.html.

6. World Bank data, found at http://data.worldbank.org/country/nigeria.

7. The variation depends on projections of informal settlement dwellers and differing estimates of household size.

8. Federal Republic of Nigeria, 2006 Census.

9. The income range designated as middle income was reported as US$6,000–US$7,000. The report featured a survey of 1,000 urban residents (Renaissance Capital 2011) http://www.fastestbillion.com/res/Research/Survey_Nigerian_middle_class-260911. pdf.

10. In contrast, for example, with Kibera, a large, dense informal settlement in Nairobi.

11. According to the WHO/UNICEF definitions, "improved" water systems include piped water systems into a dwelling, yard/plot, a public standpipe or tap, and protected wells or springs. "Unimproved" water facilities include unprotected springs/wells, surface water, bottled water, or water delivered through carts or tanker trucks. "Improved" sanitation facilities include flush toilets, septic tanks, piped sewers, flush or pour flush septic systems, and latrines that are ventilated or have a slab. "Unimproved" facilities include latrines with no slab, bucket or flush to open area, hanging toilet or latrine, or no facilities.

12. Mud and reed composites constitute a large portion of wall construction (38.4 percent); wood, bamboo, and metal sheets each constitute less than 7 percent of dwellings.

13. Palm or thatch roofs cover 15.8 percent of housing units, while slate or asbestos and earthen roofs each cover about 10 percent of housing units.

14. The head of the Nigerian Real Estate Developers Association described how his company had employed imported hydraform technology for housing construction and lowered its cost by 40 percent. http://www.vanguardngr.com/2012/04/affordable-ho using-with-bricks-you-can-reduce-cost-by-40/.

15. In contrast to the United States where the housing sector and related services are about one quarter of GDP (Dickerson 2014, 8).

16. This compares with other lower-middle income countries; 6 percent in Bolivia and Mongolia in 2011, and 17 percent in Morocco in 2014 (http://www.hofinet.org /countries/index.aspx).

17. Identifying target markets and selling housing units individually is often a difficult prospect. Professional associations, cooperatives, and labor organizations (for example, public sector unions), especially among middle-income professionals, may partner with developers to agree to purchase units in large segments, which provide more upfront finance and lower vacancy rates on new developments.

18. Additional supporting components include funding for microfinance initiatives, a mortgage guarantee program, and technical assistance.

References

Aluko, O. 2011. "Sustainable Housing Development and Functionality of Planning Laws in Nigeria: The Case of Cosmopolitan Lagos." *Journal of Sustainable Development* 4 (5): 139–50.

Arimah, C. B., and D. Adeagbo. 2000. "Compliance with Urban Development and Planning Regulations in Ibadan, Nigeria." *Habitat International* 24 (3): 279–94.

Birner, R., and A. Okumo. 2011. "Challenges of Land Governance in Nigeria: Insights from a Case Study in Ondo State." Nigeria Strategy Support Program Working Paper No. 22, International Food Policy Research Institute, Washington, DC. http://ebrary .ifpri.org/cdm/ref/collection/p15738coll2/id/126875.

Boleat, M., and S. Walley. 2008. "Nigeria: Financial System Strategy 2020." http://www .boleat.com/materials/nigerian_financial_system_strategy_2020.pdf.

Business Day. 2013. "Jos Metropolitan Development Board Generates N12.7m Revenue." January 28. http://www.businessdayonline.com/NG/index.php/news/latest/50739 -jos-metropolitan-development-board-generates-n127m-revenue.

Butler, S. 2012. "Nigerian Land Markets and the Land Use Law of 1978." *Focus on Land in Africa Brief*. Land and Natural Resource Tenure in Africa Program, World Resources Institute, and Landesa. http://landportal.info/sites/default/files/nigeria_land_markets _nov2012.pdf.

Centre for Affordable Housing Finance Africa. 2013. *Housing Finance in Africa: A Review of Some of Africa's Housing Finance Markets*. Parkview, South Africa, Centre for Affordable Housing Finance in Africa.

———. 2014. *Housing Finance in Africa: A Review of Some of Africa's Housing Finance Markets*. Parkview, South Africa, Centre for Affordable Housing Finance in Africa.

Central Bank of Nigeria. 2012. *Revised Regulatory and Supervisory Guidelines for Microfinance Banks in Nigeria*. Abuja: Central Bank of Nigeria. http://www.cenbank .org/Out/2013/CCD/Amended%20Regulatory%20and%20Supervisory%20 Guidelines%20for%20MFB.pdf.

Chiquier, L. 2009. "Housing Provident Funds." In *Housing Finance Policy in Emerging Markets*, edited by Loic Chiquier and Michael Lea. Washington, DC: World Bank.

Daphis, F., and B. Ferguson. 2004. *Housing Microfinance: A Guide to Practice*. West Hartford, CT: Kumarian.

Dasgupta, B., S. V. Lall, and N. Gracia-Lozano. 2014. *Urbanization and Housing Investment*. Washington, DC: World Bank.

DHS (Demographic and Health Survey). 2013. *Nigeria Demographic and Health Survey*. Washington, DC: USAID.

Dickerson, M. 2014. *Homeownership and America's Financial Underclass: Flawed Premises, Broken Promises, New Prescriptions*. New York: Cambridge University Press.

EFInA (Enhancing Financial Innovation & Access) and FinMark Trust. 2010. "Overview of Housing Finance System in Nigeria." Report. http://www.housingfinanceafrica.org /wp-content/uploads/2010/08/A2HF_Nigeria.pdf.

Federal Republic of Nigeria. 2006. "2006 Population and Housing Census of the Federal Republic of Nigeria." Federal Republic of Nigeria, Abuja.

Federal Republic of Nigeria. 2012. *National Urban Development Policy*. Abuja: Federal Ministry of Lands, Housing and Urban Development.

Kessides, C. 2006. *The Urban Transition in Sub-Saharan Africa: Implications for Economic Growth and Poverty Reduction Cities Alliance.* Washington, DC: Cities Alliance.

Lloyd-Jones, T., M. Theis, S. Adenekan, S. Gusah, and M. Mutter. 2014. *The Informal Housing Development Process in Nigeria: The Case of Kaduna Project Report.* London: MLC Press.

Lozano-Gracia, N., and C. Young. 2014. "Housing Consumption and Urbanization." Policy Research Working Paper 7112, World Bank, Washington, DC.

Martin, S. M., and M. Nell. 2002. *An Assessment of Rental Housing in South Africa.* Washington, DC: USAID.

Max Lock Consultancy. 2010. *Kaduna Master Plan Draft.* Consultant report.

Mutter, M., A. Lloyd-Jones, and S. Gusah. Unpublished. Part 4 of report prepared for World Bank's 2015 Stocktaking of the housing sector in Sub-Saharan Africa.

Napier, M. 2009. "FinScope SA: Restraints but No Frontiers." Finmark Trust. http://www.finscope.co.za/new/pages/default.aspx.

Oluwafemi, A., and A. O. Ayandibu. 2014. "Impact of Remittances on Development in Nigeria: Challenges and Prospects." *Journal of Sociology and Social Anthropology* 5(3): 311–18.

Omrin, M. M. 2007. "The Role of Primary Mortgage Institutions in Housing Delivery." *Housing Finance International* 22 (1).

Onyenechere, E. C. 2011. "Water and Sanitation Service Provision in Owerri City, Nigeria." Paper presented at the ECAS-4 Conference of the Nordic Africa Institute, Uppsala, Sweden, June 10.

Otubu, Tunde. 2009. "Land Use Zoning in a Changing Urban Environment." Public lecture in commemoration of the 70th birthday of Remi Makinde, Lagos, July 23.

Private Property. 2014. "7 Affordable Places to Rent a Property in Nigeria." August 22. http://www.privateproperty.co.na/news/feature/7-affordable-places-to-rent-a-property-in-nigeria.htm?id=1050.

Renaissance Capital. 2011. "A Survey of the Nigerian Middle Class." Thematic Research. http://www.fastestbillion.com/res/Research/Survey_Nigerian_middle_class-260911.pdf.

Transparency International. 2009. *Global Corruption Barometer Report.* Berlin: Transparency International.

———. 2010. *Global Corruption Barometer Report.* Berlin: Transparency International.

Ubom, A. U. and U. B. Ubom. 2014. "The Contributions of Primary Mortgage Institutions (PMIS) to Real Estate Development in Nigeria." *International Journal of Finance and Accounting* 3 (3): 157–61.

UN-Habitat (United Nations Human Settlements Programme). 2003. *The Challenge of Slums: Global Report on Human Settlements.* Nairobi: UN-Habitat.

———. 2007. *Slums: Some Definitions.* Nairobi: UN-Habitat. http://ww2.unhabitat.org/mediacentre/documents/sowcr2006/SOWCR%.

Wapwera, S. D., and C. O. Egbu. 2013. "Planning Authorities: A Review of Roles, Functions and Responsibilities in Jos Metropolis, Nigeria." *The Built and Human Environment Review* 6: 30–45.

Watson, V., and B. Agbola. 2013. "Who Will Plan Africa's Cities?" Africa Research Institute. http://www.africaresearchinstitute.org/publications/counterpoints/who-will-plan-africas-cities/.

World Bank. 2009. *World Development Report 2009: Reshaping Economic Geography.* Washington, DC: World Bank.

————. 2013a. "Doing Business: Dealing with Construction Permits in Plateau (Jos), Nigeria." *Doing Business.* http://www.doingbusiness.org/data/exploreeconomies /nigeria/sub/plateau/topic/dealing-with-construction-permits.

————. 2013b. *Access to Low Income and Affordable Housing in East Asia and the Pacific.* Washington, DC: World Bank.

————. 2014. *Doing Business: Understanding Regulations for Small and Medium-Size Enterprises.* Washington, DC: World Bank.

CHAPTER 4

Financing Nigeria's Cities

Introduction

Nigeria's rapid urban expansion has not yet found sufficient financing for the urban public goods and services needed to develop strong economies that create jobs. This chapter therefore focuses on the financing of public goods and services in larger urban centers (cities)—simply defined as relatively densely populated settlements with more than 300,000 people. Table 1.1 in chapter 1 lists the cities in all size classes that are projected to grow—42 of them in Nigeria, and most but not all state capitals.

It also looks at how and by whom financing is (or might be) mobilized and deployed, and what the challenges and opportunities are (or have been) in effectively and efficiently using such funds to "deliver the goods."

Some assumptions and qualifications need to be outlined, as major "known unknowns" and limitations exist in any data on urban finance in Nigeria.

First, detailed and robust financial and fiscal data are not always available, especially at the subnational level. Publication and disclosure of state government financial statements and reports is not, as yet, the norm; most Nigerian states do not regularly publish or make their financial reports or statements available. Federally, information on state government finances is available, but it is understandably not very disaggregated. At the federal and subnational levels, information about local government finance is even harder to access.

Second, information on subnational finance does not distinguish between urban and other revenues and expenditures: no specifically urban local government units exist in Nigeria[1] and finance data generally refer to state or local government jurisdictions as a whole. Sector-based analyses and information also tend to blur the distinction between specifically urban and general dimensions. This lack of clarity makes it difficult to analyze urban-based (as opposed to statewide, rural, or semirural) revenues, expenditures, and borrowing.

In addition, the primary focus on cities with a population of over 300,000 is based on a threefold rationale:

- These larger urban centers account for just over 50 percent of the country's urban population.[2]

- They include most state capitals and are almost all made up of more than one local government jurisdiction.
- These cities and towns typically have much higher population densities than smaller settlements.

Such cities are also very heterogeneous—not only in size, with Lagos as the singularly dominant metropolis, but also in other terms. While many are state administrative capitals, and thus include a substantial number of resident public servants, some are semi-industrial cities, a few are service-based or financial centers, others are the servicing centers for large and predominantly rural hinterlands, and others are university towns.

Some cities are located on major corridors and thrive as transport hubs; others are less connected to larger economic networks. Although all Nigerian cities have lively informal sectors and operate on the basis of informal institutional arrangements (for land tenure and housing, in particular), informality is more marked in some than others. Although all Nigerian cities face common challenges, they do so to different degrees. They also vary greatly in the resources they—or more accurately their respective states—can bring to the table.

State and Local Government in Nigeria

Nigeria's 1999 constitution provides for a three-tier governmental system: a federal government,[3] 36 state governments, and 774 local governments (often referred to as local government areas [LGAs]).

Each of the three tiers has constitutionally defined powers, rights, and responsibilities; and each tier includes an elected assembly or council (in the case of LGAs), endowed with legislative powers. The constitution explicitly specifies the names of all states and local governments. Together, the state and local government levels make up subnational government in Nigeria. Table 4.1 provides basic statistical data on state and local government populations.

States and local governments employ many people. In 2005, states and LGAs (with a combined total of about 1.16 million employees) accounted for almost 65 percent of all civilian public servants in Nigeria (USAID 2010a).

A number of important aspects of Nigeria's subnational government system need to be highlighted:

- Despite protestations to the contrary, state governments enjoy remarkable administrative autonomy relative to the federal government. While the constitution can be interpreted as formally giving the federal government strong and centralized powers, in practice states tend to operate with a great deal of latitude. In public financial and expenditure management, states operate independently of the federal government.

- State governments are constitutionally empowered to legislate on local government issues, provided that any such legislation is consistent with broad

Table 4.1 Basic Demographic Data: States and Local Governments in Nigeria (Largest States by Population)

State	State capital	No. of local governments	Population	Population density (per km²)	Percent of total national population	Surface area (km²)
Kano	Kano	44	9,383,682	460	6.7	20,389
Lagos	Ikeja	20	9,013,534	2,594	6.4	3,475
Kaduna	Kaduna	23	6,066,562	137	4.3	44,217
Katsina	Katsina	34	5,792,578	243	4.1	23,822
Oyo	Ibadan	33	5,591,589	207	4.0	27,036
Rivers	Part Harcourt	23	5,185,400	500	3.7	10,361
Bauchi	Bauchi	20	4,676,465	97	3.3	48,197
Jigawa	Dutse	27	4,348,649	186	3.1	23,415
Benue	Makurti	23	4,219,244	137	3.0	30,755
Anambra	Awka	21	4,182,032	878	3.0	4,761
Borno	Maiduguri	27	4,151,193	57	3.0	72,767
Delta	Asaba	25	4,098,391	240	2.9	17,095
Nigar	Minna	25	3,950,249	55	2.8	72,065
Imo	Owerri	27	3,934,899	766	2.8	5,135
Akwa Ibom	Uyo	31	3,920,208	578	2.8	6,788
Ogun	Abeokuta	20	3,728,098	221	2.7	16,850
Sokoto	Sokoto	23	3,696,999	115	2.6	32,146
Ondo	Akura	18	3,441,024	229	2.5	15,019
Osun	Oshogbo	30	3,423,535	399	2.4	8,585
Kogi	Lokoja	21	3,278,487	113	2.3	29,063
Zamfara	Gusau	14	3,259,846	97	2.3	33,667
Enugu	Enugu	17	3,257,298	431	2.3	7,560
Kebbi	Birnin Kebbi	21	3,238,628	89	2.3	36,320
Edo	Benin City	18	3,218,332	164	2.3	19,584
Plateau	Jos	17	3,178,712	120	2.3	26,539
Adamawa	Yola	21	3,168,101	83	2.3	37,957
Cross River	Calabar	18	2,888,966	131	2.1	22,112
Abia	Umuahia	17	2,833,999	583	2.0	4,857
Ekiti	Ado-Ekiti	16	2,384,212	411	1.7	5,797
Kwara	Ilorin	16	2,371,089	70	1.7	33,792
Gombe	Gombe	11	2,353,879	135	1.7	17,428
Yobe	Damaturu	17	2,321,591	52	1.7	44,880
Taraba	Jalingo	16	2,300,736	39	1.6	59,180
Ebonyi	Abakaliki	13	2,173,501	343	1.6	6,342
Nassarawa	Lafia	13	1,863,275	70	1.3	26,633
Bayelsa	Yanagoa	8	1,703,358	182	1.2	9,363
FCT	Abuja	6	1,405,201	186	1.0	7,569
	Total	**774**	**140,003,542**	**154**	**100.0**	**911,521**

Source: CLGF 2013.
Note: FCT = Federal Capital Territory; km2 = square kilometers.

constitutional provisions about local government. This *de jure* dominance of LGAs by their respective state governments is largely exercised in practice—in political, administrative, and fiscal terms. The clearest demonstration of this fact is the near universal state practice of appointing unelected caretaker LGA chairs and councils, rather than overseeing local government elections.

Table 4.2 Population Size of Nigerian States and Local Governments

States		Local governments	
Population	*36 States + Abuja FCT*	*Population*	*774 LGAs*
Mean	3,783,880	Mean	180,650
Median	3,423,535	Median	157,295
Max	9,383,682	Max	1,277,714
Min	1,405,201	Min	20,253

Source: National Bureau of Statistics, 2006 Census.
Note: FCT = Federal Capital Territory; LGAs = local government areas.

- In comparison to the lowest tier of subnational government in other countries, Nigerian local governments cover relatively large populations.[4] As tables 4.1 and 4.2 show, most LGAs in Nigeria (as of the 2006 census) have a population of around 160,000. Some are very large, with a population exceeding 1,000,000. The relatively large size of Nigerian LGAs suggests that they would be viable self-governing service delivery units. However, in practice, LGAs tend to operate as deconcentrated extensions of their respective state governments.

- No constitutional distinction is made between rural and urban local governments. No Nigerian municipalities exist with a specific mandate (or specific functions) to provide public goods and services in cities or towns. An LGA in an urban area has exactly the same functions, powers, and responsibilities as an LGA in a rural area. Nor is it constitutionally possible for state governments to independently legislate municipalities (as local governments) into existence—for such municipalities to be recognized as such requires a constitutional amendment.

- No subnational governments—such as metropolitan governments—exist between states and local governments. Major cities such as Lagos or Ibadan are made up of the jurisdictions of several autonomous LGAs and are not managed as city corporations. While it is formally possible for states—or indeed cooperating LGAs, with state approval—to establish coordinating or planning authorities for cities,[5] these cannot (for constitutional reasons) be recognized or considered as municipal governments with their own "fiscal" or administrative identity. By default, state governments assume the role of city managers, alongside all their other functions.

- In fiscal terms, almost all state and local governments rely heavily on their respective allocations from (or shares of) the taxes and other revenues pooled and collected by the federal government. That said, states (but not LGAs) enjoy almost complete discretionary powers over the use they make of their federally derived revenues, in much the same way as they do with respect to their own-source revenues (known as internally generated revenues [IGRs]). Conditional or earmarked grants and transfers from the federal government to the states, on the other hand, are few and far between.

- Because 75 percent of federally collected revenues are derived from oil and gas revenues (Litwack 2013), all three tiers of government are highly vulnerable to fluctuations in world energy prices. As the price of oil and gas rises or falls, so too does the size of the fiscal funding pool in which each tier of the inter-governmental system has a share. In principle, the Excess Crude Account (fiscal reserve) is intended to iron out major fluctuations in the revenues shared out to the three tiers of government; in practice and for a variety of reasons, the fiscal reserve has not been able to do so. As a result of subnational government dependence on their shares of the federal revenue pie, state and local governments can see their overall revenues and budgets fall substantially if and when oil and gas prices drop (as is currently the case).

In summary, Nigeria's subnational governance system can be characterized as dominated by relatively strong and autonomous state governments, weak and often electorally unaccountable local governments, and devoid of any meaning-fully empowered city or intermediary authorities. Fiscally, the subnational gov-ernment system as a whole relies heavily on revenue-sharing allocations from a federally collected funding pool, which varies in size with fluctuations in world energy prices.

Financing Nigeria's Urban Development

Meeting Nigeria's urban development challenges will need substantial financing.

Urban Infrastructure Investments

Although Nigeria has relatively advanced power, road, rail, and information and communication technology networks that cover extensive areas of its territory, a good deal more needs to be done to bring the stock of infrastructure up to a satisfactory level and to keep it there in both coverage and quality. For this task, development financing needs in the country are considerable.

African Development Bank (2013) estimates that infrastructure investments (and related expenditure)[6] across a broad, nationwide spectrum of sectors for 2011–20 need to be in the order of US$350 billion to meet the objectives set out in the government's medium-term Vision 20:2020. According to the report, spending on infrastructure amounted to 4.6 percent of gross domestic product (GDP) in 2011, should peak at 12.6 percent in 2016, and should then decline steadily to about 9.6 percent by 2020. Of this, about US$193 billion will be needed for *publicly* owned infrastructure and US$92 billion for *privately* owned infrastructure (such as power generation and distribution networks, communica-tions networks, and so on).

Box 4.1 Urban Transport and Water Supply: Investment Needs and Costs

Nigeria's growing cities, especially the larger agglomerations, underlie the need for significant investments in urban public transport infrastructure and services. From 2011 to 2020, it is estimated demand will increase by 5.2 million public transport trips per day. To address this rise, the African Development Bank projects the need for, among other things:

• Repairing and rehabilitating approximately 30,000 kilometers of urban and tertiary roads
• Paving and upgrading almost 15,000 kilometers of urban and tertiary roads
• Developing mass transit train and bus systems.

In all, investments of around US$40 billion in urban public transport infrastructure will be needed during 2011–20.

Rapid annual urban population growth has made it difficult for Nigeria's state water agencies—frontline service providers in the urban water sector—to meet the existing need for piped water and expand production capacity. From 2004 to 2013, while Nigeria's urban population grew from 38 percent of the total to 46 percent, urban access to improved water sources stagnated at 79 percent. Growing numbers of Nigerians living in urban areas face water scarcity as a result. Old and dilapidated piping systems are subject to frequent leakage, and newly built ones often have no water due to intermittent power supply. The African Development Bank estimates the cost of upgrading and improving urban water supply will be around US$13 billion during 2011–20.

Although the federal government will need to mobilize much of the finance required for upgrading or rehabilitating public infrastructure, subnational governments will also need to play a role. Assuming subnational public infrastructure investments need to cover about 25 percent of all spending on public infrastructure,[7] this amounts to approximately US$50 billion during 2011–21.

A significant proportion of subnational infrastructure financing will need to be targeted at investments in urban infrastructure, given that at least 50 percent of Nigeria's population is urban and that urban infrastructure typically requires more finance than rural infrastructure. An important, but unquantifiable share of federal infrastructure spending will also need to be urban. But this is an extrapolation, given that there are few specific estimates for urban infrastructure and investment needs. A more precise idea of the scale of financing required in the urban transport and urban water supply sectors is provided in box 4.1.

Although data and assessments for other urban sectors and services (such as solid waste management and housing) are not readily available, it is clear that these will also require substantial infrastructure investment to meet growing demand in cities and towns.

Other Investments and Spending on Urban Development

Although less often considered as part of urban development finance, need is growing for investments in institutional reform and capacity development and for budgetary commitments to financing operations and maintenance. Overall costs for these types of expenditure in urban areas are hard to come by—but the need to finance these costs is clear and should be factored into any overall assessment of urban finance.

Institutional Capacity Development

The urban water sector is a striking example of the need for investments in institutional reform and capacity development, as well as in new and upgraded infrastructure. The recently approved Third National Urban Water Sector Reform Project, for example, is predicated on the need for upfront institutional reforms as a prelude to further infrastructure investments. Having the right institutional framework in the urban water supply sector is an essential element underlying any coverage, quality, and value-for-money improvements of urban water supply systems, as box 4.2 illustrates.

Institutional reforms and capacity development do not come cheap. For example, 15 percent of the total budget for the new urban water supply project (which directly impacts upon three states and indirectly impacts upon nine other states) is earmarked for reform and capacity development activities. This quantum of "software" financing is probably valid across all urban infrastructure and service delivery sectors.

The need for supporting institutional capacity development and reforms is also implicitly borne out by the World Bank's Development Policy Operation loans to Lagos State government and to Edo State government (a major part of whose jurisdiction includes Benin City). All of these represent significant levels of budget support (and much of which has been or is likely to be used to finance

---

Box 4.2 Investing in the Urban Water Supply Sector: Institutional Reforms and Capacity Development Needs

"Previous interventions by Government and development partners have largely focused on addressing...physical infrastructure aspects, which alone cannot fully address the service delivery needs in a sustainable manner, unless combined with sector reforms to provide the enabling environment for sustaining services...[A]ttention has begun to shift towards addressing more institutional and governance issues such as reform of policies and legislation in combination with the physical investments ... significant challenges remain and there is a need for a sustained focus on both strategic investments and reforms at state level to meet the country's development goals."

Source: World Bank 2014d.

---

the states' ambitious infrastructure development programs), linked to bench-marked progress in local public sector management reforms World Bank 2012, 2014c). Underlying these state-level Development Policy Operations is a clear recognition of the need to finance both infrastructure and hardware improvements and, at the same time, to finance (or leverage) a steady package of agreed reforms and capacity development initiatives.

Operations and Maintenance

Nigeria is far from alone in underplaying the importance of financing operations and maintenance for its existing stock of public infrastructure—this is common to many developing and developed countries.[8] Past failures to spend enough and effectively on operations and maintenance simply result in deteriorating infrastructure and—ultimately—more costly investments in major rehabilitation or reconstruction. While the situation at the federal level is cause for concern, it is even more so at the subnational level (see box 4.3 on roads).

Urban service delivery also requires operational expenditures. Effective solid waste management in cities relies on regular financing of labor and operating costs. For example, recurrent costs accounted for almost one-third of the 2013 budget estimates for Oyo State's solid waste management authority, which is most active in the state's cities and larger towns Ogungbuyi 2013). This amount excludes recurrent spending covered by cost recovery on the part of private service providers.

Although no information is readily available on the costs of operating and maintaining Nigeria's current and future stock of urban infrastructure, good grounds exist for assuming that the consequences of not meeting such costs are likely to be considerable. In the roads sector, for example: "… *rehabilitating paved roads every 10 to 20 years is more than three times as expensive*, in cash terms, as maintaining them on a regular basis…. *Rehabilitating* gravel roads

---

Box 4.3 Subnational Road Maintenance in Nigeria

Road maintenance problems are much more severe at the subnational level (World Bank 2011). Road condition indicators for the entire national network are much worse than for the federal network. Only 67 percent of paved roads (as a whole) are in good or fair condition. Even more worrisome, only 33 percent of unpaved roads—all the responsibility of subnational governments and a good proportion in urban areas—are in good or fair condition. Road maintenance is not adequately funded or implemented at the subnational level. The World Bank report estimates that the annual maintenance and rehabilitation requirement for the subnational road network is around US$500 million, or about the same as that for the federal network. The maintenance of urban roads accounts for an important but unquantifiable share of this amount.

Source: World Bank 2011.

---

every 10 years is *twice as expensive*, in cash terms, as regular routine and periodic maintenance…" (Heggie 1995). In other words, while meeting new capital financing needs in Nigeria's cities is necessary, it should not be allowed to detract from the need for financing operations and maintenance of existing and future urban infrastructure—and the costs of this need adds considerably to overall funding requirements.

Summing Up

The public financing needs of Nigerian cities are already considerable, and will only increase as they develop and grow. Capital financing is high on the list of spending priorities, but needs to be matched by investments in institutional capacity development and by funding of operations and maintenance costs if new infrastructure and equipment is to be productive and to deliver urban services on a sustained and cost-effective basis. Putting all this together will be a formidable challenge.

Table 4.3 Public Expenditure in Nigeria, 2009–13

Item	Naira (billions)				
	2009	2010	2011	2012	2013
Federal government					
Recurrent expenditure	2,127.97	3,109.38	3,314.51	3,325.16	3,689.06
Capital expenditure	1,152.80	883.87	918.55	874.83	1,108.39
Capital as % of total federal government expenditure	35.14	22.13	21.70	20.83	23.10
Subtotal	**3,280.77**	**3,993.25**	**4,233.06**	**4,199.99**	**4,797.45**
As % of total expenditure	46.04	46.35	45.00	43.34	44.76
State governments					
Recurrent expenditure	1,426.10	1,648.40	2,055.70	1,664.40	1,723.90
Capital expenditure	1,284.20	1,522.40	1,375.20	1,965.30	2,220.00
Capital as % of total state governments expenditure	46.25	46.61	38.84	51.11	53.97
Others (deductions)	66.60	95.40	110.00	215.40	169.20
Subtotal	**2,776.90**	**3,266.20**	**3,540.90**	**3,845.10**	**4,113.10**
As % of total expenditure	38.97	37.91	37.65	39.68	38.38
Local governments					
Recurrent expenditure	704.60	823.70	1,279.80	1,345.50	1,414.00
Capital expenditure	363.00	533.00	352.10	299.40	392.90
Capital as % of total local governments expenditure	34.00	39.29	21.58	18.20	21.74
Subtotal	**1,067.60**	**1,356.70**	**1,631.90**	**1,644.90**	**1,806.90**
As % of total expenditure	14.98	15.75	17.35	16.98	16.86
Total	**7,125.27**	**8,616.15**	**9,405.86**	**9,689.99**	**10,717.45**
	100.00	100.00	100.00	100.00	100.00
Expenditure as % of nominal gross domestic product	28.70	15.90	14.90	13.60	13.40

Source: Central Bank of Nigeria Data and Statistics.

From Oil to Cities • http://dx.doi.org/10.1596/978-1-4648-0792-3

Expenditure

Expenditure Patterns

Between them, states and local governments have regularly accounted for over 50 percent of all public expenditure in Nigeria over the last decade or so. Since 2010, subnational government spending has amounted to around 7 percent of GDP (table 4.3). Whichever way you look at it, subnational public expenditure is important.[9]

On aggregate, about 35 percent of total public expenditure is spent on capital items. State governments are the biggest capital spenders—both relatively (spending roughly 50 percent of their total expenditure on capital) and absolutely (usually spending more on capital items than the federal and local government tiers taken together).

The local government tier is the least focused on capital expenditure—spending less than either the federal or state government levels on capital items and usually allocating a smaller proportion of its spending to capital expenditure than the other tiers do. In absolute per capita terms, state governments, on average, spend almost six times more than local governments on capital items (tables 4.4–4.7).

On capital expenditure, there is a good deal of variation between states and between local governments (tables 4.4–4.7).

Among state governments, Jigawa, Akwa Ibom, and Rivers stand out: in each, capital spending represented over 80 percent of all public expenditure.[10] In addition, Rivers and Akwa Ibom states were the largest per capita spenders on capital, followed by Bayelsa and Lagos.[11]

At the bottom of the league of capital spenders are Imo, Kano, and Niger states, each devoting less than 20 percent of total expenditure to capital spending. They are also the lowest capital spenders in absolute per capita terms. Most states, however, spend a little under 50 percent of their total expenditure on capital items.

The local governments that spend the highest proportion (over 40 percent) on capital items are those in Kebbi, Yobe, and Zamfara states. Equally, they were the biggest per capita spenders.[12]

The local governments spending the least capital (proportionate to total expenditure) were in Ogun, Bauchi, and Imo states; they were also, in absolute per capita terms, the LGAs that spent the least on capital. LGAs in most states spend roughly 20 percent of their total expenditure on capital items.

Levels of state and local government spending on operations and maintenance of infrastructure are difficult to determine—partly because detailed information on expenditure is not available, and partly because it is unclear as to whether maintenance spending is systematically classified and recorded as recurrent or capital.

As can be seen from tables 4.4 and 4.6, total spending by state and local governments is considerable in absolute terms. In 2013, total subnational spending amounted to about US$29.6 billion,[13] of which just over US$13.0 billion was on

Table 4.4 State Government Capital Spending as Percentage of Total Expenditure, 2013

State government	Capital spending as % of total expenditure	Capital spending per capita (Naira)
Abia	48.14	12,773
Adamawa	53.03	15,751
Akwa Ibom	84.26	67,981
Anambra	69.68	12,147
Bauchi	58.00	13,258
Bayelsa	34.16	34,109
Benue	49.58	9,907
Borno	51.56	9,539
Cross River	49.37	13,569
Delta	38.52	20,764
Ebonyi	64.16	21,164
Edo	37.71	12,584
Ekiti	39.20	13,170
Enugu	50.09	8,934
Gombe	49.03	17,248
Imo	10.76	1,372
Jigawa	85.70	18,328
Kaduna	47.32	7,434
Kano	13.17	2,217
Katsina	56.29	8,425
Kebbi	69.55	18,619
Kogi	59.19	10,706
Kwara	53.23	17,376
Lagos	66.08	28,945
Nassarawa	27.52	9,660
Niger	19.18	2,607
Ogun	28.78	3,782
Ondo	30.92	8,457
Osun	23.61	6,076
Oyo	57.58	7,815
Plateau	45.96	12,898
Rivers	80.32	72,588
Sokoto	21.24	2,786
Taraba	56.97	18,820
Yobe	60.89	14,688
Zamfara	24.16	5,276
Federal Capital Territory	60.46	33,945

Source: Central Bank of Nigeria Data and Statistics.

Table 4.5 State Government Capital Expenditure, 2013

Measure	Capital spending as % of total expenditure	Capital spending per capita (Naira)
Mean	47.98	16,101
Median	49.58	12,773
Maximum	85.70	72,588
Minimum	10.76	1,372

Source : Central Bank of Nigeria Data and Statistics.

Table 4.6 Local Government Capital Spending, 2013
(percent of total expenditure)

LGs in state	Capital spending as % of total expenditure	Capital spending per capita (Naira)
Abia	10.20	1,274
Adamawa	19.47	2,800
Akwa Ibom	11.61	1,786
Anambra	20.53	2,205
Bauchi	6.73	806
Bayelsa	23.35	2,659
Benue	20.80	2,775
Borno	35.30	5,035
Cross River	16.26	2,167
Delta	11.48	1,701
Ebonyi	35.07	4,647
Edo	20.63	2,430
Ekiti	10.29	1,351
Enugu	32.72	3,727
Gombe	11.35	1,389
Imo	8.30	1,100
Jigawa	18.31	2,412
Kaduna	11.03	1,129
Kano	24.05	2,616
Katsina	18.37	2,289
Kebbi	53.12	8,053
Kogi	11.18	1,592
Kwara	22.11	3,403
Lagos	32.59	3,547
Nassarawa	18.32	3,097
Niger	32.89	4,605
Ogun	3.85	456
Ondo	21.03	2,383
Osun	29.32	4,685
Oyo	17.71	2,202
Plateau	17.49	2,124
Rivers	12.16	1,304
Sokoto	29.56	4,030
Taraba	24.00	4,307
Yobe	50.88	9,468
Zamfara	40.81	5,095
FCT	13.43	2,562

Source : Central Bank of Nigeria Data and Statistics.
Note: FCT = Federal Capital Territory; LGs = local governments.

Table 4.7 Local Government Capital Expenditure, 2013

Measure	Capital spending as % of total expenditure	Capital spending per capita (Naira)
Mean	21.52	2,952
Median	19.47	2,430
Maximum	53.12	9,468
Minimum	3.85	456

Source: Central Bank of Nigeria Data and Statistics.

capital items. A lot of public money, then, is being spent at the subnational level: the key to assessing its contribution to meeting real needs and addressing priorities is in the ways that subnational governments spend and how effectively and efficiently they do so.

How much state and local government spending is focused on urban infrastructure and services? Unfortunately, available information on subnational public expenditure does not readily lend itself to an assessment of spending in urban areas. In highly urbanized states, it might be assumed that most (if not all) subnational government expenditure was essentially urban; however, this is misleading, simply because state governments spend on items (such as their legislatures, judiciaries, and regulatory services) that would not normally be considered "urban" public goods and services. Nonetheless, given Nigeria's urban population, it is probably safe to assume that overall subnational spending in cities amounts to a similar proportion of total expenditure.

Functional and Expenditure Assignments

The constitution provides a broad framework for functional (or expenditure) assignments across the three tiers of government, as table 4.8 shows. In addition, the Fourth Schedule of the constitution provides a more detailed listing of local government functions: these are broadly consistent with the wider framework, but also include local government revenue assignments. Additional local-government-specific functions are included in table 4.8.

In general, the constitutional assignment of functions and responsibilities to the three tiers of government is consistent with internationally accepted federal principles. But, and as with many such assignments of functions across tiers of government, room exists for overlap and duplication, and provisions are subject to interpretation.

Functional assignments are clearer in some sectors than others. Formal responsibilities in the Nigerian roads sector, for example, are shared but relatively well-defined and discrete for each tier of government, as box 4.4 illustrates.

In other sectors, however, assignments are somewhat more ambiguous. The health sector provides a trenchant illustration, as box 4.5 shows.

Another sector in which functional and expenditure assignments often lack clarity is education, as illustrated in box 4.6.

Table 4.8 Constitutional Assignment of Functions across Tiers of Government

Assignment	Federal	State	Local
Defense	National defense		
Foreign affairs	Diplomatic and consular missions, international treaties, foreign policy		
Public order	National police, security services, prisons	State public order	
Trade and commerce	Commercial policy, banking, insurance, bankruptcy, international trade, interstate trade	Intrastate trade and commerce	Local markets, slaughter houses, local economic development
Natural resources	Mines and mineral, including oil and gas surveying and mining	Natural resource development other than minerals	
Agriculture and fisheries	Promotion of agricultural research and production, fishing rights	State agricultural development	Local agriculture development
Health	Federal health policy	State health policy	Local health services
Education and science	University and professional education, scientific and technological research, national statistics	Regulation of primary education, provision of post-primary education, university and professional education, scientific and technological research	Provision and maintenance of primary school and vocational training
Transportation networks and public transportation	Aviation policy and airports, railways, federal highways	State highways, public transit	Local roads and highways, local public transit; construction and maintenance of roads, streets, street lightings, drains, and other public highways, parks, gardens
Solid waste management and sanitation			Public conveniences, sewage and refuse disposal
Vital registration			Registration of all births, deaths, and marriages

Source: Boex and Alm 2002; 1999 constitution.
Note: The constitution is curiously silent about the assignment of responsibilities for water supply. These are assigned through the National Water Supply and Sanitation Policy (2000).

Unfortunately, readily accessible data on aggregate expenditure patterns at the state and local government levels do not provide a clear indication of the extent to which formal expenditure assignments across sectors are translated into practice.

Subnational Functional Assignments and Spending on Urban Public Goods and Services: Principles and Practice

Unlike many (or most) other countries, Nigeria has no municipal or metropolitan governments; the constitution simply makes no provision for urban subnational governments. No unit of governance and coordination exists at the city or

Box 4.4 The Allocation of Functional Responsibilities in the Roads Sector

In principle, the responsibilities of each tier of government in the roads sector mirror the classification of roads themselves:

Trunk A roads (about 33,000 kilometers in total) cut across regional and state boundaries, extend to the international borders with neighboring West African countries, and make up the national road grid. Trunk A roads are under the federal government's ownership and are thus designed, constructed, maintained, and financed by the federal government through the Federal Ministry of Works. The Federal Road Maintenance Agency is in charge of carrying out maintenance of this class of roads.

Trunk B roads (about 50,000 kilometers) are the second category of main roads in Nigeria, linking major cities within states with their state capitals. State governments design, develop, finance, and maintain them through their ministries of works, transport, or infrastructure.

Trunk C roads (117,000 kilometers) are local feeder roads, are typically not asphalted or usable all year, and link villages and communities. The works departments of local governments maintain and construct these.

Source: Federal Ministry of Works 2013.

Box 4.5 Functional and Expenditure Assignments in the Health Sector

The delivery of public primary health care is the formal responsibility of local government areas (LGAs) and their respective departments of health. LGAs, for the most part, own and fund the facilities. Secondary (and some tertiary) health care, which includes several types of hospital, is the responsibility of state governments and state ministries of health. Finally, the Federal Ministry of Health is responsible for teaching hospitals in federal universities, federal medical centers, and specialized tertiary-level health care facilities.

However, public expenditure streams for the three levels of government are largely uncoordinated. In some states, the federal government funds and operates model primary care facilities overseen by national primary health care agencies. Federal, state, and local allocation and expenditure decisions are taken independently. The federal government has no constitutional power to compel other tiers of government to spend in accordance with national priorities. Finally, other federal ministries—including defense, education, and internal affairs—own and run extensive networks of health facilities—which provide treatment and care for armed forces personnel and their families, students, and prison inmates, respectively.

Source: Health Systems 20/20 2012b.

metropolitan levels to coordinate planning and budgeting or to finance the provision of urban infrastructure and services.

Instead, state and local governments are responsible for carrying out such functions. Table 4.9 provides a rough idea of how this might be expected to play

Box 4.6 Federal, State, and Local Government Assignments in Kaduna's Education System

The three tiers of government in Nigeria have concurrent responsibilities for the operation and funding of education. According to constitutional provisions, the main responsibilities of the federal government are in the realm of education policy formulation, coordination, and monitoring, and providing direct control at the tertiary level.

State governments are mainly responsible for the operation and funding of secondary education, and primary and pre-primary education provision is a local government responsibility. In practice, however, federal and state governments in Kaduna have established and managed institutions at all levels of education—pre-primary, primary, secondary, tertiary and even nonformal education centers within the same state.

Within every level of government, education systems are established and backed by their own laws and policies that are often promulgated with little or no regard to other levels. This causes endless problems. Subsequently, the mechanisms to distribute this concurrent responsibility have resulted in one of the most complex financing systems in the world.

Source: UNESCO and Kaduna State Ministry of Education 2008.

Table 4.9 Hypothetical Functional Assignments within Cities

Assignment	State government	Local government
Urban planning	Strategic planning	Local-level planning within LGA jurisdictional boundaries and providing local inputs into strategic city planning
Roads	Construction and maintenance of main city roads (and drainage), crossing cities and linking city road networks to the federal road network	Construction and maintenance of side and residential streets (and drainage)
Primary education	Setting of standards, oversight, and supervision of primary schools	Construction and maintenance of primary school facilities, payment of teachers, provision of teaching materials
Primary health care	Management of referral facilities; setting of standards, oversight, and supervision; conducting health awareness campaigns	Management of primary health centers; payment of salaries for primary health workers
Water supply	Management of city water supply systems	No function
Solid waste management	Management of waste disposal and recycling facilities; oversight and supervision of waste collection	Solid waste collection
Housing	Not known	Not known

out in Nigerian cities if functional assignments were followed as prescribed by the constitution and other national policy documents.

In practice, however, state governments have (since the promulgation of the 1999 constitution and restoration of civilian government) gradually and inexorably assumed the responsibility for most functional assignments in cities (and, indeed, for many equivalent assignments in semirural and rural areas)—both through state ministries and statewide parastatal agencies or authorities.

Local governments, largely, have become marginalized bit-players in urban infrastructure and service delivery—engaged as deconcentrated arms of the state government or delegated with carrying out "residual" tasks, such as ad hoc street maintenance. Despite their formal functional assignments, local governments play a very minor role in the provision of infrastructure, in general, and urban infrastructure, in particular. The relatively small amounts of capital expenditure that local governments control or account for reflects this (see tables 4.6 and 4.7).

Political economy factors—rather than technical considerations about the appropriateness or otherwise of formal functional assignments—have played a predominant role in the encroachment of state governments onto the formally defined functional "turf" of local governments (box 4.7).

Box 4.7 State Power and Local "Conquest" in Nigeria since 1999

Nigeria's state governments are among the most politically powerful subnational actors in Africa.

States have used their formal concurrent powers, as defined by the constitution, and capitalized on ambiguities in the constitutional division of powers to expand the scope of their authority, largely at the expense of local governments. This has enabled them to undertake extensive activities in education, health, agriculture, infrastructure development, and the administration of law and justice. The Nigerian three-tier federal design has effectively receded into a two-tier system, in which politically powerful state governments overwhelmingly dominate the subnational domain.

In practice, state-local relations in Nigeria have metamorphosed into a form of deconcentration, in which local governments have been reduced to administrative agents and political appendages of their respective state governments, in general, and state governors, in particular.

This has all made eminent political sense: party political machines are dominated by state governors and state-level actors, both keen to extend their influence and patronage. Local government appointments are prebends to be awarded to political clients (and, if at all possible, not submitted to electoral scrutiny).

Source: USAID 2010a, 2010b.

The 1999 constitution has provided state governments with the means to efface local governments, by putting states firmly in between the federal government and local governments and providing states with the power of legislating on local government.

Most importantly, the share of federally collected revenues allocated to local governments flows through their respective state governments—and provides the latter with the means to "deduct" charges (for state government expenditure) from gross local government allocations. Extensive state-level administrative control over local government personnel and staffing has reinforced the authority of state governments and diminished the autonomy of local governments, as box 4.8 discusses.

State governments also exercise control over their local governments through expenditure authorization powers. Local governments' annual budgets, for example, are subject to prior approval by state ministries of local government. In some states, these ministries also approve individual payment authorizations by LGAs above a given ceiling: in Oyo State, for example, any local government payment order for more than ₦0.5 million (about US$2,500) must be submitted to state ministries of local government for authorization.

In cities, and especially in state capitals (typically the largest cities in any state), state governments are the key subnational public actors. For most intents and purposes, state governments should be seen as the subnational institutions responsible for the provision of urban public goods and services. On paper, local governments may appear to have significant responsibility for infrastructure and service delivery; in practice, their budgetary resources are spent in accordance with decisions made by state governments.

To illustrate how this operates in the delivery and financing of public goods and services in cities, box 4.9 describes solid waste management arrangements in

---

Box 4.8 Subnational Intergovernmental Relations

Although the 1999 constitution explicitly recognizes local governments as a separate unit of government, eligible for a share of centrally pooled revenues, it limits their ability to incur expenditure.

This is due to the creation of a state and local government joint account for each state, administered by state governments into which these revenues are paid. Each state determines how funds are allocated to the local government areas (LGAs) under its jurisdiction, after deducting various amounts from gross allocations.

In the four states assessed, as in the other 32 states, data on estimates of transfers to each local government and the actual distribution of collected revenues were unavailable. LGAs lack administrative and financial autonomy and their ability to function as a unit of government was left to the discretion of the individual states.

Source: World Bank 2011.

Box 4.9   Solid Waste Management in Nigerian Cities

In Ibadan city (the Oyo State capital), the parastatal Oyo State Solid Waste Management Authority (OYOWMA) handles solid waste management. Established in 2008, with a statewide functional mandate, the authority provides urban solid waste management services in Ibadan and other (smaller) cities (such as Oyo town and Ogbomosho).

Wherever garbage collection fees can be charged, a network of 400 licensed private service providers (of whom some 300 operate in Ibadan city alone) provides waste collection services; where cost recovery is not realistic (as for some of Ibadan's poorer neighborhoods and the city's public spaces), OYOWMA is directly responsible for waste collection. The authority also provides a free-of-charge waste collection service on Thursdays.

Across the state as a whole, OYOWMA has seven operational zones, each with a representative on OYOWMA's Management Board.

OYOWMA's budget and financial statements are not publicly disclosed; nor are they accessible upon request. But informal sources (in OYOWMA) estimate that 2014 annual expenditure was in the order of ₦0.5 billion (about US$2.8 million). Of this amount, a little under ₦0.2 billion (about US$1.12 million and 40 percent of total estimated expenditure) was financed out of monthly and equal "contributions" (₦500,000 or US$2,500 per month) from each of Oyo State's 33 local governments, irrespective of whether they are urban or rural and irrespective of the amount of waste generated in their individual jurisdictions.

Assuming that Ibadan and other cities in Oyo generate larger amounts of solid waste than other parts of the state, the equal and monthly local government contribution amounts to the rural and semiurban local governments subsidizing solid waste management in the state capital (and other cities). Some local governments also have staff members seconded to OYOWMA's zonal offices. The remaining balance of OYOWMA's budget is (as far as can be understood) financed out of the state government's revenues and any cost recovery revenues.

Source: Ogungbuyi 2013; interviews with OYOWMA senior staff.

Ibadan (other Nigerian cities are similar), and how this particular public service is provided.

In short, while formal functional assignments envisage shared state and local government responsibilities for service provision in cities and elsewhere, the situation is rather different in practice. State governments are de facto responsible for the delivery of most public goods and services in cities, relying on both their own revenues and (when needed) local government revenues to finance inputs. Local governments, on the other hand, have largely residual responsibilities and enjoy little (or no) autonomy in resource allocation decisions.

From a city perspective, this is dysfunctional. Firstly, state government jurisdictions are usually considerably larger than the cities located within them, implying that state governments are expected to pay attention to more than just urban development. To that extent, states are typically less focused on purely urban priorities than would be the case, say, for municipal governments.[14] Secondly, the predominant role of state governments as de facto city managers leaves only residual roles to local governments, raising concerns about local accountability and citizen engagement.

Managing Expenditure

In discussing subnational public expenditure on urban public goods and services, it is not just the amounts or institutions involved that matter—the quality of such spending by state and local governments also needs to be taken into account.

A point worth noting here is the general paucity of information on subnational expenditure in many states and local governments. As box 4.10 shows (for the health sector), the absence of budget and spending data implies that public expenditure is poorly managed at the subnational level—even more so given that functional assignment and spending responsibilities are spread across a range of service providers and agencies.

Recent public expenditure and financial management reviews (World Bank 2011, 2013), conducted in 11 different states show that subnational planning, budgeting, budget execution, procurement, and public investment management are often well below par (box 4.11).

On the basis of what is known about subnational public expenditure and financial management, key weaknesses in infrastructure investments include the following:

- Limited subnational strategic planning in general and weak links to expenditure processes. Although a few state governments (such as Lagos and Edo) have clearly put a lot of time and energy into thinking strategically about

---

Box 4.10 Health Sector Spending at State and Local Government Levels

The complexity of fiscal transfers and financial flows in Nigeria between federal, state, and local agencies makes it difficult for governments to reconcile and track resource flows across the different levels and agencies of the health system.

In Nasarawa State, for example, spending figures reported at the local government level differed significantly from those reported at the state level, highlighting the inability of state governments to fully track and understand health expenditures within local governments.

In Sokoto, while local government budgets are broken down by sector (such as health and education), it is impossible to obtain information on LGAs' health budgets. In general, the absence of accurate and detailed records on budgets and expenditures indicates that governments at all levels do not have the means to ensure that health resources are distributed equitably, efficiently, and effectively.

Source: Health Systems 20/20 (2012b).

Box 4.11 The Quality of State Government Public Expenditure Management

Budget planning and preparation are generally weak and do not have a multiyear perspective in most states. Although some states have developed some form of medium-or long-term strategic development plan, no clear relationship exists between these plans and annual budgets.

In addition, the annual budget preparation process is not comprehensive (with significant gaps in budget coverage) and is disorganized and not run on a predetermined calendar, leading to protracted budget preparation with budgets not approved until well into the new fiscal year. While most states have clear budget calendars, compliance with the agreed timelines is generally poor.

Budget execution is also fraught with many problems. In general, credibility of the budget is low, as manifested in wide disparities between expenditure out-turns and approved figures. States typically spend less than they budgeted, usually on account of low execution rates on their capital budgets. In most states the procurement process is highly centralized, with the governor personally responsible for decisions on most large and medium-sized contracts.

Management of the capital budget is poor in most states. The budget call circulars issued to ministries, departments, and agencies during budget preparation provide only very general guidelines for the selection of capital projects for inclusion in the annual budget. No rigorous screening of project proposals takes place, and the criteria for project selection are not clearly articulated. In all the states, very few projects undergo project appraisal. Selection of specific investment projects is generally not based on formal appraisals; investment options are usually not subjected to formal cost-benefit analysis. And political considerations tend to override selection and location of most public capital projects.

Source: World Bank 2011, 2013.

---

medium and longer-term development, these are the exceptions. Insofar as other state governments have engaged in some kind of medium or long-term planning,[15] such plans are more akin to general diagnostics than to well-argued statements of intent and purpose. Moreover, no state governments have invested in long-term or strategic, citywide planning, per se. Nor is there much evidence of consistent linkage of planning and budgets.

• Public investment management is generally weak. Most state governments do not have a coherent framework within which to prioritize sectors or investments. Few if any public investment pipelines exist. Public investments in specific infrastructure projects are not subject to any rigorous scrutiny and do not seem to be robustly screened or appraised. Operations and maintenance issues are not systematically factored into any investment decisions—and are thus unlikely to be taken into account in subsequent budgets.

- Even assuming investments are well-planned and then carefully screened and appraised, subnational performance in budget execution is poor. State-level public expenditure reviews show that most states underspend—especially from their capital budgets. Low rates of capital budget execution point not only to inadequate "upstream" investment preparations, but also to procurement bottlenecks and other implementation constraints.

Given these deficiencies in state government expenditure and financial management, it would be safe to conclude that spending is both ineffective and inefficient. This would apply to any spending on urban public goods and services. All in all, it can only be concluded that subnational public expenditure in cities does not deliver "value-for-money," and that for every naira spent a great deal more could be delivered than is actually the case.

Summing Up

Absent municipal or city governments, *per se*, state governments are responsible for delivering most public goods and services in urban areas. Although assigned functions and responsibilities in the constitution, local governments (in practice) appear to play a marginal and "residual" role in urban infrastructure and service delivery.

Nonetheless, Nigerian subnational governments are big players in total public expenditure—accounting for a relatively large proportion of overall public expenditure, institutionally empowered with significant responsibilities for infrastructure and service delivery, and enjoying a great deal of discretion in the use of their fiscal resources. But their track records on managing public expenditure and finance are not reassuring.

Subnational Revenues

Overview of Subnational Government Revenues

As defined by the constitution, subnational government revenue sources in Nigeria are twofold:

- Transfers from (or shares of) the federal funding pool, made up of revenues collected by the federal government on behalf of all tiers of government; and
- Own-source revenues, known as IGRs.

Taken together, these make up the wider funding pool out of which urban public goods and services are financed. Table 4.10 summarizes all federal, state, and local government revenues during 2009–13.

As a whole, total subnational government revenues account for almost 60 percent of all public revenues, or roughly 7–8 percent of nominal GDP.

Subnational government revenues, as can be seen from table 4.10, are dominated by their shares of the federal funding pool. States and local governments rely on their federal shares for over 80 percent and over 95 percent, respectively,

Table 4.10 Federal, State, and Local Government Revenues, 2009–13

Level of government	Naira (billions)				
	2009	2010	2011	2012	2013
Federal government					
Retained revenue	2,642.98	3,089.18	3,553.54	3,629.61	4,031.83
subtotal	**2,642.98**	**3,089.18**	**3,553.54**	**3,629.61**	**4,031.83**
As % of total revenues	41.93	40.59	41.32	41.01	41.66
State governments					
Federal sources (share and others)	1,911.60	2,129.40	2,800.90	2,747.10	3,171.30
Internally generated revenues	461.20	757.90	509.30	548.10	585.90
Internally generated revenues as % of total state governments revenues	17.80	23.97	14.94	15.34	15.27
Others	217.70	275.20	99.90	277.40	79.70
subtotal	**2,590.50**	**3,162.50**	**3,410.10**	**3,572.60**	**3,836.90**
As % of total revenues	41.10	41.55	39.65	40.37	39.64
Local governments					
Federal sources (share and others)	1,023.50	1,320.30	1,569.40	1,545.80	1,768.00
State transfers to local government areas	19.70	12.70	35.20	8.70	12.80
Internally generated revenues	26.10	26.20	31.60	26.60	29.30
Internally generated revenues as % of total local governments revenues	2.44	1.93	1.93	1.61	1.62
Others	0	0	0	67.00	0
subtotal	**1,069.30**	**1,359.20**	**1,636.20**	**1,648.10**	**1,810.10**
As % of total revenues	16.97	17.86	19.03	18.62	18.70
Total	**6,302.78**	**7,610.88**	**8,599.84**	**8,850.31**	**9,678.83**
	100.00	100.00	100.00	100.00	100.00
Revenues as % of nominal gross domestic product	25.40	14.00	13.60	12.40	12.10

Source: Central Bank of Nigeria Data and Statistics.

of their total revenues. Although Nigerian subnational governments are heavily dependent on their shares of the federal funding pool, such reliance on "transfers" from central governments (or revenue sharing arrangements with higher tiers of the intergovernmental system) is not entirely exceptional.[16]

What is particular about the Nigerian case is the extent to which subnational governments (and the federal government) are reliant on shares of federal revenues that are themselves largely determined by global energy prices. Given that world oil prices have been and are likely to remain volatile, federally collected revenues are subject to the same kind of fluctuations.[17] This, in turn, exposes subnational governments to unpredictable and uncontrollable revenue flows.

Despite the establishment of an Excess Crude Account in 2004, successive drawdowns on this fiscal reserve have depleted the account balance, now reported to be about US$2.45 billion. For 2015, when global oil prices remained low, this has resulted in a diminished federal funding pool, smaller revenue shares

From Oil to Cities • http://dx.doi.org/10.1596/978-1-4648-0792-3

for state and local governments, and (according to the media) a fiscal squeeze on subnational expenditures.

Sharing Federally Collected Revenues

Prior to being shared among the three tiers of government, revenues collected by the federal government accrue to three accounts: a Federation Account, an Excess Crude Account, and a value added tax (VAT) Pool Account. Table 4.11 summarizes key features of these shared revenue accounts and the ways in which they are vertically and horizontally shared between the three tiers of government and then between states and local governments.

It is important to stress that this is a revenue-sharing arrangement—even if the end result may appear to be a system whereby intergovernmental transfers are calculated and then made to state and local governments by the federal government. State governments do not see their shares as grants but, rather, more as constitutionally sanctioned and legally enshrined shares of a common funding pool. Seen in this way, the three tiers of government are partners enjoying access to a revenue pool that is made up of taxes collected by federal authorities.

The vertical sharing arrangements between the federal and state government are well-known, frequently discussed, and highly politicized in Nigeria. However, remarkably less is known and debated about what lies beneath the state level, about how local governments access their considerable share of federal funding.

The share of the federal funding pool allocated to LGAs as a whole (20.6 percent in the case of the Federation Account and the Excess Crude Account; 30 percent in the case of the VAT pool) is determined by the Revenue Mobilization Allocation and Fiscal Commission formula and then subdivided according to the horizontal sharing formula.

Allocations to all LGAs in each state are thus calculated on the basis of the "post-derivation" formulas; these allocations are then transferred (as a single, statewide bloc) to each State Joint Local Government Account. At the state level, these accounts are managed by a Joint Accounts Allocation Committee, chaired by the state ministry of local government.

The first action the committee undertakes is to deduct a wide range of charges from the State Joint Local Government Account amount. These deductions are considerable[18] and include statutory charges (such as for pension funds, for traditional authorities, and so on), the salaries of primary school teachers, and various cost-sharing items.[19] After all deductions are made, the remaining amount is allocated to each LGA using a formula, which is often, but not always,[20] the same as the one applied for Federation Account/Excess Crude Account/VAT horizontal sharing to local governments. In practice, then, a good proportion of the "vertical" allocation set aside for local governments is effectively added to the vertical share for state governments.

Arrangements for horizontal allocations (between states) of federally collected revenues are also less frequently discussed in the public domain. While no

Table 4.11 Sharing of Revenues Collected by the Federal Government

Sharing process	Federation account	Excess crude account	VAT pool account
Revenues from	Sale of crude oil and gas, mining rents and royalties, petroleum profits tax, companies' income tax, and customs and excise duties	Oil revenues above a base amount derived from a defined oil benchmark price	VAT receipts
Amount to be shared	As above	Determined by National Economic Council	As above
Derivation	13% of both *federation account* and *excess crude account* shared among nine oil-producing states, based on a formula that uses each state's contribution to onshore total production as weights. Intended to compensate for the impact of oil exploration activities.		Not applicable
Post-derivation vertical shares	Federal government 52.68% All state governments 26.72% All local governments 20.6%	Not applicable	Federal government 15% All state governments 55% All local governments 30%
Post-derivation horizontal shares (between states and between LGAs in states)	Each state receives an allocation based on: • Equality of states (40%) • Population (30%) • Land mass and terrain (10%) • Social development (10%) • Internal revenue generation effort (10%)	Each local government receives an allocation based on: • Equality of states (40%) • Population (30%) • Land mass and terrain (10%) • Social development (10%) • Internal revenue generation effort (10%) Note: allocations to LGAs are made in a bloc for all LGAs in each state	From their respective VAT funding pools, each state and local government receives an allocation based on: • Equality of states/LGAs (40%) • Population (30%) • Derivation (20%), calculated on basis of overall state contribution to VAT Note: allocations to LGAs are made in a bloc for all LGAs in each state

Source: World Bank 2012, 2013.

Note: LGAs = local government areas; VAT = value added tax.

horizontal allocation system is ever going to be perfectly fair, the considerable weight (40 percent) given to fiscal equality in the formula through which federal shares are divided up among states and local governments appears to be inequitable.[21] State and local governments, irrespective of their different population sizes, all receive the same amount from the 40 percent of their respective vertical shares set aside for "equality."

As a consequence, there are substantial variations in the per capita allocations to states and LGAs, as tables 4.12–4.14 show—with larger subnational governments receiving smaller per capita allocations than the smaller ones.[22] Other things held constant, this is both inequitable and not responsive to aggregate needs and means that larger states and LGAs receive a disproportionately smaller share of federally collected revenues than smaller subnational governments. From the point of view of city financing, this implies that urban centers in larger states are likely to have access to lower per capita allocations than are their equivalents in smaller states.

A final issue in the way horizontal shares are allocated concerns their spatial equity outcomes. As table 4.15 shows, the generally larger (and poorer) states in the North West receive lower per capita allocations than states in other geopolitical zones. On the other hand, the oil-producing states in the South South Zone receive the largest per capita amounts from the federal funding pool—a reflection of both their 13 percent derivation shares and their

Table 4.12 Revenues per Capita by State, 2013

| State | Naira | | |
	Federal allocations	IGR	Total
Abia	21,948	3,811	25,759
Adamawa	22,632	2,367	24,999
Akwa Ibom	76,858	3,189	80,047
Anambra	15,136	1,817	16,953
Bauchi	14,691	2,780	17,470
Bayelsa	130,096	3,640	133,736
Benue	15,050	284	15,335
Borno	16,622	626	17,248
Cross River	19,765	4,396	24,161
Delta	58,047	4,075	62,122
Ebonyi	24,155	2,899	27,053
Edo	23,397	5,624	29,021
Ekiti	21,684	2,223	23,907
Enugu	17,223	1,351	18,574
Gombe	22,516	4,036	26,552
Imo	17,434	1,855	19,289
Jigawa	14,924	575	15,499
Kaduna	12,280	643	12,923

table continues next page

From Oil to Cities • http://dx.doi.org/10.1596/978-1-4648-0792-3

Table 4.12 Revenues per Capita by State, 2013 *(continued)*

State	Federal allocations	IGR	Total
	Naira		
Kano	10,007	5,328	15,335
Katsina	12,223	1,191	13,414
Kebbi	19,144	1,451	20,595
Kogi	18,057	1,617	19,674
Kwara	40,530	5,103	45,633
Lagos	15,466	17,452	32,917
Nassarawa	27,210	2,630	29,840
Niger	17,088	1,089	18,176
Ogun	15,584	7,028	22,612
Ondo	25,806	2,209	28,015
Osun	16,007	2,308	18,314
Oyo	12,894	3,058	15,953
Plateau	22,084	2,894	24,979
Rivers	47,306	16,257	63,563
Sokoto	16,635	3,165	19,800
Taraba	24,688	2,695	27,383
Yobe	24,423	3,704	28,127
Zamfara	17,700	859	18,559
FCT	54,156	7,828	61,984
Averages	**23,218**	**4,187**	**27,405**

Sources: Central Bank of Nigeria Data and Statistics; Federal Republic of Nigeria 2006.
Note: FCT = Federal Capital Territory; IGR = internally generated revenue.

Table 4.13 State Government Revenues per Capita, 2013

Measure	Federal allocations per capita	IGR per capita	Total revenue per capita
	Naira		
Mean	26,526	3,623	30,149
Median	19,144	2,780	23,907
Maximum	130,096	17,452	133,736
Minimum	10,007	284	12,923

Sources: Central Bank of Nigeria Data and Statistics; Federal Republic of Nigeria 2006.
Note: Includes 13% derivation allocations for nine oil-producing states. IGR = internally generated revenue.

Table 4.14 State Government Revenues per Capita, Non-Oil-Producing States, 2013

Measure	Federal allocations per capita	IGR per capita	Total revenue per capita
	Naira		
Mean	20,029	3,179	23,207
Median	17,088	2,367	19,674
Maximum	54,156	17,452	61,984
Minimum	10,007	284	12,923

Sources: Central Bank of Nigeria Data and Statistics; Federal Republic of Nigeria 2006.
Note: IGR = internally generated revenue.

From Oil to Cities • http://dx.doi.org/10.1596/978-1-4648-0792-3

Table 4.15 Per Capita Revenues by Geopolitical Zone and State, All States (Including Oil-Producing), 2013

Zone	States	Population (2006 census data)	Federal allocations	IGR	IGR per capita as % of total per capita	Total
North Central	Benue	4,219,244	15,050	284	1.85	15,335
	Kogi	3,278,487	18,057	1,617	8.22	19,674
	Kwara	2,371,089	40,530	5,103	11.18	45,633
	Nassarawa	1,863,275	27,210	2,630	8.81	29,840
	Niger	3,950,249	17,088	1,089	5.99	18,176
	Plateau	3,178,712	22,084	2,894	11.59	24,979
	FCT	1,405,201	54,156	7,828	12.63	61,984
	Mean	**2,895,180**	**27,739**	**3,064**	**9.95**	**30,803**
North Eastern	Adamawa	3,168,101	22,632	2,367	9.47	24,999
	Bauchi	4,676,465	14,691	2,780	15.91	17,470
	Borno	4,151,193	16,622	626	3.63	17,248
	Gombe	2,353,879	22,516	4,036	15.20	26,552
	Taraba	2,300,736	24,688	2,695	9.84	27,383
	Yobe	2,321,591	24,423	3,704	13.17	28,127
	Mean	**3,161,994**	**20,928**	**2,701**	**11.43**	**23,630**
North Western	Jigawa	4,348,649	14,924	575	3.71	15,499
	Kaduna	6,066,562	12,280	643	4.97	12,923
	Kano	9,383,682	10,007	5,328	34.75	15,335
	Katsina	5,792,578	12,223	1,191	8.88	13,414
	Kebbi	3,238,628	19,144	1,451	7.05	20,595
	Sokoto	3,696,999	16,635	3,165	15.98	19,800
	Zamfara	3,259,846	17,700	859	4.63	18,559
	Mean	**5,112,421**	**14,702**	**1,887**	**11.38**	**16,589**
South Eastern	**Abia**	2,833,999	21,948	3,811	14.79	25,759
	Anambra	4,182,032	15,136	1,817	10.72	16,953
	Ebonyi	2,173,501	24,155	2,899	10.71	27,053
	Enugu	3,257,298	17,223	1,351	7.27	18,574
	Imo	3,934,899	17,434	1,855	9.62	19,289
	Mean	**3,276,346**	**19,179**	**2,347**	**10.90**	**21,526**
South Southern	**Akwa Ibom**	3,920,208	76,858	3,189	3.98	80,047
	Bayelsa	1,703,358	130,096	3,640	2.72	133,736
	Cross River	2,888,966	19,765	4,396	18.19	24,161
	Delta	4,098,391	58,047	4,075	6.56	62,122
	Edo	3,218,332	23,397	5,624	19.38	29,021
	Rivers	5,185,400	47,306	16,257	25.58	63,563
	Mean	**3,502,443**	**59,245**	**6,197**	**9.47**	**65,442**
South Western	Ekiti	2,384,212	21,684	2,223	9.30	23,907
	Lagos	9,013,534	15,466	17,452	53.02	32,917
	Ogun	3,728,098	15,584	7,028	31.08	22,612
	Ondo	3,441,024	25,806	2,209	7.88	28,015
	Osun	3,423,535	16,007	2,308	12.60	18,314
	Oyo	5,591,589	12,894	3,058	19.17	15,953
	Mean	**4,596,999**	**17,907**	**5,713**	**24.19**	**23,620**

Sources: Central Bank of Nigeria Data and Statistics; Federal Republic of Nigeria 2006.
Notes: States indicated in bold text = oil-producing states. FCT = Federal Capital Territory; IGR = internally generated revenue.

generally smaller populations. For urban development, the implication is that South South cities have greater per capita resources than do their equivalents in the North West.

Subnational Government Revenue Assignments and Powers

The constitution and other legal instruments spell out the overall framework for revenue assignments, as well as the latitude each tier of government has in setting tax bases and tax rates. For the most part, the responsibility for setting tax rates (the amount chargeable for a given tax) and tax bases (the measure upon which tax assessments are based—such as assessed property value for property tax) lies with the senior tier of government (that is, the federal government with respect to states and states with respect to LGAs).

Table 4.16 summarizes tax assignments among the levels of government. Most federal government revenues are pooled for sharing with state and local governments.

Tax revenue sources assigned to subnational governments are limited. Although the IGRs assigned to states are not particularly expansive, they do include personal income tax, which is potentially of considerable importance. Indeed, it has been shown by Lagos State that personal income tax can generate significant amounts of revenue.

Local governments, on the other hand, have generally been assigned less important and smaller revenues. The one potentially significant local

Table 4.16 Tax Administration and Collection: Federal, State, and Local Government Responsibilities

Federal government	State government	Local government
Companies' income tax	Personal income tax (pay-as-you-earn and self-assessment)	Shops and kiosks rates
Withholding tax on companies for nonresidents and FCT Abuja	Withholding tax on individuals	Tenement rates
Petroleum profits tax	Capital gains tax on individuals	Liquor license fees
Value added tax	Stamp duties on individuals	Slaughter slab fees
Education tax	Gambling taxes	Marriage, birth, death registration fees
Capital gains tax for nonresidents, corporate bodies, and FCT Abuja	Road taxes	Street naming fees (excluding state capital)
Stamp duties for nonresidents, corporate bodies, and FCT Abuja	Business premises registration fee	Right of occupancy fees
Personal income tax for military and police personnel, nonresidents, and FCT Abuja	Development levy on individuals	Market taxes and levies
	Street naming registration fee for state capital	Motor park levies
	Right of occupancy fees	Domestic animal license fees
	Market taxes and levies	Bicycle, truck, canoe, cart fees
		Cattle tax
		Merriment and road closure levy
		Radio and television license fees
		Vehicle radio license fees
		Wrong parking charges
		Public convenience, sewage and refuse disposal fees
		Customary burial ground permit fees
		Religious places establishment permit fees
		Signboard/advertising fees

Source: Decree 21, Taxes and Levies (Approved List for Collection), September 30, 1998.
Note: FCT = Federal Capital Territory.

government revenue source is "tenement" rates, which amount to a form of property tax—but active state governments have tended to take on the responsibility for the collection of such taxes (rebaptized as land use taxes or fees).

Subnational Government Revenue Performance and Revenues
State Governments

As table 4.12 indicates, state governments, on the whole, do not raise a significant proportion of their total revenues from IGRs. On aggregate, these account for 15–20 percent of total state revenues.

But aggregates can be deceptive: there are significant variations in the performance of individual state governments. The breakdown of IGRs as a proportion of total revenues by state for 2013 (tables 4.17 and 4.18) shows that some states devote a great deal more effort than others to collecting IGRs:

- Lagos State leads all others in both the relative importance of its IGRs (53 percent of total revenues) and the absolute amount of IGR per capita (about ₦17,500).
- Six states appear to be doing considerably better than the average on IGR collection: Kano, Rivers, Ogun, Cross River, Edo, and Oyo.
- Benue State comes in at the bottom in relative importance of its IGRs (less than 2 percent of total revenues) as well as in the absolute amount collected per capita (a little under ₦300).
- Along with Benue State, six others collected IGRs amounting to less than 5 percent of their total revenues: Bayelsa, Borno, Jigawa, Akwa Ibom, Kaduna, and Zamfara.

These major variations in state fiscal effort are important to keep in mind when considering IGRs as an instrument for financing urban development.

Local Governments

IGR collection by local governments is even lower. On aggregate, IGRs account for less than 2 percent of total local government revenues (table 4.19). As with states, local governments vary considerably in their IGR collection level (when statewide local government data are assessed) (tables 4.19 and 4.20).

Even within the constraints of very limited revenue assignments, LGAs in some states are clearly doing more than others to mobilize IGRs. In Ebonyi's LGAs, for example, these account for a little over 6 percent of total revenues— and, per capita, amount to about ₦830 (the second highest per capita amount among all LGAs). In contrast, conflict-affected LGAs in Borno State collected no IGRs at all in 2013.

As with many local government finance issues, these variations in local government fiscal effort are poorly understood.

Table 4.17 State Government IGR Collection, 2013

	2013	
State government	IGR as % of total revenues	IGR per capita (Naira)
Abia	14.79	3,811
Adamawa	9.47	2,367
Akwa Ibom	3.98	3,189
Anambra	10.72	1,817
Bauchi	15.91	2,780
Bayelsa	2.72	3,640
Benue	1.85	284
Borno	3.63	626
Cross River	18.19	4,396
Delta	6.56	4,075
Ebonyi	10.71	2,899
Edo	19.38	5,624
Ekiti	9.30	2,223
Enugu	7.27	1,351
Gombe	15.20	4,036
Imo	9.62	1,855
Jigawa	3.71	575
Kaduna	4.97	643
Kano	34.75	5,328
Katsina	8.88	1,191
Kebbi	7.05	1,451
Kogi	8.22	1,617
Kwara	11.18	5,103
Lagos	53.02	17,452
Nassarawa	8.81	2,630
Niger	5.99	1,089
Ogun	31.08	7,028
Ondo	7.88	2,209
Osun	12.60	2,308
Oyo	19.17	3,058
Plateau	11.59	2,894
Rivers	25.58	16,257
Sokoto	15.98	3,165
Taraba	9.84	2,695
Yobe	13.17	3,704
Zamfara	4.63	859
Federal Capital Territory	12.63	7,828

Sources: Central Bank of Nigeria Data and Statistics; Federal Republic of Nigeria 2006.
Note: IGR = internally generated revenue.

Table 4.18 State Government IGR Collection, 2013

Measure	IGR as % of total revenues	IGR per capita (Naira)
Mean	12.70	3,623
Median	9.84	2,780
Maximum	53.02	17,452
Minimum	1.85	284

Sources: Central Bank of Nigeria Data and Statistics; Federal Republic of Nigeria 2006.
Note: IGR = internally generated revenue.

Table 4.19 Local Government IGR Collection, 2013

LGs in State	IGR as % of total revenues	IGR per capita (Naira)
Abia	0.28	35
Adamawa	3.69	537
Akwa Ibom	0.17	26
Anambra	0.44	48
Bauchi	0.74	86
Bayelsa	2.51	294
Benue	0.89	119
Borno	0	0
Cross River	1.84	242
Delta	1.78	268
Ebonyi	6.12	828
Edo	1.31	155
Ekiti	0.65	84
Enugu	1.63	184
Gombe	2.22	255
Imo	0.19	25
Jigawa	1.76	230
Kaduna	1.98	198
Kano	1.23	149
Katsina	0.84	104
Kebbi	3.96	556
Kogi	0.88	122
Kwara	0.83	127
Lagos	5.02	566
Nassarawa	1.04	161
Niger	1.33	203
Ogun	1.65	188
Ondo	0.52	58
Osun	0.57	88
Oyo	0.70	89
Plateau	0.77	94
Rivers	1.64	174
Sokoto	0.59	81
Taraba	1.04	174
Yobe	5.04	948
Zamfara	1.69	215
Federal Capital Territory	3.03	569

Sources: Central Bank of Nigeria Data and Statistics; Federal Republic of Nigeria 2006.
Note: IGR = internally generated revenue; LG = local government.

Table 4.20 Local Government IGR Collection, 2013

Measure	IGR as % of total revenues	IGR per capita (Naira)
Mean	1.64	224
Median	1.23	161
Maximum	6.12	948
Minimum	0	–

Sources: Central Bank of Nigeria Data and Statistics; Federal Republic of Nigeria 2006.
Note: IGR = internally generated revenue.

Subnational Government Revenues: Urban Shares?

Absent municipal government units and given the highly aggregated nature of information about subnational finance, it is not possible to distinguish between IGRs collected in urban areas and those collected elsewhere. Lagos is the only full-blown exception to this—there, it is probably safe to assume that virtually all IGRs (collected by both the state government and by local governments) are "municipal." It would seem likely, nonetheless, that a disproportionate share of IGRs derives from urban taxpayers—not only because of the relative size of the urban population (at least 50 percent of Nigeria's population), but also (and much more importantly) because city tax bases are invariably larger than rural tax bases.

Comments and Discussion

Several obvious points can be made about financing urban public goods and services.

First, subnational government access to its shares of the federal funding pool for revenues is double-edged. On one side, having an important share of federally collected revenues gives subnational governments access to significant fiscal resources, revenues that many of them would be unable to benefit from absent constitutionally sanctioned revenue-sharing arrangements. Subnational governments in northern Nigeria, for example, would be far worse off without their federal allocations. On the other side, reliance on federal shares means that subnational government revenues are subject to externally induced countercyclical fluctuations, due to the dependence of federal revenues on oil proceeds and the price of oil on the world market. Subnational government dependence on revenue-sharing arrangements makes for a considerable degree of budget uncertainty.

Second, states and local governments generally have a poor track record in mobilizing own-source revenues. Internally generated revenues represent a small proportion of total subnational government revenues. According to Central Bank of Nigeria data, only Lagos State's IGRs amount to more than 50 percent of total state revenues.

IGRs are important for three main reasons: (a) they lessen subnational government dependence on the vagaries and unpredictability of their federal shares, over which they have no control; (b) they give subnational governments leverage for borrowing and the means to afford loans; and, not least, (c) they strengthen downward accountability to citizens and taxpayers.

A number of factors would appear to explain the generally below par fiscal performance of subnational governments:

• Tax assignments have not provided subnational governments significant sources of revenue.
• States do not have discretion to determine either the tax base or tax rate for any of their own-source revenues—and cannot therefore increase their revenues through upward or downward adjustments to the tax base or rate.

- Outside of major cities, local economies are underdeveloped, fairly agrarian, and often very poor. And even within large cities, the highly informal nature of local economies means that a large number of potential taxpayers are fiscally "invisible." Raising significant amounts of taxes in such circumstances is no walkover.
- State and local government tax administration and collection systems are often rudimentary, corrupt, weak, and lack capacity.
- In general, Nigerians have little willingness to pay taxes or fees.
- Unwillingness to pay taxes is clearly compounded by considerable deficiencies in local service delivery. Underperforming schools, inadequate primary health facilities, unusable roads, and the like do little to encourage taxpayers (Bodea and LeBas 2013).
- The large amounts of revenue derived effortlessly from their shares of federal funds provide state and local governments with very few incentives to increase their IGRs. However, there is no hard and fast correlation between the amounts that state governments receive as their shares of the federal funding pool and their fiscal effort, measured by their IGR performance. As table 4.17 shows, the average IGR performance of the six state governments in the South South Zone (where federal shares are highest in the country) is poor. But in Cross River, Edo, and Rivers states, IGR performance is actually well above the state-wide average. Insofar as revenue-sharing arrangements may not provide state governments with positive incentives to collect IGRs, they do not necessarily crowd out subnational fiscal effort.

Despite the many factors that limit potential and actual own-source revenues at the subnational level, a good deal of room clearly exists for improvement in most states and local governments (box 4.12).

Box 4.12 Edo State: Where There's a Will, There's a Way

Although not as poor as many of Nigeria's northern states, Edo is by no means well off. It is one of the poorer states in the southern half of the country. In 2010, its per capita income was estimated to be only about US$330, compared to US$1,430 for the south and a national average of US$1,155. The population living in poverty is estimated at 44.3 percent compared to the national average of 51.6 percent and a regional average of 38.3 percent in the south. Edo also has significantly higher overall unemployment compared to both the national average and the southern region average.

Despite this, Edo State's IGRs have increased dramatically under an administration elected in 2008. Since 2008, the share of IGRs has increased, reaching 16.7 percent of total revenues in 2009 and 20.9 percent in 2010. Taxes are the largest source of IGRs, contributing close to 70 percent of the total.

Source: World Bank 2012.

Borrowing and the Private Sector: Financing Alternatives
Subnational Government Borrowing
The constitution allows subnational governments to borrow to finance their budgets. Subnational governments can borrow from external and domestic sources and from the private (commercial) and public sectors. All subnational government borrowing is subject to federal regulation of one sort or another.

Levels of Subnational Debt
Table 4.21 summarizes levels of subnational government debt in Nigeria. As can be seen, local governments borrow very little; state governments borrow significant amounts, particularly domestically. The rest of this section therefore only examines state government borrowing.

Aggregate figures for levels of state government debt, however, disguise a very high degree of variation between states, as table 4.22 shows.

Table 4.21 State and Local Government Debt (End-2013) and Ratios

Subnational government	Domestic (US$)	External (US$)	Total (US$)	Debt as % of total IGRs	Debt as % of shared federal revenues
State governments	10,624,739,488	2,816,019,272	13,440,758,760	367.0	67.8
Local governments	51,814,759	0	51,814,759	28.3	0.5
Total	10,676,554,247	2,816,019,272	13,492,573,519	350.9	43.7

Sources: Central Bank of Nigeria Data and Statistics; Debt Management Office data.
Note: IGRs: Internally generated revenues. US$1 = ₦160.

Table 4.22 Variations in State Government Debt, 2011–13

Measure	End-2013	End-2012	End-2011
State Government Domestic Debt (US$)			
Mean	287,155,121	262,103,064	208,326,799
Median	154,573,414	150,733,250	130,675,750
Maximum	1,742,919,166	1,440,205,500	1,017,641,563
Minimum	1,685,334	5,743,313	9,940,875
State Government External Debt (US$)			
Mean	76,108,629	64,437,270	58,522,900
Median	43,314,886	38,867,309	37,062,759
Maximum	938,135,518	611,253,157	491,847,296
Minimum	15,585,332	14,154,526	12,957,250
State Government All Debt (US$)			
Mean	363,263,750	326,540,335	266,849,699
Median	199,614,347	180,935,853	178,088,828
Maximum	2,681,054,684	2,051,458,657	1,476,448,296
Minimum	40,050,199	46,678,037	23,485,750

Sources: Central Bank of Nigeria Data and Statistics; Debt Management Office data.

Lagos State is by far the largest borrower among state governments, for both domestic and external debt. Indeed, it alone accounted for 15–20 percent of all state government borrowing during 2011–13 (23–33 percent of all state government external borrowing and 13–16 percent of all state government domestic borrowing).[23]

Bayelsa State is the second largest borrower, accounting for around 10 percent of all debts, mostly on the domestic market.[24] Between them, Lagos and Bayelsa account for about one quarter of all state government borrowing. In addition, a number of states—such as Akwa Ibom, Imo, Taraba—borrow very small amounts.

In addition to formal state government borrowing (for which regular official data is available), some (and perhaps many or most) states have incurred "irregular" debts (or outstanding accounts payable) in the form of arrears owed to contractors for goods, works and services, pension arrears, unpaid salaries, and the like, which can be considerable.

Domestic borrowing by state governments includes several categories: bank loans, state bonds, contractors' and other arrears. Table 4.23 breaks down the domestic debt stock of all 36 state governments and Federal Capital Territory (FCT) Abuja.

Since the end of 2011, bonds appear to have become a larger proportion of total state government debt stocks.

Regulation of Subnational Borrowing

State government domestic and external borrowing is federally regulated; states require approval from the Federal Ministry of Finance before they can borrow either on the domestic or external markets. In all cases, the national Debt Management Office is expected to carry out a debt sustainability analysis and ensure that any borrowing is within the prescribed limits. The general rule is that "the monthly debt service ratio of a subnational, including the servicing of the proposed debt issuance being contemplated, does not exceed 40 percent of its actual monthly revenue of the preceding 12 months" (DMO 2013a). Ultimately, and in one form or another, state government allocations from federally collected revenues provide loan repayment guarantees.

Table 4.23 Composition of State Governments and Federal Capital Territory Abuja Debt Stock (End-2011)

Debt category	Amount (Naira billion)	Percent of total debt stock
Bank loans	346.97	28.13
State bonds	320.23	25.97
Contractors' arrears	435.69	35.55
Pension and salary arrears	67.46	5.47
Other liabilities and debts	62.94	5.10
Total	**1,233.29**	**100.00**

Source: DMO 2012b.

In general and in official circles, regulation of state government borrowing in Nigeria is thought to be adequate and relatively effective. However, media coverage of state government borrowing is less positive[25] and often raises questions about the rigor of debt sustainability analyses, optimistic fiscal and economic scenarios, transparency, and the use of loans by states.

Purpose of State Government Borrowing

As with other financial and fiscal data, it is difficult to determine the extent to which state government domestic borrowing is being (or is) used to finance urban investments. Indeed, and with the exception of state government bonds, little information is readily available on what subnational government borrowing is intended to finance in general.

State government bond issues are intended, in part, to finance infrastructure investments. On the basis of Securities and Exchange Commission documents and bond prospectuses, a varying share of the proceeds from state bond issues is intended to finance infrastructure investments, some or many of which are in cities. For instance, the prospectus for Osun State's Series A 2012 bond issue states that of the intended ₦21.275 billion proceeds, roughly 25 percent was earmarked for several road construction and rehabilitation projects, 17 percent for commercial infrastructure, 8 percent for urban renewal, and 9.4 percent for water works. The remaining 40 percent was earmarked for refinancing (or repayment of existing loans from First Bank of Nigeria).

State government external borrowing (largely from multilateral institutions like the World Bank or African Development Bank) is usually quite clear in its purpose. Most such external borrowing is used to finance capital expenditure, often related to urban infrastructure. The only exceptions to these are the World Bank's Development Policy Operations, which are reform focused, but which enable state government borrowers to finance their budgets in many ways,[26] including on urban infrastructure and service delivery.

Levels of Debt: Sustainability Issues?

States use a significant proportion of state government borrowing to finance public investments in urban infrastructure. As a financing instrument, however, the use of borrowing to finance urban (or any other public) investments is obviously limited by the capacity of states to take on debt. In many cases, this may not be a problem. But total state government borrowing has been steadily increasing over the last decade and debt servicing is projected to take up a growing percentage of total state revenues.

Lagos State, for example, needed almost 20 percent of its total revenues in 2013 to service its external and domestic debts (World Bank 2015); other, less fiscally robust states (such as Bayelsa and Cross River States) are probably spending even more on debt servicing requirements. The overall debt situation for state governments becomes more problematic given the decline in the amounts they are allocated from federally collected revenues as world oil prices fall and any slowdown in IGRs as a result of slower economic growth. A full understanding of the sustainability (or otherwise) of state government debt requires in-depth (and case-by-case) analysis.

Public-Private Partnerships

Recognition has been growing of the potential importance of public-private partnership (PPP) financing for urban infrastructure and service delivery in Nigeria. An enabling legal and regulatory framework for PPPs is now in place at the federal level and in many states; although this can probably be improved, it is an essential precursor to on-the-ground private sector engagement in the delivery of public infrastructure and services. However, and especially for infrastructure, much of the potential of PPPs has yet to be realized.

On a small scale, PPPs have been successfully used in urban solid waste management for several years now. The Oyo State Solid Waste Management Authority, for example, has been partnering with small-scale private sector operators to collect and dump garbage in Ibadan and other cities since 2009. Private service providers, as they are known, are licensed to collect waste in specific areas, collect fees or charges from local residents and businesses, and pay for the use of public landfill sites. Similar types of arrangements for the use of private sector contractors or service providers in solid waste management are in place in other Nigerian cities, such as Lagos and Kano.

Lagos State has engaged in several substantial PPP-financed schemes for urban transport and has a pipeline of other major PPP infrastructure investments, most notably in the area of city railways. In addition, the Bus Rapid Transit (BRT) scheme and the Lekki-Oloyi Link bridge are two important projects. The BRT, operational and growing since 2008, involves the state government financing infrastructure upgrades and construction (of dedicated bus lanes, bus stops, and terminals, and so on) and then awarding management of bus fleets and routes to private sector operators, who are responsible for acquiring, running, and maintaining buses (and sharing bus fares with the Lagos Metropolitan Area Transport Authority). The operations and maintenance activities for the Lekki-Oloyi Link Bridge, construction of which was financed by the state government, are managed by a private sector operator, which charges tolls for the use of the bridge.

Outside Lagos, larger-scale PPPs in the urban sector have not been of widespread significance to date, largely due to persistent regulatory issues, high transaction costs, and low profit margins. And even within Lagos, the current PPP schemes are not free of controversy—whether driven by partisan political interests or not, there is clearly some dissatisfaction with toll charges for the Lekki-Oloyi bridge, public complaints about what is perceived to be the poor quality of the BRT bus network, and concerns about the limited degree to which PPP arrangements are pro-poor or inclusive.[27] Indeed, this kind of public dissatisfaction with the services provided through PPP arrangements is a reminder of the potential political vulnerability faced by PPP operators, adding to their risks and transaction costs.

One aspect of PPPs that has perhaps been underplayed is the extent to which they usually still require substantial public expenditure. Lagos State's better-known PPP schemes, for example, have all involved significant infrastructure investments, paid for out of either revenues or borrowing. Although PPP schemes can result in lower operating costs (as a public expenditure item), they nonetheless still rely on up-front capital spending by subnational governments—as well as the costs associated with subsequent regulation and monitoring of private sector service delivery.

Related to this, PPPs also often require a transparent and clear land-ownership framework that provides private sector investors with security and predictability and state governments with fixed public assets to bring to the table. In many Nigerian cities, such clarity is rare. In these circumstances, infrastructure PPPs (for transport, for public housing, and so on) become more difficult to agree on and implement.

Policy Actions and Institutional Strengthening

Nigeria's Urban Financing "System"

No *urban* financing system exists *per se* in Nigeria. Cities have no formal status as corporations or jurisdictions, and there are no city- or town-specific (municipal) governments that take responsibility for financing and delivering urban public goods and services. Insofar as public goods and services are provided to the residents of cities, this is done through state and local governments. State governments (with the possible exception of Lagos as a city-wide) are typically "bigger" than any one city, are expected to deliver statewide public goods and services, and certainly have constitutionally defined functions (such as the provision of judicial services) and powers (such as legislative and regulatory authority) that would generally be seen as going well beyond any municipal or metropolitan mandate. Financing a state government, in other words, encompasses rather more than financing a city, even a megacity like Lagos.

On the other hand, and although Nigerian local governments are relatively large units, they are almost always smaller than a major city (such as Zaria or Ibadan), and have constitutionally prescribed mandates and fiscal powers that are more restricted than would probably be the case for municipalities.

In addition, *realpolitik* in Nigeria has meant that, in most cases, local governments have become appendages to their respective states (and state governors)— at best, deconcentrated but active components of the state government's apparatus; at worst, largely irrelevant as governance or service delivery units. Neither states nor local governments, as they are currently described in the constitution, are city governments (however much their geographical territory might correspond to that of any given city).

Without city or municipal governments, urban public goods and services are provided and financed in a largely ad hoc or "residual" way. State governments finance and deliver city infrastructure and services as part of a wider set of

---

Box 4.13 The Politics of Metropolitan Governance

"Politics (and not economics) often dictate the ultimate structure [of metropolitan governance and coordination]. The criteria of efficiency and equity are not necessarily considered in designing a new governance structure. Both London (with the abolition of the Greater London Council in 1986) and Toronto (with the 1998 amalgamation) provide examples of cities where politics dictated the outcome."

Source: Slack 2007.

---

statewide public goods and services; local governments (insofar as they are functional) do so within their much smaller jurisdictions and in very modest ways.

From the point of view of financing cities and meeting their specific needs, this is limiting and problematic. But this is unlikely to change in the short or even medium term. Establishing a system of city or municipal government would require constitutional reforms. Moreover, city governments would quickly (and rightly) be seen by state governments (or governors) as potential rival power bases. However much Nigeria may "need" a system of municipal or city government (operating alongside state and local governments) to face the challenge (and seize the opportunities) of urban growth and development, that need is unlikely to outweigh political economy considerations, which currently favor the status quo. As box 4.13 shows, this is by no means unique to Nigeria.

Ways Forward

If nothing is done to improve the ways in which public goods and services are financed and provided in Nigeria's cities, there is a serious risk that urban growth may be far less beneficial than it ought to be. Outside of the exceptional case of Lagos, state governments are unlikely to be able to focus sufficiently on the specific requirements of individual cities or to provide appropriate finance.

The costs of "doing nothing" here are probably high: inadequate services provided inappropriately, uncoordinated or unplanned infrastructure development and the associated waste of fiscal resources, an urban citizenry faced with deteriorating conditions, and so on. As Nigeria becomes increasingly urban, and as its cities grow ever larger, the opportunity costs of the status quo increase.

Given all of the above, the financing of urban infrastructure and public services in Nigeria will need to be improved—but will likely be undertaken through the existing institutional framework or what it can accommodate. Future constitutional reform may well be indicated to establish a renewed and more efficient and effective system of municipal government and financing. In the interim, improvements will probably need to be incremental, progressive, and crafted on a case-by-case basis.

That said, a number of issues can be addressed that would contribute to improvements in urban financing.

Information and Knowledge

A first area that deserves attention is information. Quite simply, remarkably little is known about the financing and provision of urban infrastructure and services in much of Nigeria. How exactly various urban services (such as solid waste management or street maintenance) are financed in many Nigerian states is a mystery. In particular, local government finance and the ways in which it links (or does not link) into the provision of urban public goods and services is very much a black box.

If state governments do purloin or appropriate local government allocations, little is known about why and how this happens, or whether it makes sense. Next to nothing is known on a systematic basis about how local government budgets are drawn up or executed. Given that more than 20 percent of the combined Federation Account/Excess Crude Account/VAT funding pool is notionally shared with local governments, learning more about how those allocations are budgeted and then spent would be invaluable for identifying policies aimed at improving the subnational financing system.

In addition, not a great deal more is known about how most state governments allocate their revenues to sectors, to investments, and to various expenditure items. Knowing more about current state and local government finance (and how it is spent) would clearly provide a better basis upon which to identify doable and meaningful improvements in the provision of urban infrastructure and services.

Institutional Arrangements and Institutional Development

Institutional arrangements and development are a second broad area for improvement. Even given little likelihood of a "big urban bang" in Nigeria's institutional landscape, scope clearly exists for institutional changes that may sharpen the focus on tackling urban issues and more effectively and efficiently financing urban infrastructure and services.

For key service delivery functions, citywide and city-specific management and financing arrangement can be an option. For example, in some states (such as Oyo), current arrangements for solid waste management are already helping to improve sanitary conditions. But these are state government initiatives and operate on a statewide basis, which, in the case of Oyo State, may not be the best way of managing either Ibadan's particular solid waste problems or that of other cities, towns, and areas in the state. Residents of Ibadan, where population densities are higher, are probably more concerned about solid waste management than are other citizens of Oyo State and may therefore be more willing to pay or do more for better and more comprehensive services.

A potentially useful template for this kind of specifically urban institutional arrangement is the Lagos Metropolitan Area Transport Authority (box 4.14). Its mandate is to plan and coordinate public transport services and infrastructure within metropolitan Lagos; as such, it is a city-specific and single-purpose institution.

Box 4.14 Lagos Metropolitan Area Transport Authority

In response to the daunting challenge of ensuring more efficient and better public transport services in the Lagos megacity, the state government set up the Lagos Metropolitan Area Transport Authority (LAMATA), a semiautonomous public agency and corporate body.

Established by a State Act in 2002 (subsequently updated and amended in 2007), LAMATA has a broad mandate to formulate, coordinate, and implement urban transport policies in the metropolitan area. It is governed by a board made up of representatives from local transport operators, transport unions, Lagos State Government, and local government areas; and staffed by competent and competitively paid professionals. The authority's operations are financed through Lagos State budget contributions, a revenue share of the state-level Transport Fund, and loans from the World Bank.

Within the framework of a long-term transport master plan (running up until 2032), LAMATA has taken an integrated approach to the development of mass public transport systems in Lagos. Its key activities include the following:

• Establishing and regulating a Bus Rapid Transit network for key transport corridors in the city, based on publicly funded infrastructure and concessionary private sector ownership and management of rolling stock and operations.
• Upgrading and improving water transportation networks through new infrastructure and greater integration into the city's overall mass transit system.
• Overseeing the maintenance, upgrading, and rehabilitation of the city's 632 kilometer long Declared Road Network, which includes most major road arteries and corridors.
• Establishing the Light Rail Mass Transit network, on which construction work began in 2010. While the infrastructure needed for the network is being publicly funded, its rolling stock, network operations and maintenance, and day-to-day management will be undertaken by a private sector concessionaire, in line with LAMATA's public-private partnership strategy and approach.

General reviews of LAMATA's activities indicate that its integrated approach to public transport in Lagos City has reduced transport costs and journey times for many people.

Sources: Lagos Metropolitan Area Transport Authority.

Similar types of sector-specific arrangements also exist in other countries. In the public transport sector, Singapore's Land Transport Authority is responsible for all public transport planning and coordination in the city-state. Examples also exist in other sectors of city-specific and single-purpose authorities—typically for water and sanitation (such as the Hyderabad Metropolitan Water Supply and Sewerage Board).

Providing support for citywide and city-specific management boards, with a mandate to oversee the coordination of urban planning and financing; Enugu State's establishment of the Enugu Capital Territory Development Authority is an example of this kind of institutional improvement (box 4.15). That said, such

---

Box 4.15 Enugu Capital Territory Development Authority

Established by state government Law No. 5 (2009), the Enugu Capital Territory Development Authority's mandate is threefold:

1. Enforce compliance with appropriate standards by ministries, departments, and agencies with respect to municipal services in Enugu city.
2. Coordinate and monitor the provision of municipal services in Enugu city.
3. Advise the state governor on issues related to the development of Enugu city.

The authority is led by a commissioner (like other state ministers), assisted by a board that includes high-level representation from a range of ministries, departments, and agencies with urban functions (such as town planning, works and infrastructure, transport, water supply, and so on) as well as representatives from each of the three local governments within Enugu city.

While the development authority is clearly not a city government, it does appear to have a mandate similar to one—that is, with the singular exception of not being directly responsible for the delivery or provision of city infrastructure and services, but only having a regulatory and monitoring role. Nor does it have a "city budget" or access to any fiscal resources other than those for which the state government has voted appropriations. Nonetheless, the Enugu Capital Territory Development Authority is certainly an embryonic form of city manager.

Source: Enugu State Government 2009.

---

agencies are unlikely to enjoy much authority or access to finance—but they would almost certainly be more focused on urban development (and its financing) than are statewide institutions.

Outside Nigeria, several examples of this type of city management option exist, most notably in India, where a number of state governments have established metropolitan development authorities to undertake citywide planning and service coordination in major cities such as Chennai and Mumbai.

Related to all this, another potential institutional improvement might be to revive local governments in cities and to make them a more meaningful actor in identifying and prioritizing public investments and services. Local governments, in principle, have access to revenues—and could be given more opportunities to play a role in deciding where to use resources. This is not to downplay the extent to which local governments have governance deficits, accountability failings, and capacity constraints. But no other obvious candidate exists for the job of bringing public choice or voice into city development, and to thus improving "allocative efficiency."

Other institutional options certainly exist that would help sharpen public and governmental focus on cities and urban development challenges. States may already be putting some of them into practice, but they need to be documented and understood.

Given constitutional constraints and Nigeria's political economy, full-blooded and effective municipal or metropolitan governments are unlikely to emerge—in the medium term—as a framework for financing urban development. Other options need to be explored, replicated, and scaled up.

Of these options, the most promising are probably single-purpose and city-specific authorities (such as the Lagos Metropolitan Area Transport Authority [LAMATA]), empowered and mandated by state governments to manage, coordinate, and regulate key urban service sectors (such as public transport, solid waste management, and so on). Although these types of urban body are deconcentrated (rather than decentralized) institutions, they have the important virtues of (a) being focused on city functions, (b) able to maximize "within-sector" synergies and economies of scale, and (c) enjoying the authority delegated to them by state governments. Their sector specificity, on the other hand, does mean that such urban authorities may be weak on "horizontal" or "cross-sector" coordination (for example, between housing policies and solid waste or public transport management).

Greater "horizontal" coordination in urban development, however, might be improved by supporting and working through citywide development authorities (such as the Enugu Capital Territory Development Authority), operating on the basis of powers delegated by state governments, and mandated with broad planning and coordination functions for specific cities. A citywide authority like Enugu authority, on the other hand, may not provide the most robust of frameworks for urban financing and may also run the risk of becoming (yet another) relatively toothless planning agency. In practice, either or both of these institutional options for city finance would seem to be the most actionable and workable in Nigeria. And merit more thinking, with a particular focus on addressing some of their intrinsic limitations (such as weak downward accountability, "horizontal" coordination constraints, and weak financing mechanisms).

Finance and Public Financial Management

A third area for improvement is that of finance and financial management. A number of options merit discussion. Given the preponderance of revenue shares in state and local government budgets, it could be argued that changes in the way such shares are determined would be the easiest way of channeling more revenues to where they are most needed. As it stands, the formula for horizontal sharing is heavily weighted towards "equality" of states and local governments, such that each state or local government (irrespective of its size or other characteristics) receives an equal share of 40 percent of the Federation Account/Excess Crude Account/VAT funding pools. This results in smaller states/LGAs getting much higher per capita allocations than larger states/LGAs (Boex and Alm 2002). Modifying the sharing formula to give more weight to population (and less to equality) would mean larger states/LGAs receiving larger allocations, and thus more finance to fund their more populous cities. However, while this might seem to be a technically sound and logical improvement to subnational government financing, it is very unlikely to gain much traction in Nigeria's political community.

Current revenue sharing arrangements provide state governments (and, to a much lesser extent, local governments) with allocations over which they enjoy a very high degree of discretion. Subnational shares of federally collected revenues are not earmarked for spending on predetermined sectors or items. This is not going to change. But provision of additional transfers to subnational governments that are earmarked[28] for urban investments is one policy option that could be considered. To what extent such conditional grants (targeted at state governments through the federal government) would be either politically acceptable to state governments or practically workable is, of course, another matter. A variant on this would be to establish this kind of mechanism[29] at the level of an individual state, aimed at providing local governments (or other substate agencies) with access to investment-specific financing earmarked for the urban sector.

In general, and as has been seen, states and local governments have plenty of room to improve their own-source revenue (IGR) collection performance. Increases in IGRs would result in more (homegrown) finance, leverage for increased borrowing, and enhanced accountability. The Lagos and Edo state governments have shown that—given the political will and the right kind of political leadership—it is possible to increase IGRs. A number of ways exist to promote this in other states, including (a) modifying the horizontal allocation formula for Federation Account/Excess Crude Account/VAT funding pools to "reward" states that have increased their fiscal effort (which would likely be a politically unacceptable reform); (b) using development assistance instruments (such as the World Bank's Development Policy Operations Credits) to accompany and incentivize greater fiscal effort by individual states; and (c) providing demand-driven technical support to assist states (and their LGAs) in strengthening their tax collection and administration capacities. A final option here would be to give state governments more latitude to adjust their tax rates and bases—although this would probably incur substantial political transaction costs. However, increases in IGRs would not necessarily translate into more and better financing for urban public goods and services—even though such increases would probably come from city-based taxpayers.

PPPs are another urban financing option, one that is admittedly being explored with more energy than success. PPPs are potentially significant in terms of raising additional finance to cover operating expenditures—especially in Nigeria's largest cities, where the private sector has real incentives to engage. Even in smaller cities, scope exists for PPP modalities to quietly improve public services in areas like solid waste management. However, although PPPs hold some promise, they still require public spending, can be institutionally complex and transaction costly, and may not be particularly pro-poor.

Many state governments rely on borrowing to finance (or refinance) investments. But some signs suggest that state government debt is growing rapidly and that further borrowing may not be fiscally sustainable in some cases. But any policy actions on subnational government borrowing will require more information and a full assessment of subnational debt.

Last, but not at all least, one of the most sensible options for improving the financing of public goods and services in cities (and elsewhere) is to help make state and local government financial, expenditure, and investment management better. Public expenditure and public expenditure and fiscal accountability reviews of Nigerian states have consistently highlighted the poor quality of public financial, expenditure, and investment management in subnational governments, as box 4.16 shows.

What these reviews really underline is that current subnational management of public finance is unlikely to deliver value for money. Put another way, states and local governments do not spend very wisely. Improvements in the management of existing subnational finances would make for more effective spending on public goods and services, in cities and elsewhere, and make existing amounts of finance go a lot further.

Box 4.16 Subnational Public Financial, Expenditure, and Investment Management: Selected Quotes from Recent World Bank Public Expenditure Management and Financial Management Reviews in 12 States

"… the performance of the PFM systems across all the states was generally poor."

"Budget planning and preparation was generally weak in most states."

"Assessments of the efficiency of the public investment system carried out in Bayelsa, Ondo, and Plateau showed that management of the capital budget was still poor in these states."

"The capital budget system [in Lagos State 2010] is still underdeveloped … the procurement system in Lagos is generally very weak."

"Budget execution was also fraught with many problems."

"Assessments of the efficiency of public investment management in the four states revealed that management of the capital budget was quite poor in these states. The process for project development and preliminary screening in the four states has not been formalized… [Investment] project objectives, necessary justification and expected results are rarely provided and alternative options for achieving similar results are not considered in the final selection of projects. No rigorous screening of project proposals takes place … and the criteria for project selection [are] not clearly articulated in the states. In all the states, very few projects undergo project appraisal. There is no specific guidance on conducting project appraisals and the capacity … to carry out appraisals is very limited. Projects are selected based on nontransparent criteria…. The states do not carry out a periodic rationalization of the public investment program and problem projects only tend to be addressed when it is too late to apply any remedial action to make them viable."

Sources: World Bank 2010, 2011, 2013.

On a pragmatic note, one clear option here is to provide state and local governments with technical assistance and capacity support to strengthen their management of public investments and expenditure. Box 4.17 looks at an ongoing, donor-funded initiative in Nigeria that provides this type of support on a demand-driven and project-by-project basis.

Prescriptions or Menus?

A final note on how these kinds of incremental improvements might be implemented. It is tempting to take the much-lauded "Lagos megacity model" as a blueprint for changing the way other Nigerian cities are financed and managed.

Box 4.17 Nigeria Infrastructure Advisory Facility

The Nigeria Infrastructure Advisory Facility (NIAF), funded by the United Kingdom's Department for International Development, is a demand-driven technical assistance program providing support for more effective infrastructure investment to contribute to economic growth in the non-oil sector and the reduction of poverty.

NIAF provides consultancy services to federal and state governments to improve infrastructure planning and implementation. The first phase of the program ran from November 2007 to November 2011 and developed a reputation for quality. The second phase of NIAF runs until 2016.

A small team of full-time staff implements NIAF, which is in turn backstopped by a network of short-term consultants. It is designed to provide access to rapid and flexible consulting expertise to help Nigeria improve its infrastructure through policy and strategy formulation, planning, project implementation, and private sector investment. The main areas and sectors for which NIAF provides this kind of support are (a) power sector reform; (b) roads and railways sector reform; (c) improved capital program planning, financing, and implementation; (d) effective cities; (e) Northern growth; and (f) climate change.

NIAF provides support for infrastructure investment based on a clear recognition of the need for appropriate institutional and policy frameworks (such as support for the development of state mass transport policies as a prelude to the provision of technical support for subsequent infrastructure planning, financing, and implementation).

To date, NIAF has delivered over 500 "projects" (or technical assistance packages of varying scope, size, and duration), the largest proportion being in the power sector. Although many of these have been completed, some 150 are ongoing.

About 80 percent of NIAF support has been provided to the federal level (including FCT Abuja), and the remainder to states, and the total budget for these projects has been around US$100 million.

NIAF appears to be effective at improving public sector investments in infrastructure. One of its strengths lies in its demand-driven modus operandi. However, relying upon demand for technical assistance may also limit its outreach.

Source: Nigeria Infrastructure Advisory Facility website, www.niafng.org.

From Oil to Cities • http://dx.doi.org/10.1596/978-1-4648-0792-3

However, there are 35 other state governments and at least 13 cities with more than 0.5 million people—and each state has its own history, its own way of doing things, and its own subnational political economy. Cities and states share many common problems and features, but are also different to each other—and none of them are megacities like Lagos, none are "city-states" like Lagos, and very few are managed by a technically competent and genuinely reformist leadership.

What works for the Lagos megacity and the Lagos State government may therefore not work in other cities and states. Multiple options for improving institutional arrangements and urban finance may need to be presented and discussed as a menu, on a case-by-case basis, rather than as carte-blanche prescriptions. Although Lagos does show what is possible under the right political and institutional circumstances, it would be unrealistic to assume that these circumstances prevail in other states and cities in Nigeria—and it is perhaps better to start with a solid assessment of context and political economy, and then work towards actionable policies and reforms.

Notes

1. Lagos, more or less a city-state, is probably the only de facto exception here. Because the state is almost entirely composed of Lagos City (or megacity), information on state finance can be seen as very largely about city finance.

2. The official definition of an urban settlement in Nigeria is one with a population of over 20,000.

3. With its own special jurisdiction, the Federal Capital Territory of Abuja.

4. In Ghana, municipalities and districts have an average population (2010) of just over 100,000; in Uganda, sub-counties, town councils, and urban divisions had an average population in 2014 of about 25,000; in Bangladesh, Union Parishads had an average population in 2006 of about 27,000; in Vietnam, communes had an average population in 2006 of just over 10,500.

5. This has been done in Enugu State, for example, where the Enugu Capital Territory Development Authority was established by state law in 2009, with a mandate to ensure planning and coordination in Enugu city. As such, the authority acts as a citywide "apex" institution that covers the jurisdictions of three LGAs.

6. Including equipment, technical assistance, and capacity building.

7. This percentage is consistent with World Bank (2011) estimates of federal and subnational government shares of the infrastructure financing envelope.

8. As witnessed by recent debates about the condition of infrastructure in the United States. See http://www.infrastructurereportcard.org/.

9. In the 15 countries making up the European Union core, for example, subnational expenditure accounts for about 30 percent of total public spending (Eyraud and Badia) 2013. Based on data from a sample of 64 countries, it has recently been estimated that subnational government expenditure amounts to 40 percent of total public expenditure for advanced economies, compared to about 25 percent for emerging economies and developing countries (Sow and Razafimahefa 2015).

10. It is worth noting that (a) Jigawa and Akwa Ibom are also two of the six *worst* performing states in terms of IGR as a percent of total revenues; both states are highly

dependent on their share of federal revenue; and that (b) Rivers State, on the other hand, is one of the better IGR performers.

11. FCT Abuja (which is not a state government) has not been included in this ranking of capital expenditure.

12. It is worth noting that LGAs in Kebbi and Yobe are among the better IGR performers; Zamfara, however, is not, but is better than average.

13. Using an exchange rate of US$1 to ₦200 naira.

14. On the other hand, it could be argued that state governments thus provide a regional framework for urban development planning, linking cities with their suburban and economic hinterlands.

15. Such as SEEDs (State Economic Empowerment and Development plans).

16. For example, subnational governments in Botswana, Ghana, Lesotho, and Uganda derive, respectively, 66 percent, 88 percent, 90 percent, and 92 percent of total revenues from intergovernmental fiscal transfers (Fjeldstad and Heggstad 2012). In Nepal (World Bank 2014a), all local governments (districts, municipalities, and villages) currently rely on transfers from central government for about 83 percent of their total revenues.

17. See Litwack (2013) for a discussion of oil revenues and fiscal sustainability in Nigeria.

18. For example: Delta State (June 2010), 45 percent of total (USAID 2010); Borno State (2002–03), 48 percent of total (Okafor 2010); Oyo State (Tomori 2015), 80 percent (2003), 72 percent (2004), 60 percent (2005), 77 percent (2006), and 77 percent (2007).

19. For example, each of the 33 LGAs in Oyo State contributes 0.5 million naira per month to the budget of the Oyo State Solid Waste Management Authority.

20. Oyo State, for example, since 2001 has used a somewhat different horizontal formula to share out allocations to its 33 LGAs. The formula used in Oyo allocates 50 percent on the basis of equality, 30 percent on the basis of population, and 20 percent on the basis of landmass.

21. See Boex and Alm (2002) and Freinkman and Dukowicz (2008) for a much more detailed discussion of the formula for horizontal sharing.

22. This also provides incentives for the proliferation of subnational government units.

23. In 2013, Lagos State accounted for about 5.6 percent of total state government revenues, 5.4 percent of all state government shares of federally collected revenues, and 17.5 percent of all state government IGRs.

24. In 2013, Bayelsa State accounted for about 1.1 percent of total state government revenues, 1.7 percent of all state government shares of federally collected revenues, and 1.1 percent of all state government IGRs.

25. For example, see http://www.bloomberg.com/news/articles/2014-01-30/nigeria -pinching-state-bond-bonanza-before-vote-africa-credit; http://www.citizensbudget .org/index.php?option=com_contentandview=articleandid=198:rivers-state-sinks -deeper-into-debtandcatid=38:press-releasesandItemid=63; http://leadership.ng /business/1284/state-govts-raise-n565bn-from-bond-market; http://www.thisdaylive .com/articles/checking-fg-states-dominance-in-nigerias-bond-market/181788/.

26. Other than spending on items included in an agreed "negative" list.

27. See, for example: Olamide Udo-Udoma, "Transport in Lagos: Between Building and Banning," *Future Lagos*, October 29, 2013, http://futurecapetown.com/2013/10/lagos

-transport-okada-to-cable-car/#.VRJejfmUcb1; *Premium Times*, "Why BRT Buses Are in Very Bad Shape-Lagos Commissioner," September 23, 2013, http://www.premium timesng.com/news/145285-brt-buses-bad-shape-lagos-commissioner.html; Seye Olumide, Yetunde Oyebami Ojo and Wole Oyebade, "Agbaje Promises to Scrap Lekki-Epe Tollgate, Tinubu, Fashola Warn Lagosians to Shun PDP," *The Guardian*, January 14, 2015, http://www.ngrguardiannews.com/2015/01/agbaje-promises-to-scrap-lekki-epe-tollgate-tinubu-fashola-warn-lagosians-to-shun-pdp/.

28. Like the conditional grants programs for the Millennium Development Goals and basic education (Searle 2008).

29. Designed to operate as a type of Municipal Development Fund.

References

African Development Bank. 2013. *An Infrastructure Action Plan for Nigeria: Closing the Infrastructure Gap and Accelerating Economic Transformation*. Tunis: African Development Bank Group.

Bodea, C., and A. LeBas. 2013. "The Origins of Social Contracts: Attitudes toward Taxation in Urban Nigeria." CSAE Working Paper WPS/2013-02, Centre for the Study of African Economies, Oxford, U.K.

Boex, J., and J. Alm. 2002. "An Overview of Intergovernmental Fiscal Relations and Subnational Public Finance in Nigeria." Working Paper 02-1, Andrew Young School of Policy Studies, Georgia State University, Atlanta, GA.

CBN (Central Bank of Nigeria). Various years. *Annual Report and Statement of Accounts*. Abuja: CBN.

———. 2011. *Annual Statistical Bulletin—Section B*. Abuja: CBN.

———. 2012. *Statistical Bulletin—Section B*. Abuja: CBN.

———. 2013. *Statistical Bulletin—Section B*. Abuja: CBN.

CLGF (Commonwealth Local Government Forum). 2013. "The Local Government System in Nigeria." Country Profile, CLGF, London.

DMO (Debt Management Office). 2012a. "External and Domestic Borrowing Guidelines for Federal and State Governments and their Agencies."

———. 2012b. "Report on the Programme for Establishing Debt Management Departments and Domestic Debt Data Reconstruction in the 36 States of the Federation and the FCT (2008–2012)." DMO, Abuja.

———. 2013a. *National Debt Management Framework, 2013–2017*. Abuja: DMO.

———. 2013b. "To All Licensed Banks—Another Reminder: Requirement for Lending to All Tiers of Government." Circular, DMO, Abuja.

———. n.d. "Annual Summaries of External and Domestic Debt Stock of State Governments (2010–2014)." DMO, Abuja.

Eyraud, L., and M. Moreno Badia. 2013. "Too Small to Fail? Subnational Spending Pressures in Europe." Working Paper WP/13/46 International Monetary Fund, Washington, DC.

Federal Ministry of Works. 2013. *Compendium Report on Road Infrastructure and Related Development in Nigeria—an Investor's Manual*. Abuja: Pison Housing Company for the Federal Ministry of Works.

Federal Republic of Nigeria. 1999. "Constitution of the Federal Republic of Nigeria." http://www.nigeria-law.org/ConstitutionOfTheFederalRepublicOfNigeria.htm.

———. 2006. "Nigeria Population and Housing Census."

———. n.d. "National Urban Development Policy."

Fjeldstad, O.-H., and K. Heggstad. 2012. "Local Government Revenue Mobilisation in Anglophone Africa." Working Paper 7, International Centre for Tax and Development, Brighton, U.K.

Freinkman, L., and D. Dukowicz. 2008. "Statistical Analysis of Fiscal Differentiation across Nigerian States." Policy note prepared for the Nigerian Federal Ministry of Finance, the World Bank, and the U.K. Department for International Development as part of the joint Analytical Work Program on Fiscal Federalism.

Haruna, A., and G. Al-Ansar. 2013. "Nigerian Federalism and the Statutory Allocation of Funds: Analytical Review of Local Government as Third Tier of Government." *Journal of Humanities and Social Science* 11 (6): 1–9.

Health Systems 20/20. 2012a. "A Review of Public Expenditure Management in Nigeria—Cross River State Report." Report prepared for the United States Agency for International Development.

———. 2012b. "Public Budgeting and Expenditure Management in Three Nigerian States: Challenges for Health Governance." Report prepared for the United States Agency for International Development.

Heggie, I. 1995. "Management and Financing of Roads: An Agenda for Reform." World Bank Technical Paper 275, World Bank, Washington, DC.

Litwack, J. 2013. "Nigeria Economic Report." Working Paper 77684, World Bank, Washington, DC.

Mason-Jones, K., and B. Cohen. 2012. "Lagos BRT-LITE." Case study for WWF-SA, Cape Town. http://awsassets.wwf.org.za/downloads/lcf_lagos_brt_2012.pdf.

Ogungbuyi, K. 2013. "Ibadan Urban Flooding Management Project: Baseline Report on Solid Waste Management Component." Environmental Harmony Ltd.

Okafor, J. 2010. "Local Government Financial Autonomy in Nigeria: The State Joint Local Government Account." *Commonwealth Journal of Local Governance* 6: 124–131.

Searle, R. 2008. "More Resources for MDGs and Better Fiscal Coordination through Conditional Grants? Assessing the Scope for Greater Use of Incentive-Based Instruments in Nigeria." Policy Note prepared for the Nigerian Federal Ministry of Finance, the World Bank, and U.K. Department for International Development as part of the joint Analytical Work Program on Fiscal Federalism.

Slack, E. 2007. "Managing the Coordination of Service Delivery in Metropolitan Cities: The Role of Metropolitan Governance." Policy Research Working Paper 4317, World Bank, Washington, DC.

Sow, M., and I. Razafimahefa. 2015. "Fiscal Decentralization and the Efficiency of Public Service Delivery." Working Paper WP/15/59, International Monetary Fund, Washington, DC.

Tomori, M. n.d. "Urban Government Finance: Emerging Trends in Property Tax Policy in Nigeria." Unpublished.

———. 2015. "Review of Oyo State Finances in General and the City of Ibadan in Particular." Note prepared for the World Bank, Washington, DC.

United States Agency for International Development (USAID). 2010a. "Comparative Assessment of Decentralization in Africa: Nigeria Desk Study." Desk study prepared for USAID by ARD Inc., Burlington, Vermont.

———. 2010b. "Comparative Assessment of Decentralization in Africa: Nigeria In-Country Assessment Report." Report prepared for USAID by ARD Inc., Burlington, Vermont.

———. 2013. "Nigeria: Mid-Term Performance Evaluation of the Leadership, Empowerment, Advocacy and Development (LEAD) Project Final Report." Report prepared by USAID and Nigeria's Monitoring and Evaluation Project II Project, USAID, Washington, DC.

WHO (World Health Organization)/UNICEF (United Nations Children's Fund). 2014. "Joint Monitoring Programme for Water Supply and Sanitation—Nigeria." Nigeria country file. WHO/UNICEF, Geneva, New York.

World Bank. 2008. "Nigeria—A Review of the Costs and Financing of Public Education (Volume II): Main Report." Education Sector Review, World Bank, Washington, DC.

———. 2010. "Nigeria—Lagos Rolling Public Expenditure Review 1." Public expenditure review, World Bank, Washington, DC.

———. 2011. "Nigeria—State Level Public Expenditure Management and Financial Accountability Review: A Synthesis Report." For Anambra, Bayelsa, Ekiti, Kogi Niger, Ondo, and Plateau. Public expenditure review, World Bank, Washington, DC.

———. 2012. "Nigeria—First Edo State Growth and Employment Support Credit." Program Document 67031-NG, World Bank, Washington, DC.

———. 2013. "Nigeria—State Level Public Expenditure Management: A Summary Report." For Abia, Adamawa, Imo, and Kebbi states, World Bank, Washington, DC.

———. 2014a. "Local Service Delivery in Nepal." Working Paper 87922, World Bank, Washington, DC.

———. 2014b. "First Lagos State Development Policy Operation." Implementation Completion and Results Report, World Bank, Washington, DC.

———. 2014c. "Second Lagos State Development Policy Operation Program." World Bank, Washington, DC.

———. 2014d. "Nigeria—Third National Urban Water Sector Reform Project." Project Appraisal Document, World Bank, Washington, DC.

———. 2015. "Third Lagos State Development Policy Operation." Draft Program Document, World Bank, Washington, DC.

Environmental Benefits Statement

The World Bank Group is committed to reducing its environmental footprint. In support of this commitment, the Publishing and Knowledge Division leverages electronic publishing options and print-on-demand technology, which is located in regional hubs worldwide. Together, these initiatives enable print runs to be lowered and shipping distances decreased, resulting in reduced paper consumption, chemical use, greenhouse gas emissions, and waste.

The Publishing and Knowledge Division follows the recommended standards for paper use set by the Green Press Initiative. The majority of our books are printed on Forest Stewardship Council (FSC)–certified paper, with nearly all containing 50–100 percent recycled content. The recycled fiber in our book paper is either unbleached or bleached using totally chlorine-free (TCF), processed chlorine-free (PCF), or enhanced elemental chlorine-free (EECF) processes.

More information about the Bank's environmental philosophy can be found at http://www.worldbank.org/corporateresponsibility.